# Network+ CoursePrep StudyGuide/ExamGuide
## Second Edition

Tamara Dean

COURSE
TECHNOLOGY
™
THOMSON LEARNING

Australia • Canada • Mexico • Singapore • Spain • United Kingdom • United States

**COURSE TECHNOLOGY**

™

**THOMSON LEARNING**

*Network+ CoursePrep StudyGuide, Second Edition and Network+ CoursePrep ExamGuide, Second Edition* by Tamara Dean is published by Course Technology

**Product Manager:**
Amy M. Lyon

**Associate Publisher:**
Steve Elliot

**Senior Product Manager:**
Lisa Egan

**Developmental Editor:**
Ann Shaffer

**Production Editor:**
Karen Jacot

**Manufacturing Manager:**
Alexander Schall

**Marketing Manager:**
Toby Shelton

**Editorial Assistant:**
Nick Lombardi

**Cover Designer:**
Betsy Young and Abby Scholtz

ISBN 0-619-12132-7

ISBN 0-619-12133-5

# TABLE OF CONTENTS

# PREFACE

The *Network+ CoursePrep ExamGuide, Second Edition,* and *Network+ CoursePrep StudyGuide, Second Edition,* are the very best tools to use to prepare for exam day. Both products provide thorough preparation for the CompTIA Network + exam. These products are intended to be utilized with the core "Guide to" book, *Network+ Guide to Networks, Second Edition* (ISBN 0-619-06301-7) by Tamara Dean, also published by Course Technology.

## COURSEPREP EXAMGUIDE

The *Network + CoursePrep ExamGuide, Second* Edition, ISBN 0-619-12133-5, provides the essential information you need to master each exam objective. The ExamGuide devotes an entire two-page spread to each certification objective for the Network+ exam, helping you understand the objective, and giving you the bottom line information—what you *really* need to know. Memorize these facts and bulleted points before heading into the exam. In addition, there are seven practice-test questions for each objective on the right-hand page—that's over 600 questions total! CoursePrep ExamGuide provides the exam fundamentals and gets you up to speed quickly. If you are seeking even more opportunity to practice and prepare, we recommend that you consider our total solution, CoursePrep StudyGuide, which is described below.

## COURSEPREP STUDYGUIDE

For those really serious about certification, we offer an even more robust solution—the *Network+ CoursePrep StudyGuide, Second Edition,* ISBN 0-619-12132-7. This offering includes all of the same great features you get with the CoursePrep ExamGuide, including the unique two page spread, the bulleted memorization points and the practice questions. In addition, you receive a password valid for six months of practice on CoursePrep, a dynamic test preparation tool. The password is found in an envelope in the back cover of the CoursePrep StudyGuide. CoursePrep is a Web-based pool of hundreds of sample test questions. CoursePrep exam simulation software mimics the exact exam environment. The CoursePrep software is flexible and allows you to practice several ways as you master the material. Choose from Certification Mode to experience actual exam-day conditions or Study Mode to request answers and explanations to practice questions. Custom Mode lets you set the options for the practice test, including number of questions, content coverage, and ability to request answers and explanation. Follow the instructions on the inside back cover to access the exam simulation software. To see a demo of this dynamic test preparation tool, go to *www.courseprep.com.*

# FEATURES

The *Network+ CoursePrep ExamGuide* and *Network+ CoursePrep StudyGuide* includes the following features:

***Description of domains taken from the CompTIA Web site*** Each exam objective belongs to one of four domains (or broad areas) of networking knowledge. CompTIA's description of these domains helps you plan your course of study and explains the percentage of the exam devoted to each domain. For more information about Network+ exams, visit the CompTIA Web site at *www.comptia.org*.

***Detailed coverage of the certification objectives in a unique two-page spread*** Study strategically by really focusing in on the Network+ certification objectives. To enable you to do this, each certification objective is explained in a two-page format. The left-hand page provides the critical facts you need, while the right-hand page features practice questions relating to that objective. You'll find the certification objective(s) and sub-objectives(s) at the top of each left-hand page.

An overview of the objective is provided in the ***Understanding the Objective*** section. Next, ***What You Really Need to Know*** lists bulleted, succinct facts, skills, and concepts about the objective. Memorizing these facts will be important for your success when taking the exam. ***Objectives on the Job*** places the objective in an industry perspective and tells you how you can expect to incorporate the objective on the job. This section also provides troubleshooting information.

***Practice Test Questions*** Each right-hand page contains seven practice test questions designed to help you prepare for the exam by testing your skills, identifying your strengths and weaknesses, and demonstrating the subject matter you will face on the exam and how it will be tested. These questions are written in a similar fashion to real Network+ exam questions. The questions test your knowledge of the objectives described on the left-hand page and also the information in the *Network+ Guide to Networks, Second Edition* (0-619-06301-7). You can find answers to the practice test questions in the answer key at the back of the book and on the CoursePrep Web site (*www.courseprep.com*), where you can also find additional Web-based exam preparation questions.

***Glossary*** Boldfaced terms used in the book and other terms that you need to know for the exams are listed and defined in the glossary.

# How to use this book

The *Network+ CoursePrep ExamGuide, Second Edition*, and *Network+ CoursePrep StudyGuide, Second Edition*, are all you need to successfully prepare for the CompTIA Network+ exam if you have some experience and working knowledge of supporting and maintaining networks. This book is intended to be used with a core text, such as *Network+ Guide to Networks, Second Edition* (ISBN 0-619-06301-7), also published by Course Technology. If you are new to this field, use this book as a roadmap of where you need to go to prepare for certification, and use *Network+ Guide to Networks, Second Edition,* to give you the knowledge and understanding that you need to reach your goal. Course Technology publishes a full series of network and Network+ products. For more information, visit our website at *www.course.com* or contact your sales representative.

# Acknowledgments

I could not have completed this guide without the support and planning of the ever-capable and efficient Course Technology staff, especially Amy Lyon, Product Manager, Lisa Egan, Senior Product Manager, and all those who contributed to further refining the text and creating the finished product. Many thanks to Ann Shaffer, the Developmental Editor, for doing a superb job of ensuring clarity and consistency and always being a joy to work with. Thanks also to the technical editor, James Conrad, who scrutinized the content and helped to make the guide more accurate and complete, and to Karen Jacot, Course Technology Production Editor, for helping to transform the manuscript into a published book. For additional help with technical material, I'm grateful to my smart, generous colleagues, Peyton Engel, Michael Grice, and David Klann. Thanks to Paul and Jan Dean, Nancy Dale, Sara, Bridget, Sandhya, Ann, Stacy, Jen, Lea, Kris, Susan, Carol, Paula, Alicia, and Sandy for being strong and good-humored allies.

# Network+ Objectives

The following descriptions of the Network+ Objective domains are taken from the CompTIA Web site at *www.comptia.org*. Each objective belongs to one of four domains (or broad areas) of networking knowledge. For example, the objective of recognizing an RJ-45 connector belongs to the "Media and Topologies" domain, which accounts for 20 percent of the exam's content.

## Domain 1.0: Media and Topologies — 20 percent of examination

This domain requires knowledge of cabling and connector types, physical topologies (such as the star topology), and logical topologies (such as Ethernet and Token Ring) that make up a network. It also includes an understanding of network connectivity devices such as hubs, routers, switches, and gateways. Many of the topics in this domain comply with industry standards, such as IEEE's working group standards for Physical and Data Link layer network access. Although the topics in this domain are highly technical, they are also relatively straightforward.

## Domain 2.0: Protocols and Standards — 25 percent of examination

This domain requires knowledge of protocols and standards, the means by which two computers communicate. Given that the most popular network protocol currently used on networks is TCP/IP, this domain pays particular attention to the protocols and subprotocols in the TCP/IP suite. In addition to protocols, this domain covers the OSI Model, a popular theoretical construct used to describe computer-to-computer communication. Much of the knowledge in this domain refers to networking at the most fundamental, data-bit level.

## Domain 3.0: Network Implementation — 23 percent of examination

This domain requires understanding of the most popular networking clients and network operating systems (NOSs). It covers not only the features of each, but also how to integrate different clients with different NOSs. In addition, this domain requires knowledge of good networking practices to ensure that data is safe and always available and that network access is never interrupted.

## Domain 4.0: Network Support — 32 percent of examination

This domain requires the ability to diagnose and troubleshoot common network problems relating to client connectivity, remote connectivity, topology, hardware, and media. It requires knowledge of troubleshooting utilities and methodology. This domain emphasizes practical knowledge that will prove invaluable in a networking career.

# OBJECTIVES

## 1.1 Recognize the following logical or physical network topologies given a schematic diagram or description:

### STAR/HIERARCHICAL PHYSICAL TOPOLOGY

### UNDERSTANDING THE OBJECTIVE

Every network depends on a physical layout, or topology. The **physical topology** describes how servers, workstations, printers, and other devices are physically connected in a **local-area network (LAN)** or **wide-area network (WAN)**. While most modern networks contain a combination of topologies, all combinations rely on a few fundamental topologies: bus, star, and ring. Because each individual topology has particular advantages and disadvantages, different situations may require different topologies. The most common physical topology used on modern networks is a star, or hierarchical, topology.

### WHAT YOU REALLY NEED TO KNOW

◆ In a **star topology**, every node on the network is connected through a central device, such as a hub, in a star configuration, as shown in the following diagram:

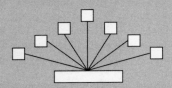

◆ In a star topology network, each device transmits its data to the hub, which repeats the data to all other devices on the segment. The recipient node then picks up the data addressed to it.

◆ Any single physical wire on a star network only connects two devices, so a cabling problem will only affect two nodes. Devices such as workstations or printers transmit data to the hub, which then retransmits the data to the network segment where the destination node is located, so the destination node can pick it up.

◆ Star topologies are more fault-tolerant and provide better performance than bus or ring topologies. On Ethernet networks, a single cable or node fault will not immobilize a star-wired network. However, star networks require more cabling and devices and are generally more expensive than bus or ring networks.

◆ Star networks can be easily upgraded, moved, and interconnected with other networks.

◆ Star topology networks that divide workstation groups and connectivity devices into layers are known as **hierarchical**.

### OBJECTIVES ON THE JOB

The star topology forms the basis of the most popular type of network in use today. Because it is so popular, you should be familiar with the way connectivity devices and nodes are arranged in this topology. As your experience with star topology networks increases, you will also learn how to troubleshoot and add to them.

# PRACTICE TEST QUESTIONS

1. **Which of the following is an advantage to using star topology networks over using bus or ring topology networks?**
    a. Star topology networks are more scalable.
    b. Star topology networks are less expensive to install.
    c. Star topology networks are easier to install.
    d. Star topology networks are more secure.

2. **What would happen if a node in a star-wired Ethernet network failed?**
    a. Performance over the entire network would suffer slightly.
    b. Only the failed node would be unable to transmit or receive data.
    c. Data could no longer be transmitted or received at any point in the network.
    d. The failed node would broadcast errors to the rest of the network.

3. **What is the function of a hub in a star-wired network?**
    a. to reduce RF emissions that may result in security breaches
    b. to increase available bandwidth by sending multiplexed signals
    c. to arbitrate addressing conflicts between sending nodes
    d. to repeat signals to all nodes on the segment

4. **In a network using the star topology, five workstations and a hub would be connected via how many physical cables?**
    a. three
    b. four
    c. five
    d. six

5. **In which of the following networks would it make the most sense to implement a hierarchical topology?**
    a. a LAN that connects two local lumber yards
    b. a WAN that connects freelance writers across the nation
    c. a LAN that connects multiple departments, offices, and employees in an insurance company
    d. a WAN that connects multiple churches within a city

6. **What would happen to a star network if one of its workgroup hubs failed?**
    a. All nodes connected to that hub would be unable to communicate with nodes on other segments, but they could communicate with each other.
    b. All nodes connected to that hub would be unable to communicate with nodes on other segments as well as nodes on their own segment.
    c. Nodes would be able to communicate with the network, as they would automatically connect to an alternate hub on the backbone.
    d. Communication on the entire LAN would halt.

7. **What type of terminator is used on a star-wired network?**
    a. 20-ohm resistor
    b. 50-ohm resistor
    c. 100-ohm resistor
    d. Terminators are not used on star-wired networks.

## 1.1 Recognize the following logical or physical network topologies given a schematic diagram or description (continued):

### BUS PHYSICAL TOPOLOGY

### UNDERSTANDING THE OBJECTIVE

A bus topology is one in which multiple nodes share a single channel. By sharing that channel, they also share a fixed amount of bandwidth. Bus topologies are used on 10Base5 and 10Base2 Ethernet networks.

### WHAT YOU REALLY NEED TO KNOW

♦ A **bus topology** consists of a single cable connecting all nodes on a network without intervening connectivity devices and appears as follows in a network diagram:

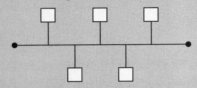

♦ Since every node on a bus topology network shares the same channel for data transmission, adding nodes on a bus network impairs performance.

♦ A bus topology can be considered a peer-to-peer topology because every device on the network shares the responsibility for getting data from one point to another.

♦ Bus topologies require 50-ohm resistors known as **terminators** at each end of the bus to prevent **signal bounce**, a phenomenon in which data travels endlessly between the two ends of the network.

♦ The bus topology is the least fault-tolerant of any topology, because one break in the cable can take down the entire network, and bus topology faults are difficult to find.

♦ A bus topology is the least expensive and simplest topology to install.

### OBJECTIVES ON THE JOB

If you use a bus topology, chances are you are working on a Thinnet (10Base2) network. Bear in mind that if one of the nodes fails, the entire network will lose connectivity. For this reason, and because the addition of more nodes will cause performance problems, it may be wise to upgrade a bus topology network to a star topology network.

# PRACTICE TEST QUESTIONS

1. **On a bus topology, terminators eliminate the possibility of:**
   a. crosstalk.
   b. noise.
   c. signal bounce.
   d. EMI.

2. **How many nodes share a single channel on a bus topology?**
   a. all connected nodes
   b. one
   c. two
   d. four

3. **Which two of the following types of networks use a bus topology?**
   a. 10BaseT
   b. 100BaseT
   c. 10Base5
   d. 10Base2

4. **What is one advantage of using a network based on the bus topology over a network based on the star or mesh topologies?**
   a. Bus topologies are more fault tolerant.
   b. Bus topologies allow faster throughput.
   c. Bus topologies are more secure.
   d. Bus topologies are simpler to install and maintain.

5. **What type of terminator is used on a bus network?**
   a. 20-ohm resistor
   b. 50-ohm resistor
   c. 20-ohm transistor
   d. 50-ohm transistor

6. **You are the administrator for a LAN that uses the bus topology to connect seven workstations. Each workstation runs Windows 2000 Professional. What would you need to do if you wanted to add a workstation to the network and enable other workstations to read data from the new workstation's hard disk?**
   a. Apply shared access to the appropriate folders on the new workstation.
   b. Modify the sharing services parameters in the domain controller's operating system.
   c. Modify the file sharing properties on each workstation on the network so that each can read from the added workstation.
   d. Add the new workstation's account to a folder-sharing group on the network.

7. **What would happen to the entire network if one of the nodes in a bus-wired network failed?**
   a. Performance would suffer slightly.
   b. The failed node could not transmit data, but other nodes would be fine.
   c. Data would no longer be transmitted to or from any node.
   d. Errors would be broadcast to every node.

## 1.1 Recognize the following logical or physical network topologies given a schematic diagram or description (continued):

### MESH PHYSICAL TOPOLOGY

### UNDERSTANDING THE OBJECTIVE

In a LAN, a mesh topology is one in which at least some of the nodes are connected via more than one link. In a WAN, a mesh topology is one in which some of the locations are connected via more than one link. Mesh topologies are most commonly used in WANs.

### WHAT YOU REALLY NEED TO KNOW

♦ A **mesh topology** is one in which nodes or locations are directly interconnected with multiple other nodes or locations on the network.

♦ A network may use a **full-mesh topology**, in which each node is connected directly to each other node, as shown in the following diagram:

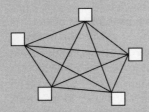

♦ Full-mesh topologies are the most expensive physical topologies because they require the most equipment, connectivity, setup, and maintenance. However, they are also the most fault-tolerant physical topologies.

♦ A less expensive, yet still fault-tolerant alternative to full-mesh topologies is a **partial-mesh topology**, in which only some of the nodes on a network are directly connected to other nodes, as shown in the following diagram:

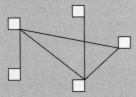

♦ Mesh topologies are typically used in the context of wide-area networks (WANs). A location in a WAN topology is equivalent to a node in a LAN topology.

### OBJECTIVES ON THE JOB

If you are designing a WAN that must be fault tolerant, a mesh topology is a wise choice. In designing a partial mesh, arrange the redundant links so that they connect the most critical locations on the network.

## PRACTICE TEST QUESTIONS

1. **Which of the following advantages does a partial-mesh topology provide?**
   a. All nodes have multiple connections to the network.
   b. At least some nodes have multiple connections to the network.
   c. Any node can be taken down without affecting network performance.
   d. Network performance will be similar, no matter what kind of link is used between nodes.

2. **Which of the following is the most fault-tolerant WAN topology?**
   a. partial mesh
   b. full mesh
   c. ring
   d. hierarchical

3. **If a full-mesh WAN consists of four locations, how many separate connections does it contain?**
   a. two
   b. four
   c. six
   d. eight

4. **If a partial-mesh WAN consists of four locations, how many separate connections might it contain? (Choose all that apply.)**
   a. two
   b. three
   c. four
   d. five

5. **Which of the following organizations is most likely to use a full-mesh WAN?**
   a. a school district
   b. a regional charitable organization
   c. a regional power company
   d. a local chain of grocers

6. **What would happen to the entire network if one of the nodes in a full-mesh WAN failed?**
   a. Performance for all locations on the WAN would suffer.
   b. The failed location would be unable to transmit or receive data, but other locations could communicate without a problem.
   c. Data would no longer be transmitted to or from any of the locations.
   d. The failed location would broadcast errors to every other location.

7. **A mesh WAN could connect LANs that use the bus topology. True or false?**

## 1.1 Recognize the following logical or physical network topologies given a schematic diagram or description (continued):

### RING PHYSICAL TOPOLOGY

### UNDERSTANDING THE OBJECTIVE

A ring topology connects nodes using a single channel in a ring. In order to determine which node can transmit data at any given time, ring networks use tokens that circulate on the network and are reserved by the transmitting node.

### WHAT YOU REALLY NEED TO KNOW

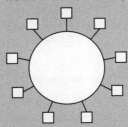

- ◆ In a **ring topology**, each node is connected to the two nearest nodes so that the entire network forms a circle, as shown in the following diagram:

- ◆ Data is transmitted in one direction (unidirectionally) around the ring. Each workstation accepts and responds to packets addressed to it, then forwards the other packets to the next workstation in the ring.
- ◆ Because there are no ends to a ring network and because data stop at their destination, ring networks do not require terminators.
- ◆ Ring topologies often use the **token passing** technique, in which a node that wants to send data picks up the constantly circling token, adds its data, sends the packet, and when the recipient accepts the packet, releases the token so that other nodes can transmit.
- ◆ A disadvantage of the ring topology is that one defective node can take down the network.
- ◆ Another disadvantage with the ring topology is that, as with a bus topology, adding more nodes to a ring network can detract from performance.
- ◆ A popular hybrid topology used on Token Ring networks is the star-ring hybrid topology.

### OBJECTIVES ON THE JOB

If you work with a Token Ring network, bear in mind that it will use the star-ring hybrid topology, not a simple ring topology. Still, you must be aware of the scalability limitations of this type of topology.

# PRACTICE TEST QUESTIONS

1. **In which two of the following topologies will the addition of more nodes detrimentally affect the network's performance?**
   a. bus
   b. star
   c. ring
   d. mesh

2. **At any given time, how many tokens circulate on a simple ring network?**
   a. one
   b. five
   c. ten
   d. There are no limits on the number of tokens that may circulate.

3. **What is the function of a token on a token-passing ring network?**
   a. It signals to the rest of the network to listen for traffic.
   b. It signals to the rest of the network that the MAU is receiving an excessive number of errors.
   c. It enables multiple nodes on the network to transmit data simultaneously.
   d. It enables one node on the network to transmit data at any one time.

4. **A modern day Token Ring network actually uses which of the following hybrid topologies?**
   a. star-bus
   b. ring-bus
   c. ring-tree
   d. star-ring

5. **In how many directions is data transmitted on a ring network?**
   a. one
   b. two
   c. It depends on the number of nodes on the network.
   d. It depends on the location of the nodes on the network.

6. **What would happen to the entire network if one of the nodes in a simple ring network failed?**
   a. Performance over the entire network would suffer slightly.
   b. The failed node would be affected, but other nodes would be fine.
   c. Data would no longer be transmitted to or from any nodes.
   d. Errors would be broadcast to every node.

7. **What type of terminator is used on a ring network?**
   a. 20-ohm resistor
   b. 50-ohm resistor
   c. 20-ohm transistor
   d. Terminators are not used on ring networks.

## 1.1 Recognize the following logical or physical network topologies given a schematic diagram or description (continued):

### WIRELESS PHYSICAL TOPOLOGY

### UNDERSTANDING THE OBJECTIVE

Wireless network devices, which can interconnect with wire-bound networks, are represented on a network diagram by an antenna radiating concentric waves from one point to many points.

### WHAT YOU REALLY NEED TO KNOW

◆ Nodes on a wireless network use special NICs with infrared or radio frequency transmitters (typically internal antennae) to issue signals to a base station.

◆ A wireless device's base station, or access point, allows it to connect and communicate with wire-bound devices on a LAN, such as servers and hubs.

◆ The use of base stations allows clients with wireless NICs to roam. Thus, the client does not have a static physical location on the network, as a node on a wire-bound network would have.

◆ When a large number of mobile clients are used, or when clients must communicate over a large geographical range, the number of access points must increase.

◆ When using base stations, nodes transmit signals in a broadcast fashion in order to ensure that the base station receives them. On a network diagram, this may be represented by an antenna radiating concentric waves from one point to many other points.

◆ Broadcast transmission is susceptible to eavesdropping. Thus, security is a concern in wireless networking. Using spread-spectrum radio frequency transmission is one way of improving wireless communications security.

◆ In some cases, wireless nodes may communicate directly with each other. By communicating directly, the nodes avoiding having to transmit first to a base station, then relying on the base station to repeat signals to another access point on the LAN.

◆ Wireless standards currently support data throughput at both 1 Mbps and 2 Mbps. At the 1 Mbps wireless data rate, it is possible to transmit over a greater range with less total throughput. At the 2 Mbps wireless data rate, it is possible to achieve greater throughput within a smaller range.

### OBJECTIVES ON THE JOB

If you are installing or maintaining a wireless network, be certain to understand the nature of atmospheric transmission as well as the type of mobility your clients will require. This will help you determine the quantity and positioning of base stations in the network's topology.

# PRACTICE TEST QUESTIONS

1. Which of the following networks could integrate wireless devices?
   - a. Token Ring
   - b. 10BaseT
   - c. 100BaseT
   - d. all of the above

2. What is required for a NIC to transmit to a base station?
   - a. RJ-45 connector
   - b. vampire tap
   - c. antenna
   - d. multiplexer

3. As the distance between wireless mobile users and a wire-bound connectivity device increases,
   - a. the necessary quantity of base stations also increases.
   - b. the possibility for eavesdropping on its signals also increases.
   - c. the power required by the wireless node's NIC also increases.
   - d. the possibility for incorrect data delivery also increases.

4. What is another term for a base station?
   - a. antenna
   - b. RF generator
   - c. CSU/DSU
   - d. access point

5. Rather than using a base station, a wireless node may communicate directly with another wireless node. True or false?

6. Which of the following data transmission methods does a wireless NIC use?
   - a. duplex
   - b. point-to-point
   - c. broadcast
   - d. unicast

7. Which IEEE committee has specified standards for wireless LANs?
   - a. 802.2
   - b. 802.3
   - c. 802.10
   - d. 802.11

## 1.2 Specify the main features of networking technologies, including speed, access, method, topology, and media:

### 802.2 (LLC)

### UNDERSTANDING THE OBJECTIVE

Everything in the networking field, from hardware to protocols, relies on standards to ensure that components from different manufacturers can be easily integrated. IEEE is the body that sets standards at the Physical and Data Link layers of the OSI Model for computer networking. The most well-known IEEE standards are those set by the 802 Committee.

### WHAT YOU REALLY NEED TO KNOW

- The **Institute of Electrical and Electronic Engineers (IEEE)**, or "I-triple-E," is an international society composed of engineering professionals. It maintains a standards board that establishes its own standards for the electronics and computer industry and contributes to other standards-setting bodies, such as ANSI.

- IEEE's committees set standards that apply to different layers of the OSI Model, including the Physical and Data Link layers, and therefore correspond to different network access methods and network media.

- The most well-known IEEE committee is the 802 committee. Among its popular standards are 802.3, which governs Ethernet networks; 802.5, which governs Token Ring networks; and 802.11, which governs wireless networks.

- To accommodate shared access for multiple network nodes (as opposed to simple point-to-point communication), the IEEE expanded the OSI Model by separating the Data Link layer into two sublayers: the Logical Link Control (LLC) sublayer and the Media Access Control (MAC) sublayer.

- The 802.2 standards apply to the **Logical Link Control sublayer (LLC)**, the upper sublayer in the Data Link layer, which provides a common interface and supplies reliability and flow control services.

- The **Media Access Control (MAC)** sublayer, the lower sublayer within the Data Link layer, appends the physical address of the destination to data frames.

- IEEE's specifications for Ethernet (802.3) and Token Ring (802.5) technology apply to the MAC sublayer of the Data Link layer. Thus, the 802.2 standards are independent but work in tandem with the 802.3 and 802.5 specifications.

### OBJECTIVES ON THE JOB

All modern networks rely on the foundation of 802.2 LLC standards in order to frame data and ensure reliable delivery. You should be aware of how these standards are applied in your particular network, whether it uses Ethernet or Token Ring MAC sublayer standards.

# PRACTICE TEST QUESTIONS

1. **The 802.2 standards apply to what sublayer of the Data Link layer?**
   a. the MAC sublayer
   b. the Logical Link Control sublayer
   c. the Access Method sublayer
   d. the Network Transmission sublayer

2. **To which other standards body does IEEE contribute its recommendations?**
   a. ISO
   b. OSI
   c. ITU
   d. ANSI

3. **In what year was the IEEE 802 committee formed?**
   a. 1980
   b. 1990
   c. 1995
   d. 1998

4. **Which of the following MAC sublayer specifications can work with the 802.2 sublayer specification? Choose all that apply.**
   a. 802.2
   b. 802.3
   c. 802.5
   d. 802.15

5. **Which of the following functions is handled by the 802.2 sublayer?**
   a. issuing electrical signals onto the wire
   b. appending a physical address to a data frame
   c. appending a logical address to a data frame
   d. ensuring appropriate flow control for a group of data frames

6. **The 802.2 specifications apply to the lower sublayer of the Data Link layer of the OSI Model. True or false?**

7. **What was the primary reason the IEEE divided the OSI Model's Data Link layer into two sublayers?**
   a. to account for the variety of functions required for point-to-point data communication
   b. to simplify the process of ensuring proper addressing between sending and receiving nodes
   c. to better articulate the difference between transmission and reception
   d. to accommodate evolving encryption techniques

## 1.2 Specify the main features of networking technologies, including speed, access, method, topology, and media (continued):

### 802.3 (ETHERNET)

### UNDERSTANDING THE OBJECTIVE

IEEE 802.3 standards specify the MAC sublayer requirements for Ethernet standards, including its network access method, Carrier Sense Multiple Access/Collision Detection (CSMA/CD), which allows multiple nodes to share a single channel on an Ethernet network.

### WHAT YOU REALLY NEED TO KNOW

◆ The 802.3 standards define elements of Ethernet networks in the MAC sublayer (of the Data Link layer)

◆ 802.3 specifies the **Carrier Sense Multiple Access/Collision Detection (CSMA/CD)** method of network access, allowing multiple nodes to share a single Ethernet channel.

◆ The term "Carrier Sense" refers to the fact that Ethernet NICs listen on the network and wait until they detect (or sense) that no other nodes are transmitting data over the signal (or carrier) on the communications channel before they begin to transmit. The term "Multiple Access" refers to the fact that several Ethernet nodes can be connected to a network and can monitor traffic, or access the media, simultaneously.

◆ In CSMA/CD, when a node wants to transmit data, it must first access the transmission media and determine whether the channel is free. If the channel is not free, it waits and checks again after a random (but brief) amount of time. If the channel is free, the node transmits its data.

◆ If two nodes simultaneously check the channel, determine that it's free, and begin to transmit, their two transmissions will interfere with each other; this is known as a **collision**. In this event, the network performs a series of steps known as the collision detection routine. If a station's NIC determines that its data has been involved in a collision, it will first propagate the collision throughout the network by using a **jamming** signal, ensuring that no other station attempts to transmit. Then the NIC remains silent for a random period of time. After waiting, the node will determine if the line is again available; if it is available, the line will retransmit its data.

◆ IEEE's 802.3 standards apply to all wire-based Ethernet network types, including 10Base2, 10Base5, 10BaseT, 100BaseT, and Gigabit Ethernet. These networks may use bus, star, or star-wired bus physical topologies.

### OBJECTIVES ON THE JOB

Since the IEEE 802.3 standard forms the basis of the most popular networks in use today, you should be thoroughly familiar with its specifications. In particular, you should understand CSMA/CD, its advantages and disadvantages, and how it pertains to network performance on both 10BaseT and Fast Ethernet networks.

# PRACTICE TEST QUESTIONS

1. **Which network access method is defined by IEEE 802.3?**
    a. CSMA/CA
    b. demand priority
    c. token passing
    d. CSMA/CD

2. **A network that follows 802.3 specifications would use which of the following topologies? Choose all that apply.**
    a. bus
    b. star
    c. ring
    d. cube

3. **At what sublayer of the Data Link layer do 802.3 standards operate?**
    a. MMC sublayer
    b. LLC sublayer
    c. MAC sublayer
    d. Ethernet sublayer

4. **In the network access method specified by 802.3, which of the following are likely to occur?**
    a. collisions
    b. sags
    c. multiplexing
    d. token arbitrations

5. **What network component is responsible for applying 802.3 standards to an electrical signal?**
    a. RJ-45 connector
    b. AUI connector
    c. NIC
    d. multimeter

6. **Which of the following networks would use 802.3 standards? Choose all that apply.**
    a. 10BaseT
    b. 10Base5
    c. 100BaseVG-AnyLAN
    d. 100BaseT

7. **At what data transmission speed is a modern 802.3-based network likely to run?**
    a. 1 Mbps
    b. 4 Mbps
    c. 16 Mbps
    d. 100 Mbps

## 1.2   Specify the main features of networking technologies, including speed, access, method, topology, and media (continued):

### 802.5 (TOKEN RING)

### UNDERSTANDING THE OBJECTIVE

IEEE 802.5 specifications describe the MAC sublayer elements of Token Ring networks, including its network access method known as token passing.

### WHAT YOU REALLY NEED TO KNOW

◆ The 802.5 standards define the MAC sublayer (of the Data Link layer) elements of networks using the Token Ring transmission method.

◆ Traditional Token Ring networks transmit data at either 4 Mbps or 16 Mbps over shielded or unshielded twisted-pair wiring.

◆ The 100 Mbps Token Ring standard, finalized in 1999, is known as **high-speed Token Ring (HSTR)**. HSTR can use either twisted-pair or fiber-optic cable as its transmission medium. While it is as reliable and efficient as Fast Ethernet, it is less common because of its more costly implementation.

◆ Token Ring networks use the token-passing network access method and a star-ring hybrid physical topology.

◆ According to the 802.5 standards, on a Token Ring network, one workstation, called the active monitor, acts as the controller for token passing. Specifically, the **active monitor** maintains the timing for ring passing, monitors token and frame transmission, detects lost tokens, and corrects errors when a timing error or other disruption occurs. Only one workstation on the ring can act as the active monitor at any given time.

◆ In token passing, a 3-byte token circulates around the network. When a station has something to send, it picks up the token, changes it to a frame, and then adds the header, information, and trailer fields. Each node reads the frame as it traverses the ring to determine whether it is the intended recipient. If a node is the recipient, it picks up the data, then retransmits the frame to the next node on the ring. When the frame reaches the originating station, it reissues a free token that can then be reused.

◆ The token-passing control scheme ensures high data reliability (no collisions) and an efficient use of bandwidth. It also does not impose distance limitations on the length of a LAN segment, unlike CSMA/CD.

### OBJECTIVES ON THE JOB

In the early 1990s, the Token Ring architecture competed strongly with Ethernet to be the most popular logical topology. Since that time, the economics, speed, and reliability of Ethernet have greatly improved, making Token Ring seem less desirable. Thus, you are much more likely to work with Ethernet networks than Token Ring networks.

# PRACTICE TEST QUESTIONS

1. **Which of the following data transmission speeds would be used on 802.5 networks? Choose all that apply.**
   a. 1 Mbps
   b. 4 Mbps
   c. 10 Mbps
   d. 16 Mbps

2. **What network access method is specified by the 802.5 standard?**
   a. CSMA/CA
   b. demand priority
   c. token-passing
   d. CSMA/CD

3. **What type of media could be used by a network that relies on the 802.5 standard? Choose all that apply.**
   a. coaxial cable
   b. UTP
   c. STP
   d. single-mode fiber

4. **At which sublayer of the Data Link layer do 802.5 standards operate?**
   a. MMC sublayer
   b. MAC sublayer
   c. LLC sublayer
   d. TMC sublayer

5. **What network component is responsible for applying 802.5 standards to an electrical signal?**
   a. RJ-45 connector
   b. AUI connector
   c. cabling
   d. NIC

6. **Why is the 802.3 standard more popular than the 802.5 standard?**
   a. The 802.3 standard is more reliable than the 802.5 standard.
   b. The 802.3 standard is not subject to collisions and, therefore, suffers less data corruption than the 802.5 standard.
   c. The 802.3 standard can offer greater speed at lower overall cost than can the 802.5 standard.
   d. The 802.3 standard is more compatible with evolving security standards than the 802.5 standard.

7. **What type of topology would be used on an 802.5 network?**
   a. bus
   b. star-wired bus
   c. star-wired ring
   d. cube

## 1.2   Specify the main features of networking technologies, including speed, access, method, topology, and media (continued):

### 802.11B (WIRELESS)

### UNDERSTANDING THE OBJECTIVE

The purpose of the IEEE 802.11b standard is to provide a wireless connectivity system that standardizes access to one or more frequency bands for LAN communications. Wireless standards were first proposed by IEEE in 1997 with the aim of facilitating interoperability between different manufacturers' wireless networking devices.

### WHAT YOU REALLY NEED TO KNOW

◆ The IEEE 802.11b standard defines protocols necessary for atmospheric-based transmission between nodes on a LAN. As with 802.3 and 802.5, the 802.11b specifications apply to data transmissions between the MAC sublayer and the LLC sublayer of the Data Link layer.

◆ Typically, wireless LAN communication is issued by a radio NIC to an access point, such as a base station. Application of the 802.11b standard takes place at the NIC.

◆ The 802.11b standard supports the continuation of service according to other MAC sublayer standards, such as Ethernet (802.3). This enables those parts of a LAN that rely on wireless transmission to connect with a wire-based Ethernet LAN, for example.

◆ Wireless standards are designed to be used within buildings, such as warehouses, hospitals, office buildings, malls, and residences. The 802.11b specifications are particular to LANs, but may be used in small WANs, such as outdoor parks.

◆ Wireless LANs transmit data across a broad area (unlike wire-bound LANs). Therefore, data privacy is a concern with this type of transmission. Using spread-spectrum radio frequency and standard security measures addresses this concern.

◆ The 802.11b standard uses the **Carrier Sense Multiple Access/Collision Avoidance (CSMA/CA)** network access method, not CSMA/CD, as in Ethernet. Nodes using CSMA/CA signal their intent to transmit before actually doing so. In this way, collisions and the need for data retransmittals are (mostly) avoided.

◆ A spectrum range of 2.4 gigahertz (GHz) is used for 802.11b spread spectrum transmission. This band was selected because it is available license-free in most parts of the world.

◆ Data are transmitted at either 1, 2, or 11 Mbps using the 802.11b standards.

### OBJECTIVES ON THE JOB

Although IEEE's 802.11 standards have been established for some years, wireless networking equipment is still evolving. When specifying or purchasing such equipment, be certain that it is 802.11b-compliant and interoperable with your existing network components.

# PRACTICE TEST QUESTIONS

1. **What networking component is responsible for applying 802.11b standards to an electrical signal?**
   a. NIC
   b. portal
   c. base station
   d. antenna

2. **Which of the following media is the least secure?**
   a. fiber-optic cable
   b. UTP
   c. direct infrared
   d. spread-spectrum RF

3. **A modern wireless LAN is most likely to transmit data at which of the following speeds?**
   a. 2 Mbps
   b. 25 Mbps
   c. 16 Mbps
   d. 100 Mbps

4. **Which radio frequency band is specified for use by the 802.11b standard?**
   a. 1.5 GHz
   b. 2.4 GHz
   c. 5.5 GHz
   d. 6.2 GHz

5. **Which of the following network access methods do 802.11b devices use?**
   a. CSMA/CA
   b. demand priority
   c. token-passing
   d. CSMA/CD

6. **In which of the following situations would the use of 802.11b standards be most appropriate?**
   a. a WAN that connects 25 university department buildings
   b. a LAN that connects 50 inventory control personnel in a warehouse to a database server
   c. a WAN that connects 120 mobile sales people with their corporate headquarters
   d. a MAN that connects four bank branches across a large metropolitan area

7. **At what layer of the OSI Model do 802.11b standards operate?**
   a. Physical layer
   b. Data Link layer
   c. Network layer
   d. Transport layer

## 1.2 Specify the main features of networking technologies, including speed, access, method, topology, and media (continued):

### FDDI

### UNDERSTANDING THE OBJECTIVE

Fiber Distributed Data Interface (FDDI) is a logical topology whose standard was originally specified by ANSI in the mid-1980s. It uses a double fiber-optic ring to transmit data at speeds of up to 100 Mbps.

### WHAT YOU REALLY NEED TO KNOW

◆ **FDDI (Fiber Distributed Data Interface)** is a logical topology whose standard was originally specified by ANSI in the mid-1980s and later refined by ISO.

◆ FDDI ( pronounced "fiddy") uses a double ring of multimode or single-mode fiber to transmit data at speeds of up to 100 Mbps.

◆ FDDI was developed in response to the throughput limitations of Ethernet and Token Ring technologies used at the time. In fact, FDDI was the first network transport system to reach the 100 Mbps threshold. For this reason, you will frequently find it supporting network backbones that were installed in the late 1980s and early 1990s.

◆ A popular implementation of FDDI involves connecting LANs located in multiple buildings, such as those on college campuses. FDDI links can span distances as large as 62 miles.

◆ Because Ethernet technologies have developed faster transmission speeds and are more compatible with other existing network technologies, FDDI is no longer the much-coveted technology that it was in the 1980s.

◆ Its reliance on fiber-optic cable ensures that FDDI is more reliable and more secure than transmission methods that depend on copper wiring. Another advantage of FDDI is that it works well with Ethernet 100BaseTX technology.

◆ One drawback to FDDI technology is its high cost relative to Fast Ethernet (costing up to 10 times more per switch port than Fast Ethernet).

◆ FDDI is based on a ring physical topology similar to a Token Ring network. It also relies on the same token-passing routine that Token Ring networks use. However, unlike Token Ring technology, FDDI runs on two complete rings. During normal operation, the primary FDDI ring carries data, while the secondary ring is idle. The secondary ring will assume data transmission responsibilities should the primary ring experience Physical layer problems.

### OBJECTIVES ON THE JOB

If you work on a university or other campus-wide network, you may be required to work with FDDI technology. FDDI is a separate standard from Ethernet or Token Ring, and as such, it uses different network access methods, connectivity equipment, and signaling techniques.

# PRACTICE TEST QUESTIONS

1. **On what type of physical topology is a FDDI network based?**
   - a. star
   - b. ring
   - c. bus
   - d. tree

2. **Why is FDDI considered more reliable than Ethernet or Token Ring?**
   - a. It uses more sophisticated error-checking protocols.
   - b. It uses more reliable sequencing and flow-control techniques.
   - c. It is designed to better withstand data collisions.
   - d. It uses duplicate sets of transmission media.

3. **On which of the following networks is FDDI most likely to be found today?**
   - a. a VPN that connects 120 satellite sales offices with a company's headquarters
   - b. a LAN that connects 200 workstations, 5 servers, and 15 printers within an office building
   - c. a WAN that connects seven manufacturing plants across the nation
   - d. a WAN that connects 18 buildings on a college campus

4. **Which of the following agencies originally specified the FDDI standard?**
   - a. ANSI
   - b. IEEE
   - c. ISO
   - d. ITU

5. **Which of the following network technologies is the most compatible with FDDI?**
   - a. 10Base2
   - b. 10Base5
   - c. 10BaseT
   - d. 100BaseFX

6. **Why is Ethernet preferred over FDDI for modern networks?**
   - a. It can achieve faster throughput at lower overall cost.
   - b. It works better with today's popular TCP/IP protocol.
   - c. It is more reliable.
   - d. It is better suited for evolving security measures.

7. **Which of the following would be found on a FDDI network?**
   - a. collisions
   - b. tokens
   - c. amplifiers
   - d. vampire taps

## 1.3   Specify the characteristics (e.g., speed, length, topology, cable type, etc.) of the following technologies:

### 802.3 (ETHERNET) STANDARDS

### UNDERSTANDING THE OBJECTIVE

The Ethernet (802.3) standard, including the specification of CSMA/CD as a network access method, applies to several types of networks, including 10Base2, 10Base5, 10BaseT, 100BaseT, and 100BaseF.

### WHAT YOU REALLY NEED TO KNOW

◆ All types of wire-bound Ethernet use the CSMA/CD network access method.

◆ 10Base2 (Thinnet) and 10Base5 (Thicknet) versions of Ethernet use coaxial cable and rely on the bus physical topology. Both are capable of transmitting data up to 10 Mbps.

◆ 10BaseT is a standard that uses unshielded twisted-pair wiring, uses a star-based physical topology, and is capable of transmitting data at a maximum speed of 10 Mbps.

◆ 10BaseT networks may connect up to five network segments with up to four connectivity devices. Only three of the connected segments can contain hosts. The maximum segment length on a 10BaseT network is 100 meters.

◆ 100BaseT is a standard that uses unshielded twisted-pair or fiber-optic cable in a star-wired bus physical topology and is capable of transmitting data at a maximum speed of 100 Mbps. 100BaseT comes in at least two varieties: 100BaseTX and 100Base4.

◆ **100BaseTX** achieves its speed by sending the signal 10 times faster and condensing the time between digital pulses as well as the time a station must wait and listen for a signal. 100BaseTX requires Category 5 or higher unshielded twisted-pair cabling. 100BaseTX is capable of full duplexing.

◆ **100BaseT4** is different from 100BaseTX in that it uses all four pairs of wires in a UTP cable, and therefore it can use Category 3 wiring. It breaks the 100 Mbps data stream into three streams of 33 Mbps each. These three streams are sent over three wire pairs. The fourth wire pair is used for signaling. Because 100BaseT4 technology uses all four wire pairs for unidirectional signaling, it cannot support full duplexing.

◆ **100BaseFX** is a version of Ethernet that uses fiber-optic cable as its transmission medium. 100BaseFX and 100BaseT, both of which are considered **Fast Ethernet**, may coexist on the same network.

### OBJECTIVES ON THE JOB

On any modern network, you will probably find some type of Ethernet technology. You should be familiar with the differences between Ethernet versions, and most importantly, which versions are incompatible with one another.

# PRACTICE TEST QUESTIONS

1. **Which of the following Ethernet technologies can transmit data at no more than 10 Mbps? Choose all that apply.**
   a. 10BaseT
   b. 100BaseT
   c. 10Base2
   d. 100BaseFX

2. **Which of the following Ethernet technologies uses CSMA/CD?**
   a. 10Base5
   b. 10BaseT
   c. 100BaseTX
   d. all of the above

3. **Which of the following share the same maximum segment length?**
   a. 10Base2 and 10Base5
   b. 10BaseT and 10BaseF
   c. 10BaseT and 100BaseT
   d. 100BaseT and 100BaseFX

4. **Which of the following Ethernet technologies uses coaxial cable? Choose all that apply.**
   a. 10Base2
   b. 10Base5
   c. 10BaseT
   d. 100BaseFX

5. **Which of the following Ethernet technologies uses a star-wired bus physical topology? Choose all that apply.**
   a. 10Base2
   b. 10Base5
   c. 10BaseT
   d. 100BaseFX

6. **Which of the following IEEE standards specifies CSMA/CD?**
   a. 802.2
   b. 802.3
   c. 802.5
   d. 802.11

7. **Which of the following differentiate 100BaseTX and 100BaseT4? Choose all that apply.**
   a. their network access method
   b. their maximum throughput
   c. the number of wire pairs they utilize
   d. their method of achieving faster throughput

## 1.3   Specify the characteristics (e.g., speed, length, topology, cable type, etc.) of the following technologies (continued):

### 10BASET

### UNDERSTANDING THE OBJECTIVE

10BaseT is an Ethernet specification that uses baseband transmission and enables data rates of up to 10 Mbps. 10BaseT networks can use unshielded or shielded twisted-pair cable, both of which require RJ-45 connectors. 10BaseT is limited to a maximum segment length of 100 meters and uses a star topology.

### WHAT YOU REALLY NEED TO KNOW

◆ **10BaseT** uses baseband transmission (thus the "Base" in its name) and twisted-pair cabling (thus, the letter "T" in its name) and a star topology to transmit data at 10 Mbps (thus, the "10" in its name).

◆ As with all Ethernet networks, 10BaseT follows a set of communication rules called Carrier Sense Multiple Access with Collision Detection (CSMA/CD). CSMA/CD allows multiple nodes to share one data channel while minimizing the possibilities for data collisions.

◆ 10BaseT networks use unshielded twisted pair, including Category 3, 4, 5, and higher cables. Unshielded twisted pair is the same kind of wiring used for telephone connections, and for this reason, 10BaseT networks historically fit well into an organization's existing physical infrastructure.

◆ Nodes on a 10BaseT Ethernet network connect to a central hub or repeater in a star fashion. Typical of a star topology, a single network cable only connects two devices. This characteristic makes 10BaseT networks more fault tolerant than 10Base2 or 10Base5, which use the bus topology.

◆ Because 10BaseT networks use a star topology, they are easier to troubleshoot than 10Base2 or 10Base5 networks, because you can better isolate problems.

◆ Each node on a 10BaseT network uses RJ-45 connectors to connect the network cable with the NIC at the workstation end and with the hub at the network end.

◆ The maximum distance a 10BaseT segment can traverse is 100 meters.

◆ 10BaseT networks can contain up to five sequential segments connected by four hubs or switches.

### OBJECTIVES ON THE JOB

Modern networks often can use both 10BaseT and 100BaseT on the same network. Bear in mind that all NICs and ports on such connectivity devices as routers or hubs must be compatible with the transmission technology your network uses (such as 10BaseT). Even if your network runs only 10BaseT now, it is wise to purchase devices that can automatically sense whether the network is running 10BaseT or 100BaseT and then adjust to that rate.

# PRACTICE TEST QUESTIONS

1. **What is the maximum segment length for a 10BaseT network?**
   a. 100 meters
   b. 85 meters
   c. 10 meters
   d. 10 feet

2. **Which two of the following types of wiring might a 10BaseT network use?**
   a. CAT5
   b. CAT3
   c. CAT2
   d. CAT1

3. **What does the "Base" in 10BaseT represent?**
   a. basic
   b. basal
   c. base 10
   d. baseband

4. **What kind of connector is used in a 10BaseT network?**
   a. BNC
   b. AUI
   c. RJ-45
   d. RJ-52

5. **On what topology are 10BaseT networks based?**
   a. bus
   b. star
   c. ring
   d. mesh

6. **What other technology can run on the same network with 10BaseT technology?**
   a. 10Base2
   b. 10Base5
   c. 100BaseT
   d. Gigabit Ethernet

7. **What is the maximum throughput of a 10BaseT network?**
   a. 10 Kbps
   b. 10 Mbps
   c. 10 Gbps
   d. 10 Tbps

### 1.3 Specify the characteristics (e.g., speed, length, topology, cable type, etc.) of the following technologies (continued):

#### 100BASET AND 100BASETX

### UNDERSTANDING THE OBJECTIVE

100BaseT is an Ethernet transmission technology that can achieve data rates up to 100 Mbps. The most popular version of 100BaseT is the 100BaseTX specification, which can be easily added to an existing 10BaseT network and can take advantage of full duplexing.

### WHAT YOU REALLY NEED TO KNOW

- ◆ **100BaseT** is specified in the IEEE 802.3 (Ethernet) standard. It uses baseband transmission (thus the "Base" in its name) and twisted-pair cabling (thus, the letter "T" in its name) and transmits data at 100 Mbps (thus, the "100" in its name).
- ◆ 100BaseT relies on a star-wired bus or hierarchical topology, just like 10BaseT.
- ◆ For best performance, 100BaseT requires CAT5 or better twisted-pair cabling with RJ-45 data connectors.
- ◆ 100BaseT upgrades can be easy and inexpensive to accomplish for an organization that currently uses the popular 10BaseT technology.
- ◆ The length between a node and its hub for 100BaseT networks cannot exceed 100 meters.
- ◆ Because of the speed on a 100BaseT network, the window of time for the NIC to detect and compensate for errors is very small. To minimize undetected collisions, 100BaseT buses can only practically support a maximum of three network segments connected with two hubs.
- ◆ **100BaseTX** is the most popular version of 100BaseT, largely because it is compatible with technology used for 10BaseT and therefore requires little investment to upgrade.
- ◆ 100BaseTX uses two of the four wire pairs in a CAT5 or better cable and is capable of full-duplexing.
- ◆ 100BaseTX sends signals 10 times faster than a 10BaseT network and condenses the time between digital pulses, as well as the time a station is required to wait and listen in CSMA/CD.
- ◆ 100BaseT and 100BaseTX may also be called **Fast Ethernet**.

### OBJECTIVES ON THE JOB

The most popular form of fast LAN transmission technology in use today is 100BaseTX, a variation of the 100BaseT Ethernet standard. It is likely that 100BaseTX will continue to be preferred. Eventually, Fast Ethernet technologies will likely be replaced by Gigabit Ethernet, which is capable of data transmission rates up to 1 Gbps.

# PRACTICE TEST QUESTIONS

1. **What is the maximum number of segments that can be connected in serial on a 100BaseT network?**
   a. two
   b. three
   c. four
   d. five

2. **Why has 100BaseTX become the most popular form of Fast Ethernet?**
   a. Its transmission methods are more sophisticated than other forms of Fast Ethernet.
   b. It provides better security than other forms of Fast Ethernet.
   c. It requires minimal investment to upgrade to 100BaseTX from the popular 10BaseT technology.
   d. It relies on the ring topology, which is already popular in most organizations.

3. **What is the maximum segment length on a 100BaseTX network?**
   a. 10 meters
   b. 85 meters
   c. 100 meters
   d. 185 meters

4. **Which of the following network access methods is used by 100BaseT?**
   a. demand priority
   b. CSMA/CA
   c. CSMA/CD
   d. token-passing

5. **What type of connector is used on a 100BaseT network?**
   a. RJ-11
   b. RJ-45
   c. AUI
   d. SC

6. **Which two of the following cable types could be used for a 100BaseTX network?**
   a. CAT7
   b. CAT5e
   c. CAT3
   d. CAT1

7. **How many wire pairs does the 100BaseTX standard require?**
   a. one
   b. two
   c. four
   d. eight

## 1.3 Specify the characteristics (e.g., speed, length, topology, cable type, etc.) of the following technologies (continued):

### 10BASE2

### UNDERSTANDING THE OBJECTIVE

10Base2 is a form of Ethernet network that provides 10 Mbps throughput over coaxial cabling. Also known as Thin Ethernet, or "Thinnet," 10Base2 was popular for LANs in the 1980s but has largely been replaced by more modern Ethernet technologies (such as 10BaseT or 100BaseT) that require less expense, afford simpler installation, and rely on more scalable topologies.

### WHAT YOU REALLY NEED TO KNOW

- ◆ IEEE has designated **Thinnet** as **10Base2** Ethernet. The "10" represents its data transmission rate of 10 Mbps, "Base" stands for baseband transmission, and "2" represents its maximum segment length of 185 (or roughly 200) meters.
- ◆ Thinnet's sheath is typically black, and its cable diameter is approximately 0.64 cm. It is more flexible and easier to handle than Thicknet.
- ◆ Because of its black sheath, Thinnet may also be called "black Ethernet."
- ◆ Thinnet usually connects the wire to network devices with BNC T connectors. A BNC connector with three open ends attaches to the NIC at the base of the "T" while attaching to the Thinnet cable at its two sides. BNC barrel connectors (with only two open ends) are used to join two Thinnet cable segments.
- ◆ Like Thicknet, Thinnet relies on the bus topology and therefore requires terminators to avoid signal bounce.
- ◆ Thinnet can accommodate a maximum of 30 nodes per segment. Its total maximum network length is just over 550 meters.
- ◆ To minimize interference, devices on a Thinnet network should be separated by at least 0.5 m.
- ◆ Because of its insulation and shielding, Thinnet is more resistant to noise than twisted-pair wiring. However, it is not as resistant as Thicknet.
- ◆ Thinnet is less expensive than Thicknet and fiber-optic cable, but it is more expensive than twisted-pair wiring. For this reason, Thinnet is sometimes called "cheapernet."

### OBJECTIVES ON THE JOB

Thinnet is occasionally used on modern networks, but more often you will see it on networks installed in the 1980s. The major advantages to Thinnet are its very low cost and ease of use. If you work with Thinnet, pay particular attention to the restrictions of its bus topology, including the need for terminators and the practical drawbacks of having all nodes share a single channel.

## PRACTICE TEST QUESTIONS

1. **In the IEEE designation 10Base2, what does the 2 represent?**
   - a. 2 feet
   - b. 2 Mbps
   - c. 200 feet
   - d. 185 meters

2. **What color is typically used for the sheath of a Thinnet cable?**
   - a. yellow
   - b. black
   - c. green
   - d. red

3. **What is a BNC barrel connector used for?**
   - a. connecting a Thinnet workstation to the network
   - b. connecting a Thicknet workstation to the network
   - c. connecting two Thinnet cable segments
   - d. connecting a Thinnet segment to a Thicknet segment

4. **What is the maximum throughput on a Thinnet network?**
   - a. 1 Mbps
   - b. 4 Mbps
   - c. 10 Mbps
   - d. 100 Mbps

5. **On what physical topology does 10Base2 depend?**
   - a. bus
   - b. ring
   - c. star
   - d. mesh

6. **Why is the maximum segment length for Thicknet longer than for Thinnet?**
   - a. Thicknet is more noise-resistant than Thinnet.
   - b. Thicknet is more flexible than Thinnet.
   - c. Thicknet has a higher throughput than Thinnet.
   - d. Thicknet is more heat-resistant than Thinnet.

7. **On a 10Base2 network, how many nodes share one signal channel?**
   - a. one
   - b. two
   - c. four
   - d. all connected nodes

## 1.3   Specify the characteristics (e.g., speed, length, topology, cable type, etc.) of the following technologies (continued):

### 10BASE5

### UNDERSTANDING THE OBJECTIVE

10Base5 is another form of Ethernet that provides 10 Mbps throughput over coaxial cabling. Prior to the acceptance of Thinnet, many LANs used the 10Base5 standard, also known as Thick Ethernet, or Thicknet.

### WHAT YOU REALLY NEED TO KNOW

◆ **Thicknet** cabling is a rigid coaxial cable, approximately 1 cm thick, used for the original Ethernet networks. Because it is often covered with a yellow sheath, it may be called "yellow Ethernet."

◆ IEEE designates Thicknet as **10Base5** Ethernet. The "10" represents its throughput of 10 Mbps, the "Base" stands for baseband transmission, and the "5" represents the maximum segment length of a Thicknet cable, 500 meters.

◆ To minimize the possibility of interference between stations, network devices on a Thicknet network should be separated by at least 2.5 m.

◆ Thicknet is less expensive than fiber-optic cable but more expensive than twisted-pair cable. It is also more expensive than other types of coaxial cabling, such as Thinnet, because it contains more materials.

◆ Thicknet requires a combination of a vampire tap to connect to a transceiver on the backbone plus a drop cable to connect network devices.

◆ In Thicknet, the port on the device's NIC is connected with the drop cable via either an AUI connector or an n-series connector (or n-connector).

◆ **AUI (Attachment Unit Interface)** is an Ethernet standard that establishes physical specifications for connecting coaxial cables with transceivers and networked nodes.

◆ An **n-connector** uses a screw-and-barrel arrangement to securely connect coaxial cable segments and devices.

◆ Thicknet can accommodate a maximum of 100 nodes per segment. Its total maximum network length is 1500 meters. Thicknet's high resistance to noise allows its transmissions to travel longer distances without repeating than Thinnet.

### OBJECTIVES ON THE JOB

If you are working with Thicknet, you should be familiar with its unique connectors, including AUI connectors, vampire taps, and n-connectors. You should also be aware that Thicknet is the least flexible networking medium, and as a result, it may present unique installation challenges. However, Thicknet is rarely used on modern networks, and it is unlikely that you will ever need to work with it.

## PRACTICE TEST QUESTIONS

1. **What is the maximum throughput on a Thicknet network?**
   a. 1 Mbps
   b. 10 Mbps
   c. 100 Mbps
   d. 1 Gbps

2. **In the IEEE designation 10Base5, what does the "5" represent?**
   a. 5 meters
   b. 5 feet
   c. 50 meters
   d. 500 meters

3. **What two elements of a Thicknet network does a drop cable connect?**
   a. a network node and a transceiver
   b. a transceiver and the backbone
   c. a transceiver and a MAU
   d. a network node and another network node

4. **Based on its required medium, which of the following Ethernet technologies is the most expensive to install and maintain?**
   a. 10Base2
   b. 10Base5
   c. 10BaseT
   d. 100BaseFX

5. **On what type of physical topology does Thicknet depend?**
   a. bus
   b. star
   c. ring
   d. mesh

6. **Which of the following media is the most expensive?**
   a. Thicknet
   b. Thinnet
   c. UTP
   d. STP

7. **According to IEEE standards, what is the maximum number of nodes that can be connected to a Thicknet segment?**
   a. 10
   b. 50
   c. 100
   d. No limit is specified.

## 1.3 Specify the characteristics (e.g., speed, length, topology, cable type, etc.) of the following technologies (continued):

### 100BASEFX

### UNDERSTANDING THE OBJECTIVE

100BaseFX is another form of Fast Ethernet, or Ethernet that is capable of 100 Mbps throughput. Unlike 100BaseT, which uses unshielded twisted-pair cabling, 100BaseFX uses fiber-optic cable. It is an expensive but highly reliable and noise-resistant networking technology.

### WHAT YOU REALLY NEED TO KNOW

◆ The **100BaseFX** standard specifies a network capable of 100 Mbps throughput that uses baseband transmission and fiber-optic cabling.

◆ 100BaseFX requires multimode fiber containing at least two strands of fiber. One strand is used for data transmission, while the other strand is used for reception, making 100BaseFX a full-duplex technology.

◆ 100BaseFX networks require one of several types of connectors, including the two most popular connectors: SC and ST.

◆ Its maximum segment length is 400 meters, with a maximum of two repeaters allowed to connect segments.

◆ The 100BaseFX standard uses a star topology, with its repeaters connected through a bus. The use of a star topology makes this standard highly scalable and fault-tolerant.

◆ 100BaseFX, like 100BaseT, is also considered "Fast Ethernet."

◆ Organizations converting from UTP to fiber media can combine 100BaseTX and 100BaseFX within one network. For this to occur, connectivity devices must have both RJ-45 and SC or ST ports. Alternately, a 100BaseTX to 100BaseFX media converter may be used at any point in the network to interconnect the different media and convert the signals of one standard to signals that work with the other standard.

◆ Since fiber does not conduct electrical current to transmit signals, 100BaseFX is unaffected by either EMI or RFI.

◆ 100BaseFX is significantly more expensive than 100BaseT. Not only is the cable itself more expensive than twisted pair, but fiber-optic NICs and hubs can cost as much as five times more than NICs and hubs designed for UTP networks. In addition, hiring skilled fiber cable installers costs more than hiring twisted-pair cable installers.

### OBJECTIVES ON THE JOB

If you work on a network that uses 100BaseFX, chances are that some of the network (such as the backbone) uses this fiber-based technology, while other parts of the network (such as workstation connections) use the UTP-based 100BaseT technology. Thus, you should be familiar with integrating the different types of hardware required for these different Fast Ethernet standards.

# PRACTICE TEST QUESTIONS

1. **On what physical topology does the 100BaseFX standard depend?**
   a. bus
   b. ring
   c. star
   d. mesh

2. **Which of the following connectors could be used on a 100BaseFX network?**
   a. AUI
   b. RJ-11
   c. RJ-45
   d. SC

3. **What is the maximum segment length for a 100BaseFX network?**
   a. 200 meters
   b. 400 meters
   c. 1200 meters
   d. 2 miles

4. **How does a 100BaseFX network achieve full duplexing?**
   a. It multiplexes a single channel on one strand of fiber into multiple subchannels.
   b. It uses two fiber strands, one for transmission and one for reception.
   c. It relies on switching and routing equipment to arbitrate sessions and avoid collisions.
   d. It uses different encoding for each transmission, so multiple signals can be issued over the same strand of fiber.

5. **100BaseFX is most likely to coexist with what other Ethernet technology on the same network?**
   a. 10Base2
   b. 10Base5
   c. 10BaseT
   d. 100BaseT

6. **What is the single greatest disadvantage to using 100BaseFX?**
   a. It is expensive.
   b. It is not highly scalable.
   c. Its standards are not stable.
   d. It is less secure than other types of Ethernet networks.

7. **What type of fiber-optic cable is specified for use with 100BaseFX?**
   a. single-mode
   b. duplex-mode
   c. reverse-mode
   d. multimode

# OBJECTIVES

## 1.3 Specify the characteristics (e.g., speed, length, topology, cable type, etc.) of the following technologies (continued):

### GIGABIT ETHERNET

### UNDERSTANDING THE OBJECTIVE

As you would probably guess, the evolution of Ethernet has not stopped with the development of the 100 Mbps standard. Through its 802.3z project, IEEE established specifications for an Ethernet version that runs at 1000 Mbps, called 1 Gigabit Ethernet.

### WHAT YOU REALLY NEED TO KNOW

- ◆ **1 Gigabit Ethernet** can technically run over unshielded twisted-pair (UTP) cable, but it performs much better over multimode fiber.
- ◆ 1 Gigabit Ethernet is defined by IEEE's 802.3z committee.
- ◆ Though UTP is rare on 1 Gigabit Ethernet networks, a segment of 1 Gigabit Ethernet running on UTP can span a maximum of 100 meters.
- ◆ A segment of 1 Gigabit Ethernet running on fiber-optic cable can span a maximum of 550 meters.
- ◆ A Gigabit Ethernet network that uses fiber-optic cable requires either SC or ST connector types.
- ◆ Like Fast Ethernet, a fiber-based, 1 Gigabit Ethernet network uses the CSMA/CD network access method, relies on the star physical topology, and is capable of full duplexing.
- ◆ In March 1999, representatives from the networking industry began discussing a **10 Gigabit Ethernet** standard, which would provide 10,000 Mbps throughput. The standards for 10 Gigabit are currently being defined by the IEEE 802.3ae committee and will include full duplexing and multimode fiber requirements.
- ◆ IEEE aims to make the 10 Gigabit standard compatible with the Physical layer standards for 1 Gigabit Ethernet to allow organizations to easily upgrade their networks.
- ◆ The 1- and 10-Gigabit technologies compete directly with other fast networking solutions, such as Asynchronous Transfer Mode (ATM).

### OBJECTIVES ON THE JOB

You will most likely encounter 1 Gigabit Ethernet as part of a network's backbone. It is well suited to connecting multiple buildings on a single campus, for example. Currently, this scheme would not be appropriate for connecting workstations to hubs, for example, because workstations' NICs and CPUs could not process data fast enough to make the cost worthwhile. In the near future, however, PCs will be equipped with adequate hardware and processing power to take advantage of 1 Gigabit Ethernet.

# PRACTICE TEST QUESTIONS

1. **Which of the following media is preferred for 1 Gigabit Ethernet?**
   a. coaxial cable
   b. UTP
   c. STP
   d. fiber-optic cable

2. **Which of the following IEEE committees is responsible for establishing 1 Gigabit Ethernet standards?**
   a. 802.3a
   b. 802.3z
   c. 802.5
   d. 802.11b

3. **Which of the following network access methods does a 1 Gigabit Ethernet network use?**
   a. CSMA/CD
   b. CSMA/CA
   c. demand priority
   d. token-passing

4. **Which of the following technologies compete directly with 1 Gigabit Ethernet?**
   a. FDDI
   b. Token Ring
   c. 100VG-AnyLAN
   d. ATM

5. **What is the maximum segment length for a 1 Gigabit Ethernet network running over fiber-optic cable?**
   a. 50 meters
   b. 55 meters
   c. 500 meters
   d. 550 meters

6. **What part of a network is most likely to use 1 Gigabit Ethernet?**
   a. work area
   b. horizontal wiring
   c. backbone
   d. drop cables

7. **Which of the following types of connectors could be used on a 1 Gigabit Ethernet network?**
   a. BNC
   b. AUI
   c. n-connector
   d. SC

# OBJECTIVES

## 1.4 Recognize the following media connectors and/or describe their uses:

### RJ-11, RJ-45, AUI, AND BNC

### UNDERSTANDING THE OBJECTIVE

Different Ethernet technologies require different connectors, such as RJ-11, RJ-45, AUI, and BNC. The most common is the RJ-45 connector, used on 10BaseT and 100BaseT LANs.

### WHAT YOU REALLY NEED TO KNOW

◆ **RJ-11**, which stands for **registered jack-11**, is the standard interface for phone (or modem) connections and is illustrated below.

◆ An RJ-11 jack contains four or six wires. Prior to the advent of CAT5 cabling, RJ-11 plugs and jacks could be used for LAN communications as well as phone communications.

◆ **RJ-45**, which stands for **registered jack-45,** identifies the Ethernet 10BaseT and 100BaseT interfaces.

◆ An RJ-45 jack, illustrated below, typically contains eight wires (four wire pairs) and looks like a large telephone jack.

◆ Common network interfaces are BNC or RJ-45 connectors. **BNC**, which stands for **British Naval Connector**, identifies the Ethernet 10Base2 interface and is illustrated below.

◆ An **AUI (Attachment Unit Interface)** connector is a type of data bus connector that contains 15 pins, as illustrated below, and is an Ethernet 10Base5 standard for connecting coaxial cables with transceivers and networked nodes.

### OBJECTIVES ON THE JOB

On most modern networks, you will work with RJ-45 connectors. Not only should you be able to recognize these plugs, you should also be able to terminate a UTP patch cable with one, using the proper networking tools.

# PRACTICE TEST QUESTIONS

1. **What type of network would use an AUI interface?**
    a. 10Base2
    b. 10Base5
    c. 10BaseT
    d. 100BaseFX

2. **What type of UTP could be used on a LAN that had RJ-11 connectors on the ends of its patch cables?**
    a. CAT3
    b. CAT5
    c. CAT6
    d. CAT7

3. **How many wire pairs are typically terminated in an RJ-45 connector?**
    a. two
    b. three
    c. four
    d. five

4. **What kind of connector would you find on the end of a CAT5 patch cable?**
    a. RJ-11
    b. RJ-45
    c. AUI
    d. BNC

5. **What type of connector would be found on a Thinnet cable?**
    a. RJ-11
    b. RJ-45
    c. AUI
    d. BNC

6. **What is another term for an AUI connector?**
    a. vampire tap
    b. DB-15
    c. n-connector
    d. barrel connector

7. **Which of the following connectors is often used to connect a modem to a phone jack?**
    a. RJ-11
    b. RJ-45
    c. AUI
    d. BNC

## 1.4  Recognize the following media connectors and/or describe their uses (continued):

### ST AND SC

### UNDERSTANDING THE OBJECTIVE

Networks that use fiber-optic cabling may use any of 10 different types of connectors. Currently, the two most popular connector types for fiber-optic–based networks are ST and SC connectors.

### WHAT YOU REALLY NEED TO KNOW

◆ An ST connector terminates multimode fiber media and is illustrated below.

◆ An SC connector terminates multimode fiber media and is illustrated below.

◆ ST and SC connectors are used with fiber-based networks, such as 10BaseF or 100BaseF.

◆ When used with 10BaseF or 100BaseF networks, each cable is terminated with a pair of SC or ST connectors, as illustrated below. One of the connectors handles data transmission while the other handles data reception, allowing for a full-duplex connection.

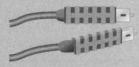

◆ Although fiber-optic cable may be terminated with one of several different types of connectors, SC or ST connectors are the most popular ones in use on modern LANs.

### OBJECTIVES ON THE JOB

Bear in mind that most networks currently use fiber-based technologies only on parts of their networks, and 100BaseF is likely to coexist with 100BaseT on the same network. When combining 100BaseF and 100BaseT technologies on the same network, you must use equipment capable of accepting both SC or ST connectors and RJ-45 connectors.

## PRACTICE TEST QUESTIONS

1. **Why do ST connectors terminate in pairs?**
   a. Half of the pair is used for transmission, while the other half is used for reception.
   b. Half of the pair is used for transmission and reception, while the other half is used as a fail-over cable for greater reliability.
   c. Both connectors in the pair are used to transmit and receive data simultaneously, resulting in higher throughput.
   d. One-half of the pair is used for CSMA/CD network access and the other half is used for CSMA/CA network access.

2. **Which of the following types of networks might use an SC connector?**
   a. 10BaseT
   b. 10Base5
   c. 100BaseTX
   d. 100BaseFX

3. **Which of the following connectors is most likely to be found on a network that uses ST connectors?**
   a. RJ-11
   b. RJ-45
   c. BNC
   d. AUI

4. **A network could use both ST and SC connectors. True or False?**

5. **What kind of fiber-optic cable is likely to be found inside an ST connector?**
   a. duplex-mode
   b. single-mode
   c. iso-mode
   d. multimode

6. **Which of the following physical topologies would most likely be used with SC and ST connectors?**
   a. bus
   b. star-wired bus
   c. star-wired ring
   d. ring

7. **ST and SC connectors are the only types of connectors that may be used on 100BaseF networks. True or false?**

## 1.5 Choose the appropriate media type and connectors to add a client to an existing network.

### UNDERSTANDING THE OBJECTIVE

Understanding the type of medium and connector required by a network technology is fundamental to understanding how to install and maintain networks.

### WHAT YOU REALLY NEED TO KNOW

◆ **Connectors** are the pieces of hardware that connect the wire to the network device, be it a file server, workstation, switch, or printer. Every networking medium requires a specific kind of connector. The types of connectors you use will affect the cost of installing and maintaining the network, the ease of adding new segments or nodes to the network, and the technical expertise required to maintain the network.

◆ BNC connectors are used with Thinnet, or 10Base2 Ethernet networks, which rely on coaxial cabling as their transmission medium.

◆ AUI connectors are used with Thicknet, or 10Base5 Ethernet networks, which rely on coaxial cabling as their transmission medium.

◆ The AUI standard calls for male connectors with 15 pins to connect to the MAU and female connectors with openings for 15 pins to connect to the network node's Ethernet interface.

◆ AUI connectors may also be called DB-15 or DIX connectors. **DIX** stands for Digital, Intel, and Xerox, the three companies that together pioneered Thicknet technology. **DB-15** is a more general term for connectors that use 15 metal pins to complete a connection between devices. "DB" stands for "Data bus," while the number 15 indicates how many pins are used to make the connection.

◆ RJ-11 connectors may be used with older Ethernet networks that rely on twisted-pair cabling, such as 10BaseT. However, since they are not compatible with newer UTP cable types, they are rarely found on modern networks.

◆ RJ-45 connectors are the most popular type of network connector. They may be used on both Token Ring and Ethernet networks that rely on twisted-pair cabling, including different types of 10BaseT and 100BaseT technology.

◆ ST and SC connectors are the two most popular types of connectors used with fiber-based networks, such as 10BaseF and 100BaseF.

### OBJECTIVES ON THE JOB

The type of connector and medium type required by a particular network will be obvious once you begin working on the network. However, if you are designing a network from scratch, you should be careful to specify the proper medium and connector types. The most popular combination in use on modern networks is unshielded twisted-pair cabling with RJ-45 connectors.

# PRACTICE TEST QUESTIONS

1. **Which of the following connectors could be used with CAT3 cable? Choose all that apply.**
   a. BNC
   b. AUI
   c. RJ-11
   d. RJ-45

2. **Which of the following connectors could be used on a 100BaseFX network?**
   a. ST
   b. AUI
   c. RJ-45
   d. DIX

3. **What type of medium is used with BNC connectors?**
   a. coaxial cable
   b. unshielded twisted-pair cable
   c. shielded twisted-pair cable
   d. fiber-optic cable

4. **Which of the following connectors would be used on a 10Base5 network?**
   a. BNC
   b. AUI
   c. RJ-11
   d. RJ-45

5. **What type of medium does a 10BaseT network use?**
   a. coaxial cable
   b. unshielded twisted-pair cable
   c. shielded twisted-pair cable
   d. fiber-optic cable

6. **On a 100BaseTX network, how many wire pairs within the cable are used?**
   a. one
   b. two
   c. four
   d. six

7. **What type of topology would a network that requires RJ-45 cabling use? Choose all that apply.**
   a. bus
   b. star-wired ring
   c. star-wired bus
   d. ring

## 1.6   Identify the purpose, features, and functions of the following network components:

### HUBS

### UNDERSTANDING THE OBJECTIVE

Hubs are simple connectivity devices that belong to the Physical layer of the OSI Model. Their primary purpose is to regenerate (or repeat) digital signals from one node to the rest of a network segment. Because they do not perform sophisticated functions, such as those that a router performs, hubs are less intricate and less expensive than higher-layer connectivity devices.

### WHAT YOU REALLY NEED TO KNOW

◆ At its most primitive, a **hub** is a multiport repeater, or a device that regenerates the digital signals it receives from one node to the rest of the nodes on a network segment. A hub often connects multiple workstations to each other and to the network's backbone.

◆ Hubs belong to the Physical layer of the OSI Model.

◆ On Ethernet networks, hubs typically serve as the central connection point for branches of a star or star-based hybrid topology.

◆ On Token Ring networks, hubs are called **Multistation Access Units (MAUs)** and are used to connect nodes in a star-based ring topology.

◆ Hubs come in many different varieties and are specific to the type of technology a network uses—for example, 10BaseT versus Token Ring.

◆ On a hub, the **uplink port** is the receptacle used to connect one hub to another hub in a daisy chain or hierarchical fashion.

◆ On a hub, the **backbone port** is the receptacle used to connect a hub to the network's backbone, and it should only be used for this purpose.

◆ Some hubs have internal processing capabilities that allow them to process data, provide troubleshooting information, and monitor traffic. Such hubs are known as **intelligent hubs** or **managed hubs**.

◆ On Ethernet networks, hubs have collision lights (or LEDs), which can indicate the volume of collisions that segment is experiencing by blinking.

◆ The **link LED** is the light on a port that indicates whether it is in use. If a connection is live, this light should be solid or blinking green.

### OBJECTIVES ON THE JOB

Hubs can be found on even the smallest networks, and they certainly perform critical functions on larger networks. While working as a networking professional, you should be familiar with specifying, installing, maintaining, and troubleshooting hubs. As with all network equipment, hub functionality varies from one model and manufacturer to another, so be certain to read the documentation that ships with the hub in order to properly perform these functions.

# PRACTICE TEST QUESTIONS

1. **What is the main difference between a hub and a multistation access unit (MAU)?**
   a. Hubs can extend a network, while MAUs cannot.
   b. MAUs can be used in a star-bus topology, while hubs cannot.
   c. Hubs are typically used with Ethernet networks, while MAUs are used with Token Ring networks.
   d. Because of their multiport design, hubs are more fault-tolerant than MAUs.

2. **What can you view to determine whether a hub port is receiving information from a workstation's NIC?**
   a. the uplink LED
   b. the collision LED
   c. the link LED
   d. the backbone LED

3. **Which of the following characteristics do hubs and MAUs share?**
   a. Both can connect multiple workstations to the network's backbone.
   b. Both can translate between IPX and IP traffic.
   c. Both forward and/or filter frames based on their MAC address.
   d. Both interpret Network layer addresses to determine where to deliver data.

4. **Which of the following is probably the least expensive connectivity device?**
   a. switch
   b. router
   c. bridge
   d. hub

5. **What is used to connect one hub to another hub in a daisy-chain fashion?**
   a. their uplink ports
   b. their backbone ports
   c. their punch-down ports
   d. their collision ports

6. **In which two of the following types of networks would viewing a hub's collision LED be useful for troubleshooting?**
   a. 10BaseT
   b. 100BaseVG-AnyLAN
   c. Token Ring
   d. 100BaseFX

7. **What is the maximum number of hubs that can be connected in serial on a 10BaseT network?**
   a. two
   b. three
   c. four
   d. five

## 1.6 Identify the purpose, features, and functions of the following network components (continued):

### SWITCHES AND BRIDGES

### UNDERSTANDING THE OBJECTIVE

Bridges are devices that connect two LANs or LAN segments using one port per segment. Bridges listen to all network traffic and, based on the packets' MAC addresses, determine whether to forward the packets to another segment or discard them. Bridges keep track of which MAC addresses should be forwarded to which port in a filtering database.

### WHAT YOU REALLY NEED TO KNOW

◆ **Bridges** are devices that move frames between two LANs or LAN segments.

◆ Bridges are similar to repeaters in that they do not modify the contents of a packet. But they are more sophisticated than repeaters, because they interpret addressing information and filter packets.

◆ Because they can selectively filter packets, bridges can be useful for separating LAN segments, thus reducing the possibility that errors on one segment will affect transmission on the other segment.

◆ Bridging occurs at the Data Link layer of the OSI Model, which encompasses flow control, error handling, and physical addressing.

◆ Bridges read the destination MAC address of each frame and decide whether to forward (retransmit) the packet to another segment on the network or, if it belongs to the same segment as the source address, filter (discard) it.

◆ As nodes on a network transmit data through the bridge, the bridge establishes a **filtering database** of known MAC addresses and their location on the network. (This filtering database is also known as a **forwarding table**.) The bridge uses its filtering database to determine whether a packet should be forwarded or filtered.

◆ **Switches**, which subdivide a network into smaller logical pieces (or collision domains), can be described as multiport bridges. Switches operate at the Data Link layer of the OSI Model and interpret MAC address information.

◆ Both switches and bridges can connect networks that use dissimilar network access methods, such as Token Ring and Ethernet.

◆ Because they have multiple ports, switches can make better use of limited bandwidth and prove more cost-efficient than bridges. Each port on the switch acts like a bridge, and each device connected to a switch effectively receives its own dedicated channel.

### OBJECTIVES ON THE JOB

Since bridges and switches only interpret addressing information at the Data Link layer of the OSI Model, they can connect networks that use different Network layer protocols (for example, IPX and IP). Both can be useful for extending and interconnecting multiple LAN segments.

# PRACTICE TEST QUESTIONS

1. **Which of the following do bridges and hubs have in common?**
   a. Both operate at the Physical layer of the OSI Model.
   b. Both can interpret MAC addresses and forward or filter frames based on this information.
   c. Both repeat signals in order to allow data to reach their destination.
   d. Both can interpret Network layer addresses to efficiently forward data to their destination.

2. **Which of the following is associated with a MAC address in a bridge's filtering database?**
   a. bridge port number
   b. IP address
   c. protocol
   d. subnet mask

3. **Why is a switch generally faster than a router?**
   a. because it does not interpret Data Link layer information
   b. because it does not acknowledge data transmission errors
   c. because it accepts only connectionless protocols
   d. because it does not pay attention to Network layer information

4. **What IEEE standard describes bridging?**
   a. 802.1
   b. 802.2
   c. 802.3
   d. 802.5

5. **What is one advantage of using a switch over a bridge?**
   a. Since switches have multiple ports, fewer are necessary to make the same number of connections between multiple segments.
   b. Switches are less expensive to install and maintain.
   c. Switches are inherently more secure than bridges.
   d. Since switches can interpret Network layer addresses, they can more efficiently forward data to their destination.

6. **Under what conditions will a bridge filter a packet?**
   a. when it detects an incorrect checksum
   b. when it detects a damaged header
   c. when the packet's destination MAC address belongs to the port on which the bridge received it
   d. when the packet's source MAC address belongs to the port on which the bridge received it.

7. **Switches provide the foundation for which of the following types of networks?**
   a. VPNs
   b. VLANs
   c. MANs
   d. WANs

## 1.6 Identify the purpose, features, and functions of the following network components (continued):

### ROUTERS

### UNDERSTANDING THE OBJECTIVE

Routers use Network layer addressing information to intelligently route data between LANs. They are used to connect dissimilar LANs in the case of WANs or LAN segments in the case of LANs.

### WHAT YOU REALLY NEED TO KNOW

◆ **Routers** are devices that connect multiple LANs or LAN segments and direct data between nodes using the best possible route. A router has multiple ports and can connect dissimilar LANs and WANs running at different transmission speeds and using a variety of protocols.

◆ Routers belong to the Network layer of the OSI Model. In order for a protocol to be routable, it must contain Network layer information. IPX/SPX, TCP/IP, and AppleTalk are routable protocols, while SNA and NetBEUI are nonroutable.

◆ The best path between nodes on a network depends on the number of hops between nodes, the current network activity, unavailable links, varying network transmission speeds, and topology.

◆ When used in networking, the term **route** means to intelligently direct data based on addressing, patterns of usage, quality of service, and network availability.

◆ Unlike bridges, routers are protocol-dependent. They must be designed or configured to recognize protocols on the network.

◆ A typical router has an internal processor, its own memory and power supply, input and output jacks for different types of network connectors (depending on the network type), and usually, a management console interface.

◆ To determine the best path between two nodes, routers communicate with each other through **routing protocols**. Examples of routing protocols are EIGRP and BGP.

◆ In **static routing**, a router contains routing tables (instructions on how to forward packets) that are manually programmed by a network administrator. Since the location of devices on a network and the best paths between them can change often, static routing is not a flexible or efficient technique.

◆ In **dynamic routing**, a router calculates the best path between nodes and automatically updates its routing tables if it detects network congestion or failures. Dynamic routing is faster and more reliable than static routing.

### OBJECTIVES ON THE JOB

Routers are common devices used to connect two different LANs. They are sophisticated and flexible. However, the more sophisticated the device, the more complex it is to install, configure, and maintain. Careful thought must be put into designing a network with routers.

## PRACTICE TEST QUESTIONS

1. **What resource does a router use to help it determine the best path between two nodes?**
   a. filtering database
   b. routing table
   c. SNMP database
   d. DNS records

2. **What is one advantage of dynamic routing over static routing?**
   a. It is more reliable.
   b. It is more secure.
   c. It prevents network administrators from having to configure the router.
   d. It can interpret both IP and IPX addresses.

3. **Which of the following addresses could a router interpret?**
   a. 506.78.34.110
   b. AE:09:35:00:BF:34
   c. AA:01:01:46:34:29:80
   d. 128.92.35.117

4. **Which two of the following factors do routers consider when selecting the best path for data to travel between two nodes?**
   a. network transmission type
   b. network congestion
   c. network protocol
   d. data priority

5. **What is the function of a routing protocol?**
   a. to enable communications between routers
   b. to facilitate translation between the Network and Transport layers of the OSI Model
   c. to convert nonroutable protocols into routable protocols
   d. to ensure that encapsulated protocols are routed properly

6. **Which of the following cannot forward NetBEUI packets?**
   a. repeater
   b. bridge
   c. brouter
   d. router

7. **What is one of a router's primary functions?**
   a. to determine the best path for forwarding data to its destination
   b. to regenerate attenuated signals
   c. to separate groups of network devices into broadcast domains
   d. to filter traffic according to subnet

## 1.6   Identify the purpose, features, and functions of the following network components (continued):

### GATEWAYS AND CSU/DSU

### UNDERSTANDING THE OBJECTIVE

Gateways connect two dissimilar networks or subnetworks. Gateways are combinations of software and hardware, and as such, they operate at multiple layers of the OSI Model. CSU/DSUs form the terminating equipment for a T-carrier, connecting the incoming line and the multiplexer.

### WHAT YOU REALLY NEED TO KNOW

- ◆ In general, a **gateway** is a computer running special software or a connectivity device that acts as a translator between two dissimilar systems. It may connect networks running different protocols, architecture, or formatting.

- ◆ Gateways operate at multiple layers of the OSI Model, including Application, Session, Transport, and Network. They repackage incoming information so the destination network can read it. They may also perform security and filtering functions.

- ◆ Gateways can exist on servers, PCs, or mainframes. In the case of connecting two large networks, a gateway is often a specialized router or router interface.

- ◆ Gateways are much slower than bridges or normal routers because of the complex translations they conduct. Because they are slow, gateways have the potential to cause extreme network congestion.

- ◆ The most common type of gateway is the e-mail gateway, which translates messages from one type of system to another.

- ◆ An Internet gateway allows and manages access between LANs and the Internet. It can restrict the kind of access LAN users have to the Internet and vice versa.

- ◆ A LAN gateway allows segments of a LAN running different protocols or network access methods to communicate with each other.

- ◆ A **CSU/DSU** is the termination point for a T-carrier line at the customer's site, connecting the line with a multiplexer.

- ◆ Although CSUs (channel service units) and DSUs (data service units) are actually two separate devices, they are typically combined into a single box called a CSU/DSU.

- ◆ The **CSU** provides termination for the digital signal and ensures connection integrity through error correction and line monitoring. The **DSU** converts the digital signal used by bridges, routers, and multiplexers into the digital signal sent via the cabling.

### OBJECTIVES ON THE JOB

Chances are, if you work on a LAN that connects to the Internet (two dissimilar networks), you will need to understand gateways. Since gateways can be very different, you must be certain to understand the functions and requirements of your particular gateway before installing, configuring, or maintaining it.

# PRACTICE TEST QUESTIONS

1. **Why are gateways slower than bridges?**
   a. because they must read the source and destination MAC addresses
   b. because they must manage sessions, translate encoded data, and interpret logical and physical addresses
   c. because they must assign new IP addresses to every packet
   d. because they must interpret application programming interface output

2. **What type of gateway would connect Token Ring and Ethernet networks within one building?**
   a. e-mail gateway
   b. IBM host gateway
   c. LAN gateway
   d. Internet gateway

3. **Which two of the following could be considered gateways?**
   a. router
   b. switch
   c. bridge
   d. firewall

4. **Which two of the following could host an e-mail gateway?**
   a. server
   b. PC
   c. bridge
   d. hub

5. **When acting as an e-mail gateway, in which OSI Model layers does a gateway perform most of its functions?**
   a. Data Link and Physical
   b. Transport and Network
   c. Transport and Session
   d. Application and Presentation

6. **What does "CSU" stand for?**
   a. communications service unit
   b. channel service unit
   c. communications session unit
   d. cable session unit

7. **A CSU/DSU connects an incoming T-carrier line with which of the following devices?**
   a. router
   b. modem
   c. multiplexer
   d. laser

## 1.6 Identify the purpose, features, and functions of the following network components (continued):

### NETWORK INTERFACE CARDS/ISDN ADAPTERS/SYSTEM AREA NETWORK CARDS AND WIRELESS ACCESS POINTS

### UNDERSTANDING THE OBJECTIVE

Network interface cards, wireless access points, and ISDN adapters are components of a network that connect individual devices to media and perform data transmission and reception.

### WHAT YOU REALLY NEED TO KNOW

◆ A **transceiver** is a device that receives and transmits signals. In most modern networks, a transceiver can only be found in the network interface card (NIC), ISDN adapter, or wireless access point, depending on the type of network.

◆ **Network Interface Cards (NICs)** are connectivity devices that enable a workstation, server, printer, or other node to receive and transmit data over the network media. NICs are also sometimes called **network adapters**.

◆ All network adapters have their own circuitry, a system board interface, and at least one receptacle for a connection to the network. They may be external or internal to a device.

◆ NICs belong to the Physical layer of the OSI Model because they transmit data signals but do not (in general) analyze the data from higher layers.

◆ NICs come in a variety of types depending on network transport system (Ethernet vs. Token Ring), network transmission speed (for example, 10 Mbps vs. 100 Mbps), connector interfaces (for example, BNC vs. RJ-45), type of system board (for example, PCI or ISA) or device (for example, workstation or printer) they suit, and of course, manufacturer.

◆ Typically, a wireless NIC uses an antenna to exchange signals with a base station transceiver or other wireless NIC adapters. This type of connectivity suits environments where cabling cannot be installed or clients who need to be mobile.

◆ From the telephone company's lines, the ISDN channels connect to a Network Termination 1 device at the customer's site. The **Network Termination 1 (NT1)** device connects the twisted-pair wiring at the customer's building with the ISDN terminal equipment via RJ-11 or RJ-45 data jacks. The ISDN **terminal equipment (TE)** may include cards or standalone devices used to connect computers to the ISDN line (similar to a network adapter used on Ethernet or Token Ring networks).

◆ So that the ISDN line can connect to analog equipment, the signal must first pass through a terminal adapter. An **ISDN adapter** converts digital signals into analog signals for use with ISDN phones and other analog devices.

### OBJECTIVES ON THE JOB

It's a good idea to use the same NIC vendor, if not the same make and model, for all devices on a network. This makes support and maintenance easier. Because Token Ring networks are becoming rare and because modern Token Ring NICs include RJ-45 receptacles, it is unlikely that you will need to use Token Ring media filters unless you are working on an older network.

# PRACTICE TEST QUESTIONS

1. **Which of the following do all NICs have in common?**
   a. antenna
   b. RJ-11 receptacle
   c. RJ-45 receptacle
   d. a means for connecting to the system board

2. **What type of NIC is best suited for inventory control personnel who must quickly travel through a large warehouse entering data into their networked workstation?**
   a. PCMCIA
   b. PCI
   c. infrared
   d. USB

3. **Which two of the following features that can be found on a sophisticated NIC (such as one found in a server) improves the performance of the NIC?**
   a. diagnostic LEDs
   b. Direct Memory Access (DMA)
   c. SNMP capabilities
   d. on-board CPU

4. **Which of the following is one function of an ISDN adapter?**
   a. to convert incoming digital signals into analog signals
   b. to convert outgoing digital signals into analog signals
   c. to convert outgoing baseband signals into broadband signals
   d. to convert incoming baseband signals into broadband signals

5. **What types of receptacles would be found on an ISDN adapter?**
   a. BNC and AUI
   b. RJ-11 and RJ-45
   c. AUI and n-connector
   d. RJ-45 and RJ-52

6. **Which of the following types of NICs are you most likely to find on a modern desktop computer?**
   a. PCI
   b. PCMCIA
   c. infrared
   d. parallel port

7. **Which two of the following might be terminating equipment connected to an ISDN adapter?**
   a. fax machine
   b. multiplexer
   c. media filter
   d. telephone

## 1.6   Identify the purpose, features, and functions of the following network components (continued):

### MODEMS

### UNDERSTANDING THE OBJECTIVE

Like a NIC, a modem must have unique and appropriate IRQ, I/O address, and memory address range settings. Among other parameters, a modem's maximum port speed can be configured through the operating system. The throughput of modern modems is limited to 56 Kbps.

### WHAT YOU REALLY NEED TO KNOW

◆ The word **modem** is derived from its function as a MODulator/DEModulator. A modem converts a computer's digital pulses into analog signals for the PSTN (because not all of the PSTN is necessarily capable of digital transmission), then converts the analog signals back into digital pulses at the receiving computer's end.

◆ On modern computers, modems are typically connected to the machine's system board through an expansion slot. However, if an external modem is used, it may connect to the PC's serial port, PCMCIA slot, or USB port.

◆ Often the default values assigned when the modem is installed are correct. However, the ISP a user dials might prefer different port settings (including parity, data bits, and stop bits). You can configure these values through the operating system of any personal computer.

◆ To use FIFO buffers, a modem must have a 16550 UART compatible chip. The higher the buffer settings, the faster data will be transmitted; however, less data correction will be employed.

◆ The IRQ, I/O base address, and memory range for a modem on a modern PC is initially assigned in the BIOS, but it can be modified through the operating system. IRQ 4 is commonly assigned to the COM1 or COM3 serial ports, which are used for modem connections.

◆ A modem's speed is measured in bits per second. The fastest modem transmission possible with current technology is 56 Kbps.

◆ A **dial-up** connection uses a PSTN or other line to access a remote server via modems at both the source (for example, the salesperson's computer) and destination (for example, the office's LAN server).

### OBJECTIVES ON THE JOB

For networking professionals, knowledge of modems is often required when establishing or troubleshooting remote connectivity. In such a situation, it is necessary to understand how the modem interacts with the operating system and how to fine-tune a modem connection. Fortunately, however, all types of modems are similar and not nearly as complex as other connectivity devices, such as routers.

# PRACTICE TEST QUESTIONS

1. **What IRQ number is commonly assigned to a computer's internal modem?**
   a. 1
   b. 3
   c. 4
   d. 9

2. **What is the most likely means for a modem to connect to a desktop computer's system board?**
   a. serial port
   b. PCMCIA slot
   c. parallel port
   d. expansion slot

3. **If a user configures her modem's maximum port speed to 115,200 bps in her operating system, at what speed is she most likely to connect to her ISP?**
   a. 576,000 bps
   b. 115,200 bps
   c. 52,600 bps
   d. 11,520 bps

4. **In a remote networking situation, who or what dictates the proper connection preferences, including data bits and parity bit?**
   a. the remote access server
   b. the client's modem
   c. the LAN manager
   d. the client's operating system

5. **From what two words does the term "modem" originate?**
   a. modulator/demodulator
   b. modifier/demodifier
   c. moderate/demoderate
   d. modiplexer/demodiplexer

6. **What type of chip is needed for a modem to support FIFO buffering?**
   a. 3000 UART or better
   b. 10000 UART or better
   c. 16550 UART or better
   d. 56000 UART or better

7. **Which of the following is one function of a modem?**
   a. to convert incoming digital signals into analog signals
   b. to convert outgoing digital signals into analog signals
   c. to convert outgoing baseband signals into broadband signals
   d. to convert incoming baseband signals into broadband signals

## 2.1 Given an example, identify a MAC address.

### UNDERSTANDING THE OBJECTIVE

A MAC address is the unique hexadecimal number assigned to a NIC at the manufacturer's factory. The MAC address operates in the MAC sublayer of the Data Link layer of the OSI Model. It provides the interface between the Physical layer and the Logical Link Control sublayer of the Data Link layer.

### WHAT YOU REALLY NEED TO KNOW

- The Data Link layer is subdivided into the Logical Link Control and the MAC sublayers.
- The **MAC sublayer** appends the physical address of the destination to the data frame, thus creating a connection between the Physical layer and the Logical Link Control sublayer of the Data Link layer.
- **Data Link layer addresses** are fixed numbers associated with the networking hardware and are usually assigned to the network adapter at the factory. These addresses are also called **MAC addresses**, after the Media Access Control (MAC) sublayer, or **physical addresses**.
- MAC addresses are 12-digit hexadecimal numbers guaranteed to be unique because industry standards govern what numbers each manufacturer can use.
- As an example, NICs manufactured by the 3Com Corporation begin with the following sequence of six characters: 00608C. The part of the MAC address unique to a particular vendor is called the **Block ID**. The remaining six characters in the sequence are added at the factory, based on the NIC's model and manufacture date, and together are called the **Device ID**. An example of a Device ID assigned by a manufacturer might be 005499. Together, this Block ID and Device ID would result in a unique MAC address of 00608C005499.
- You can view the MAC address of a device or client's NIC through the NIC diagnostic utility, or on a Windows 9x computer through the WINIPCFG utility, or on a Windows NT or 2000 computer through the IPCONFIG utility, or on a UNIX computer through the IFCONFIG utility. It may also be printed on the NIC's circuit board.
- MAC addresses are used by some connectivity devices, such as bridges, to determine how to forward data over the network.

### OBJECTIVES ON THE JOB

MAC addresses, which are key pieces of information in troubleshooting, should never be changed (and it is difficult to do so). For example, you need to know how to recognize and interpret MAC addresses to resolve other addressing conflicts (such as IP or IPX conflicts).

# PRACTICE TEST QUESTIONS

1. **Which of the following is an example of a valid MAC address?**
   a. 128.7.99.24
   b. AE:09:33:00:23:B5
   c. 92:CG:50:28:K3:48
   d. 247.34.188.203

2. **What part of a MAC address would all like-model Ethernet NICs have in common?**
   a. Port ID
   b. Node ID
   c. Block ID
   d. Host ID

3. **Which of the following devices depends on MAC addresses to forward packets?**
   a. bridges
   b. routers
   c. hubs
   d. firewalls

4. **How can an end user discover a Windows 2000 workstation's MAC address?**
   a. by checking the TCP/IP properties
   b. by running WINIPCFG /all at the command prompt
   c. by running IPCONFIG /all at the command prompt
   d. by checking the network adapter properties in the Devices tab of the System properties dialog box

5. **Which of the following terms is used interchangeably with "MAC address"?**
   a. LLC sublayer address
   b. Physical address
   c. Logical address
   d. Network address

6. **What does MAC stand for?**
   a. median axis channel
   b. multiple access carrier
   c. media access control
   d. multiple arbitrator channel

7. **Which of the following occurs at the MAC sublayer?**
   a. An address is appended to the data packet.
   b. Checksum data is added to the data packet.
   c. Flow control data is added to the data packet.
   d. Packets are padded if they do not meet the minimum packet size.

## 2.2 Identify the seven layers of the OSI Model and their functions:

### LAYERS 1 THROUGH 3

### UNDERSTANDING THE OBJECTIVE

The Open Systems Interconnection (OSI) Model is a theoretical construct that separates the functions of a network into seven layers. Each layer is associated with different protocols, hardware, or software. Layers 1 through 3 include the Physical, Data Link, and Network layers. Services that operate at these layers include electrical pulses (Physical layer), physical addressing (Data Link layer), and logical addressing and routing (Network layer).

### WHAT YOU REALLY NEED TO KNOW

- ◆ The OSI Model is a theoretical representation of what happens between two nodes on a network. It does not stipulate hardware or software.

- ◆ The **Physical layer** is the lowest, or first, layer of the OSI Model. This layer contains the physical networking medium, such as cabling, connectors, and repeaters. Protocols at the Physical layer are responsible for generating and detecting voltage in order to transmit and receive signals carrying data.

- ◆ The Physical layer handles the data transmission rate and monitors data error rates, but does not handle error correction.

- ◆ The second layer of the OSI Model, the **Data Link layer**, controls communication between the Network layer and Physical layer. Its primary function is to divide data it receives from the Network layer into distinct frames that can then be transmitted by the Physical layer.

- ◆ Bridges and switches work in the Data Link layer, because they decode frames and use the frame information to transmit data to its correct recipient.

- ◆ The primary function of the **Network layer**, the third layer, is to translate network addresses into their physical counterparts and decide how to route data from the sender to the receiver.

- ◆ The Network layer determines the best route between nodes by considering delivery priorities, network congestion, quality of service, and cost of alternative routes.

- ◆ Services that work in the Network layer include IP and IPX.

### OBJECTIVES ON THE JOB

Knowledge of the OSI Model helps you identify and fix errors on a network. It also helps you understand higher-level networking concepts such as addressing. A deep understanding of what functions occur at each layer of the OSI Model helps you install, configure, and troubleshoot routers, switches, bridges, and other networking equipment.

# PRACTICE TEST QUESTIONS

1. **At what layer of the OSI Model would a network be affected if a coaxial cable were severed?**
   a. Physical
   b. Data Link
   c. Network
   d. Transport

2. **Which of the following functions belongs to the Network layer of the OSI Model?**
   a. bridging
   b. repeating
   c. routing
   d. error correction

3. **At what layer of the OSI Model are MAC addresses interpreted?**
   a. Physical
   b. Data Link
   c. Network
   d. Transport

4. **If a printer can interpret physical addresses but cannot interpret an IP address, at what layer is it failing?**
   a. Physical
   b. Data Link
   c. Network
   d. Transport

5. **Which of the following is not considered when a router chooses the best path from one node to another on a network?**
   a. network congestion
   b. quality of service
   c. time to send data
   d. geographical distance between nodes

6. **At which layer of the OSI Model is data packaged into frames?**
   a. Physical
   b. Data Link
   c. Network
   d. Transport

7. **Which of the following functions belongs to the Physical layer?**
   a. applying electrical charges to a wire
   b. determining which segment a node is on, based on its MAC address
   c. determining which segment a node is on, based on its IPX address
   d. determining whether a packet has been damaged between its source and target

## 2.2   Identify the seven layers of the OSI Model and their functions (continued):

### LAYERS 4 THROUGH 7

### UNDERSTANDING THE OBJECTIVE

Layers 4 through 7 deal with higher-level functions, such as managing traffic on a network, encoding and encrypting data, and establishing a user interface. Examples of these functions include HTTP and e-mail (the Application layer), data encryption (the Presentation layer), session negotiation (the Session layer), and error correction (Transport layer).

### WHAT YOU REALLY NEED TO KNOW

◆ The **Transport layer**, the fourth layer of the OSI Model, is responsible for ensuring that data is transferred from point A to point B reliably, in the correct sequence, and without errors.

◆ Transport protocols also handle **flow control**, the method of gauging the appropriate rate of transmission based on how fast the recipient can accept data.

◆ Services that work in the Transport layer include TCP and SPX.

◆ The **Session layer**, the fifth layer of the OSI Model, is responsible for establishing and maintaining communication between two nodes on the network for the session's duration. Other Session layer functions include synchronizing the dialog between the two nodes, determining whether communication has been cut, and if it has been cut, where to restart transmission.

◆ The Session layer also sets the terms of communication by deciding which node communicates first and how long a node can communicate.

◆ The **Presentation layer**, the sixth layer in the OSI Model, serves as a translator between the application and the network. At the Presentation layer, data is formatted in a schema that the network can understand.

◆ The Presentation layer also takes care of data encryption and decryption, such as the scrambling of system passwords.

◆ The top, or seventh, layer of the OSI Model is the Application layer. The **Application layer** provides interfaces to the software that enable programs to use network services, but it does not refer to a particular program.

◆ Some of the services provided by the Application layer include file transfer, file management, and message handling for electronic mail.

### OBJECTIVES ON THE JOB

Problems that occur in the higher layers of the OSI Model are more apt to be related to software than hardware or firmware. For example, if you have ruled out physical connectivity problems when you are unable to dial in to your ISP's modem pool, you might find a problem at the Session layer (which handles communication).

# PRACTICE TEST QUESTIONS

1. **Which layer of the OSI Model is also known as the traffic cop because it manages communication between nodes?**
   a. Transport
   b. Session
   c. Presentation
   d. Application

2. **Which of the following is a true statement?**
   a. MS Word resides at the Application layer.
   b. The MSMQ API resides at the Application layer.
   c. The network operating system resides at the Application layer.
   d. The MAC address resides at the Application layer.

3. **At which layer of the OSI Model does data encryption take place?**
   a. Transport
   b. Session
   c. Presentation
   d. Application

4. **Which layer of the OSI Model is responsible for sequencing?**
   a. Transport
   b. Session
   c. Presentation
   d. Application

5. **With which layer of the OSI Model is a programmer likely to be most familiar?**
   a. Transport
   b. Session
   c. Presentation
   d. Application

6. **Which layer of the OSI Model takes care of error correction?**
   a. Transport
   b. Session
   c. Presentation
   d. Application

7. **Which of the following is an example of a Transport layer protocol?**
   a. IP
   b. IPX
   c. TCP
   d. FTP

## 2.3 Differentiate between the following network protocols in terms of routing, addressing schemes, interoperability, and naming conventions:

### TCP/IP

### UNDERSTANDING THE OBJECTIVE

Transmission Control Protocol/Internet Protocol (TCP/IP) is the most popular protocol in use today and is used exclusively by Internet services. IP in the TCP/IP suite contains addressing information; therefore, it belongs to the Network layer of the OSI Model and is routable.

### WHAT YOU REALLY NEED TO KNOW

◆ **TCP/IP** is a routable protocol (or suite of protocols). It is the protocol of choice for most modern networks, including the Internet.

◆ Two core protocols of TCP/IP are the Transmission Control Protocol (TCP) and the Internet Protocol (IP).

◆ **TCP**, a connection-oriented protocol, belongs to the Transport layer of the OSI Model and ensures that data is received whole, in sequence, and error-free. **Connection-oriented** means that TCP verifies that a connection is sound before it transmits data.

◆ **IP** operates at the Network layer of the OSI Model and provides information about how and where data should be delivered. IP is the subprotocol that enables TCP/IP to **internetwork**—that is, to traverse more than one LAN segment and more than one type of network through a router—and thus, makes it routable.

◆ In the currently used version of IP, **IP version 4 (IPv4),** each IP address is a unique 32-bit number, divided into four groups of **octets**, or 8-bit bytes, that are separated by periods.

◆ IP address data is sent across the network in binary form. For example, the IP address 131.127.3.22 (in **dotted-decimal notation**) is the same as the binary number 10000011 01111111 00000011 00010110.

◆ In order to communicate via the Internet, organizations must register for a group of IP addresses that are associated with their domain name. Available IP addresses belong to one of three classes: A, B, or C.

◆ TCP/IP is compatible with every modern desktop and network operating system, including Macintosh, NetWare, Windows 9x, Windows 2000, Windows NT, and UNIX.

### OBJECTIVES ON THE JOB

Since the Internet and many different applications rely on TCP/IP and probably will for a long time, the need to understand this protocol will continue to be critical. You should know the addressing conventions of this protocol, as well as the addresses that have special meaning, such as the loopback address. You should also know how to recognize addressing conflicts and to help avoid them.

# PRACTICE TEST QUESTIONS

1. Which protocol in the TCP/IP suite is responsible for addressing?
   a. UDP
   b. TCP
   c. ARP
   d. IP

2. At what layer of the OSI Model does TCP reside?
   a. Data Link
   b. Network
   c. Transport
   d. Session

3. Which of the following is not a valid IP address?
   a. 127.0.0.1
   b. 10.10.10.10
   c. 199.220.37.18
   d. 392.89.32.5

4. Which of the following is a connection-oriented subprotocol of the TCP/IP suite?
   a. TCP
   b. IP
   c. UDP
   d. ICMP

5. Which of the following subprotocols allows TCP/IP to be routable?
   a. TCP
   b. IP
   c. UDP
   d. ICMP

6. On a UNIX server, what command could you type to determine the IP address of your network interface?
   a. ipconfig /all
   b. ifconfig /all
   c. winipcfg /all
   d. inetcfg /all

7. On what version of TCP/IP does most of the Internet currently rely?
   a. 2
   b. 4
   c. 6
   d. 8

## 2.3 Differentiate between the following network protocols in terms of routing, addressing schemes, interoperability, and naming conventions (continued):

### IPX/SPX

## UNDERSTANDING THE OBJECTIVE

The Internetwork Packet Exchange/Sequenced Packet Exchange (IPX/SPX) protocol suite was originally designed by Xerox. Novell modified it in the 1980s for its NetWare NOS. IPX contains Network layer addressing information; therefore, the IPX/SPX protocol is routable.

## WHAT YOU REALLY NEED TO KNOW

◆ IPX operates at the Network layer of the OSI Model and provides routing and internetwork services.

◆ IPX is a **connectionless** service. It does not require that a session be established before transmitting, and it does not guarantee that data will be delivered error-free.

◆ SPX is a connection-oriented protocol that belongs to the Transport layer of the OSI Model. It verifies that data is received whole, error-free, and in sequence.

◆ Because it contains addressing information, IPX/SPX is routable.

◆ IPX/SPX is required for Novell NetWare versions 3.x and lower. In versions 4.x and higher, IPX/SPX is optional, and it has often been replaced by TCP/IP.

◆ Other operating systems, such as Windows 2000, Windows 9x, Macintosh, and UNIX, can use IPX/SPX to internetwork with Novell NetWare systems.

◆ IPX addresses contain two parts: the network address and the node address.

◆ An IPX network address must be an 8-bit hexadecimal address, which means that each of its bits can have a value of either 0–9 or A–F. An example of a valid network address is 000008A2. The network address then becomes the first part of the IPX address on all nodes that use that server as their primary server.

◆ An IPX node address is equal to a device's MAC (or physical) address. Because MAC addresses are preassigned to all NICs, using IPX/SPX means a network administrator does not need to manually assign node addresses to each device.

## OBJECTIVES ON THE JOB

If you are establishing or maintaining an IPX/SPX network, become familiar with the addressing conventions of this protocol. Node addresses depend on MAC addresses (which should never change), but network addresses are assigned manually. If they are improperly assigned, the server and all of its clients will be unable to communicate on the network.

# PRACTICE TEST QUESTIONS

1. **What company originally designed the IPX/SPX protocol?**
   a. IBM
   b. Xerox
   c. Microsoft
   d. Cisco

2. **Which of the following protocols belonging to the IPX/SPX suite verifies that data is received error-free?**
   a. IPX
   b. SAP
   c. SPX
   d. NCP

3. **Two workstations on the same network running IPX/SPX will have the same**
   a. host address.
   b. network address.
   c. node address.
   d. MAC address.

4. **To what layer of the OSI Model does IPX belong?**
   a. Data Link
   b. Network
   c. Transport
   d. Session

5. **Which of the following is not a valid network address when using the IPX/SPX protocol?**
   a. 11111111
   b. AB0045099
   c. ABCABCAB
   d. F29FF034

6. **Which of the following is a connectionless protocol?**
   a. IPX
   b. SPX
   c. SAP
   d. RIP

7. **Which of the following network operating systems requires the use of IPX/SPX?**
   a. IntraNetWare
   b. NetWare 5.0
   c. NetWare 4.11
   d. NetWare 3.11

## 2.3 Differentiate between the following network protocols in terms of routing, addressing schemes, interoperability, and naming conventions (continued):

### NETBEUI

### UNDERSTANDING THE OBJECTIVE

Network Basic Input Output System (NetBIOS) is a protocol designed by IBM to provide Transport and Session layer services for applications running on small, homogenous networks. Microsoft adopted NetBIOS as its foundation protocol and added an Application layer component on top of NetBIOS called the NetBIOS Enhanced User Interface (NetBEUI).

### WHAT YOU REALLY NEED TO KNOW

◆ Microsoft adopted IBM's NetBIOS as its foundation protocol, initially for networks using Windows for Workgroups, and added an Application layer component on top of NetBIOS called the NetBIOS Enhanced User Interface (NetBEUI).

◆ **NetBEUI** is a fast and efficient protocol that consumes few network resources, provides excellent error correction, and requires little configuration. NetBEUI is the easiest type of protocol to set up.

◆ Neither NetBIOS nor NetBEUI provides services at all the OSI Model layers, though NetBEUI roughly corresponds to the Presentation and Session layers.

◆ NetBEUI can only support up to 254 connections and does not allow for good security. It is therefore not appropriate for use on large networks. In practice, using the maximum of 254 nodes would result in very poor performance. Therefore, NetBEUI networks usually contain many fewer nodes.

◆ Because NetBEUI lacks network addressing information, it is not routable by itself.

◆ NetBIOS does not contain a Network layer with addressing information, but to transmit data between network nodes, NetBIOS needs to know how to reach each workstation. Network administrators must assign each workstation a NetBIOS name.

◆ The NetBIOS name can be any combination of 16 or fewer alphanumeric characters, including special characters.

◆ Once NetBIOS has found a workstation's NetBIOS name, it discovers the workstation's MAC address and uses it for further communication with the workstation.

◆ If you are running both TCP/IP and NetBIOS on your network, it's a good policy to make the NetBIOS name identical to the TCP/IP host name.

### OBJECTIVES ON THE JOB

Today, NetBEUI is most commonly used in small Microsoft-based networks to integrate legacy, peer-to-peer networks. In newer networks, TCP/IP has become the protocol of choice because it is routable and more flexible and scalable than NetBEUI. Therefore, mastering NetBEUI is useful for administrators working on older Microsoft networks, but it is a skill rarely needed when administering modern networks.

# PRACTICE TEST QUESTIONS

1. **What is the relationship between NetBIOS and NetBEUI?**
   a. NetBEUI encrypts NetBIOS on the network.
   b. NetBEUI enables NetBIOS to be routed.
   c. NetBEUI adds an Application layer to NetBIOS.
   d. NetBEUI is the IBM version of NetBIOS.

2. **To which layers of the OSI Model does NetBEUI correspond?**
   a. Physical and Network
   b. Session and Transport
   c. Transport and Network
   d. Presentation and Session

3. **What does NetBEUI use to identify workstations on the network?**
   a. host name
   b. node address
   c. network address
   d. NetBIOS name

4. **What company originally designed NetBIOS?**
   a. IBM
   b. Microsoft
   c. Sun
   d. Cisco

5. **Why is NetBEUI not suitable for large networks?**
   a. It can only support dumb terminals.
   b. It suffers poor performance when more than a hundred nodes are connected.
   c. It cannot support shared devices such as printers.
   d. It can only support up to 512 NetBIOS names.

6. **Under what circumstances can NetBIOS be routed?**
   a. if it's encapsulated by another protocol
   b. if it's bound to multiple NICs
   c. if it traverses LAN segments
   d. if it's assigned appropriate node addresses

7. **What is the maximum number of characters in a NetBIOS name?**
   a. 8
   b. 16
   c. 32
   d. 64

## 2.3   Differentiate between the following network protocols in terms of routing, addressing schemes, interoperability, and naming conventions (continued):

### APPLETALK

### UNDERSTANDING THE OBJECTIVE

AppleTalk is the protocol designed by Apple, Inc. to network Macintosh computers. It has largely been replaced by newer, more flexible protocols such as TCP/IP.

### WHAT YOU REALLY NEED TO KNOW

◆ **AppleTalk** is the protocol suite used to interconnect Macintosh computers. AppleTalk is a complete protocol suite containing services that fit into each layer of the OSI Model. Since it contains Network layer addressing information, AppleTalk is routable.

◆ Although AppleTalk was originally designed to support peer-to-peer networking among Macintoshes, it can now be routed between network segments and integrated with NetWare- or Microsoft-based networks.

◆ An AppleTalk network is separated into logical groups of computers called **AppleTalk zones**. Each network can contain multiple zones, but each node can belong to only one zone.

◆ AppleTalk zones enable users to share file and printer resources on one another's Macintoshes.

◆ Zone names are not subject to the same strict naming conventions that TCP/IP and IPX/SPX networks must follow. Instead, zone names typically describe a department or other group of users who share files. An example of a zone name is "Sales and Marketing."

◆ **AppleShare** is the AppleTalk subprotocol that provides file sharing services, print queuing services, password access to files or folders, and user accounting information.

◆ An **AppleTalk node ID** is a unique 8-bit or 16-bit number that identifies a computer on an AppleTalk network. AppleTalk assigns a node ID to each workstation when the workstation first connects to the network. The ID is randomly chosen from a group of currently available addresses. Once a device has obtained an address, it stores it for later use.

◆ An **AppleTalk network number** is a unique 16-bit number that identifies the network to which a node is connected. Its use allows nodes from several different networks to communicate.

### OBJECTIVES ON THE JOB

Although Apple has improved AppleTalk's ability to use different network models and span network segments, it remains unsuited to large LANs or WANs. Even Apple has begun supporting the TCP/IP protocol to integrate Macintoshes with other networks, including the Internet.

# PRACTICE TEST QUESTIONS

1. **What is a logical group of computers on an AppleTalk network called?**
   a. a workgroup
   b. a zone
   c. a share
   d. a segment

2. **An AppleTalk network number is similar to what IPX/SPX number?**
   a. host address
   b. node ID
   c. network address
   d. login ID

3. **What company developed the AppleTalk suite of protocols?**
   a. Apple
   b. Macintosh
   c. Microsoft
   d. IBM

4. **Which of the following protocols are routable? Choose all that apply.**
   a. AppleTalk
   b. TCP/IP
   c. IPX/SPX
   d. NetBEUI

5. **Which of the following AppleTalk subprotocols provides print queuing functions?**
   a. AppleTalk Transaction Protocol
   b. Zone Information Protocol
   c. AppleTalk Filing Protocol
   d. AppleShare

6. **AppleTalk can be used with which of the following network operating systems? Choose all that apply.**
   a. Windows NT
   b. NetWare 3.11
   c. Windows 98
   d. DOS

7. **Which of the following networks is most likely to use AppleTalk?**
   a. a WAN that connects 25 departments on a university campus
   b. a group of three Macintosh graphics computers in a home-based business
   c. a LAN that connects 120 mobile salespeople with their corporate headquarters
   d. a MAN that connects 50 city and county government offices across a large city

# OBJECTIVES

## 2.4  Identify the OSI layers at which the following network components operate: HUBS, SWITCHES, BRIDGES, ROUTERS, NETWORK INTERFACE CARDS

### UNDERSTANDING THE OBJECTIVE

The higher the OSI Model layer at which a network component operates, the more sophisticated its functions. Hubs and repeaters, which simply regenerate signals, operate at the Physical layer. NICs operate at both the Physical and Data Link layers. Bridges and traditional switches operate at the Data Link layer. Routers and Layer 3 switches, which interpret logical addressing information, operate at the Network layer. Gateways operate at multiple layers of the OSI Model.

### WHAT YOU REALLY NEED TO KNOW

- ◆ Network devices operate at the Physical layer of the OSI Model, which handles voltage detection and signaling. Such devices include hubs and repeaters.

- ◆ Hubs and repeaters are not capable of interpreting any type of address—either physical or logical—but instead simply regenerate a signal on a network segment.

- ◆ Network Interface Cards (NICs) operate at both the Physical and Data Link layers of the OSI Model, because they are responsible for both applying signals to a network medium and packaging data into frames.

- ◆ Bridges operate at the Data Link layer of the OSI Model. Because of this, they are only capable of interpreting MAC (or physical) addresses, not logical addresses.

- ◆ Most switches also operate at the Data Link layer of the OSI Model. Like bridges, switches rely on MAC address information to determine how to direct packets to their destination.

- ◆ **Layer 3 switches**, so called because they can function at Layer 3 of the OSI Model (the Network layer) are capable of interpreting logical as well as physical addresses.

- ◆ Routers, because they rely on logical addresses to determine how to forward data to their destination, belong to the Network layer of the OSI Model.

- ◆ Gateways operate at several layers of the OSI Model, since they are a combination of hardware and software. Gateways are most likely to operate in the Network, Transport, Session, and Presentation layers.

### OBJECTIVES ON THE JOB

Understanding the layers at which each component of a network operates is vital to properly designing a network. It is also very important in troubleshooting. For example, you may recognize errors on a network that are due to late collisions on an Ethernet network, leading you to realize that at some point on the network, data signals are not being timed properly. Because signaling belongs to the Physical layer of the OSI Model, you can then begin to examine hubs, repeaters, and NICs for the source of the problem.

# PRACTICE TEST QUESTIONS

1. Which of the following perform functions that belong to the Network layer of the OSI Model? Choose all that apply.
   a. hubs
   b. routers
   c. gateways
   d. NICs

2. Which of the following is responsible for assigning Data Link layer information to a packet?
   a. hub
   b. repeater
   c. NIC
   d. router

3. At what layer of the OSI Model do bridges operate?
   a. Physical
   b. Data Link
   c. Network
   d. Transport

4. If a workstation on a network that relies solely on TCP/IP begins issuing IPX/SPX-based data packets, what device will recognize this problem?
   a. hub
   b. bridge
   c. switch
   d. router

5. Which of the following devices could perform functions at the Session layer of the OSI Model?
   a. hub
   b. switch
   c. gateway
   d. router

6. A Layer 3 switch is capable of performing functions at what two layers of the OSI Model?
   a. Physical and Data Link
   b. Data Link and Network
   c. Physical and Network
   d. Network and Transport

7. What kind of addresses does a traditional switch interpret?
   a. MAC addresses
   b. IP addresses
   c. logical addresses
   d. static addresses

## 2.5 Define the purpose, function and/or use of the following protocols within TCP/IP:

### IP, TCP, AND UDP

### UNDERSTANDING THE OBJECTIVE

IP, TCP, and UDP are all core protocols in the TCP/IP protocol suite. IP resides at the Network layer, while TCP and UDP are Transport layer protocols.

### WHAT YOU REALLY NEED TO KNOW

- The **Internet Protocol (IP)** is a core protocol in the TCP/IP suite that resides at the Network layer of the OSI Model. Its primary purpose is to add logical addresses to data frames, providing information on how and where data should be delivered.

- Because IP provides addressing, logical addresses in the TCP/IP suite are known as **IP addresses**.

- IP is considered connectionless because it does not require that a session be established before it begins transmission, and it does not guarantee that data will be delivered in sequence or error-free.

- The **Transport Control Protocol (TCP)** belongs to the Transport layer of the TCP/IP suite and provides reliable data delivery services. TCP sits on top of the IP subprotocol and makes up for IP's reliability deficiencies with its checksum, flow control, and sequencing information.

- TCP is a connection-oriented subprotocol, which means it requires that a connection be established between communicating nodes before it transmits data.

- A TCP segment contains several components that ensure data reliability, including acknowledgment, code, urgent pointer, and flow control fields.

- The **User Datagram Protocol (UDP)**, like TCP, also sits in the Transport layer of the OSI Model and relies on IP. Unlike TCP, UDP is a connectionless transport service. UDP offers no assurance that packets will be received in the correct sequence. In fact, this protocol does not guarantee that the packets will be received at all.

- UDP's lack of sophistication is an advantage in situations where data must be transferred quickly, such as live audio or video transmissions over the Internet. In these cases, TCP, with its acknowledgments, checksums, and flow control mechanisms, would add too much overhead to the transmission and bog it down.

### OBJECTIVES ON THE JOB

In optimizing and troubleshooting networks, it is critical to understand that TCP is connection-oriented, while UDP is connectionless. Different higher-level TCP/IP subprotocols rely on either TCP or UDP, using UDP when efficiency is their primary criterion or TCP when reliability is more important. For example, TCP should never be used to send live video feeds over the Internet, because its error-correction and flow control mechanisms will cause transmission delays.

# PRACTICE TEST QUESTIONS

1. **Which of the following protocols is responsible for providing information on where data should be delivered?**
   a. TCP
   b. IP
   c. HTTP
   d. UDP

2. **What is the function of the Acknowledgment field in the TCP datagram?**
   a. It confirms receipt of the data in a return message to the sender.
   b. It confirms the size of the datagram to the recipient, proving that the datagram was not corrupted en route.
   c. It confirms the sequence of the datagrams to the recipient.
   d. It confirms the length of the datagram's header in a return message to the sender.

3. **What is an advantage of using UDP over TCP?**
   a. It is more reliable.
   b. It is more secure.
   c. It is more widely compatible.
   d. It is more efficient.

4. **Which of the following protocols are connectionless? Choose all that apply.**
   a. TCP
   b. IP
   c. UDP
   d. HTTP

5. **Which of the following fields would be found in both a UDP and a TCP datagram? Choose all that apply.**
   a. Acknowledgment
   b. Source Port
   c. Sequence Number
   d. Destination Port

6. **What Transport layer protocol does Telnet use?**
   a. TCP
   b. IP
   c. UDP
   d. ICMP

7. **What Network layer protocol does TCP use?**
   a. TCP
   b. UDP
   c. IP
   d. ICMP

## 2.5 Define the purpose, function and/or use of the following protocols within TCP/IP (continued):

### FTP AND TFTP

### UNDERSTANDING THE OBJECTIVE

FTP is the basic file transfer utility used most often to download programs and data from the Internet, and to upload data to Web pages or other TCP/IP hosts. FTP relies on TCP at the Transport layer. TFTP also transfers files but relies on the UDP protocol at the Transport layer.

### WHAT YOU REALLY NEED TO KNOW

◆ The **File Transfer Protocol (FTP)** is an Application layer protocol in the TCP/IP suite that enables a client and server to directly exchange data through a series of commands. FTP manages file transfers between TCP/IP hosts.

◆ At the Transport layer, FTP depends on the TCP protocol, and is, therefore, connection-oriented.

◆ FTP is a popular way to distribute files over the Internet. Some software sites allow users to download programs through a process called "anonymous FTP" in which their FTP host does not require a secure log on.

◆ FTP transfers are separated into two channels: one for data and one for control information. FTP data is exchanged over TCP port 20, and the FTP control commands are sent and received through TCP port 21.

◆ Although FTP is simple, it lets you show file and directory structures, manage files and directories, send data in binary or ASCII format, compress files, and append files.

◆ The **Trivial File Transfer Protocol (TFTP)** is similar to FTP in that it is a TCP/IP Application layer protocol that enables file transfers between computers. TFTP, however, relies on UDP at the Transport layer. Its use of UDP means that TFTP is connectionless and does not guarantee reliable delivery of data.

◆ TFTP does not actually log on to the remote host before enabling file transfers. Instead, when using TFTP, a computer issues a read request or a write request to the remote host. The remote host responds with an acknowledgment, after which the two computers begin transferring data. Each time a packet of data is transmitted to the host, the local workstation waits for an acknowledgment from the host before issuing another packet.

◆ TFTP uses port 69.

### OBJECTIVES ON THE JOB

Before the Web provided an easier means of transferring files, FTP commands were regularly used to exchange data between machines. You can still use FTP commands without using browser software or special client software, that is, from the operating system's command prompt. As a network professional, you may need to use these commands to download software (such as NOS patches or client updates) from hosts.

# PRACTICE TEST QUESTIONS

1. **To connect to the Netscape FTP site (ftp.netscape.com) from an FTP> prompt, what command would you type?**
   a. `ftp netscape.com`
   b. `login ftp.netscape.com`
   c. `ftp.netscape.com`
   d. `open ftp.netscape.com`

2. **What Transport layer protocol does TFTP rely on?**
   a. TCP
   b. IP
   c. UDP
   d. ICMP

3. **What port is used by FTP for data transfer?**
   a. 20
   b. 21
   c. 22
   d. 23

4. **What can you type at the FTP prompt to see a list of available commands?**
   a. ?
   b. query
   c. list commands
   d. commands/H

5. **If an FTP site allows unrestricted access, what user name can you probably type to log in to the site?**
   a. your e-mail address
   b. anonymous
   c. guest
   d. anyone

6. **Which of the following functions cannot be performed via FTP?**
   a. sending a file to a server
   b. changing to another directory
   c. retrieving a file from a server
   d. changing the permissions on a file

7. **What port does TFTP use?**
   a. 21
   b. 23
   c. 45
   d. 69

## 2.5 Define the purpose, function and/or use of the following protocols within TCP/IP (continued):

### SMTP, POP3, AND IMAP

### UNDERSTANDING THE OBJECTIVE

Together, POP3 and SMTP form the routine that enables clients to pick up e-mail from a server. While SMTP transfers mail between servers, POP3 accepts the mail from SMTP and holds it until e-mail clients retrieve it. A newer subprotocol, Internet Mail Access Protocol (IMAP), is replacing POP3 in many cases.

### WHAT YOU REALLY NEED TO KNOW

◆ The **Simple Mail Transfer Protocol (SMTP)** moves messages from one e-mail server to another over TCP/IP networks. SMTP is a subprotocol of the TCP/IP suite.

◆ SMTP provides the basis for Internet e-mail service and relies on higher-level programs for its instructions. Such services as the UNIX sendmail software provide a more user-friendly and sophisticated mail interface while using SMTP for transport.

◆ Requests to receive and send mail go through port 25 on SMTP servers.

◆ The **Post Office Protocol (POP)** relies on SMTP. POP is a subprotocol of the TCP/IP suite that provides centralized storage for e-mail messages. POP also assigns error messages in the case of undeliverable mail.

◆ The current and most widely used version of POP is POP3.

◆ A POP server is necessary to store messages because users are not always logged on to the network and available for receiving messages from the SMTP server.

◆ Both SMTP and a service such as POP3 are necessary for a mail server to receive, store, and forward messages.

◆ When configuring clients to use Internet e-mail, the SMTP and POP3 server names must be specified within the e-mail client.

◆ A small organization can use one POP server for all its users' mail. Very large corporations can have several POP servers, one for each department. Internet service providers typically have one large POP server for all their clients.

◆ POP3 does not let users keep the mail on the server after they retrieve it, which can be a disadvantage for users who move from machine to machine. A newer protocol that is replacing POP3, **Internet Mail Access Protocol (IMAP)**, does let users read messages and keep them on the mail server.

### OBJECTIVES ON THE JOB

If a company's SMTP server is down, mail cannot leave the organization, but it can be exchanged within the organization. If a POP3 server is down, clients cannot pick up mail because the SMTP server cannot transfer mail to it. Most companies have one SMTP server and one or more POP3 servers for storing mail.

## PRACTICE TEST QUESTIONS

1. **If all users in a multinational organization can send and receive mail to and from colleagues, except for those in the Marketing department, what is probably the source of the problem?**
    a. the company's SMTP server
    b. the company's POP server
    c. the Marketing department's SMTP server
    d. the Marketing department's POP server

2. **What port does SMTP use?**
    a. 20
    b. 21
    c. 25
    d. 28

3. **Which of the following is one advantage of using POP over IMAP?**
    a. It requires fewer resources on the server.
    b. It allows clients to save unread messages on the server.
    c. It allows clients to selectively delete messages on the server before downloading them.
    d. It is more reliable.

4. **What does the S in SMTP stand for?**
    a. system
    b. selective
    c. secure
    d. simple

5. **Where must a client identify its SMTP server to properly send and receive mail?**
    a. within the e-mail client software
    b. within the operating system's TCP/IP configuration
    c. within the NIC device settings
    d. within the CMOS settings

6. **Which protocol is responsible for interpreting the following type of address: user@mailserver.com?**
    a. SMTP
    b. POP
    c. IMAP
    d. SNMP

7. **Which of the following is one advantage of using IMAP over POP?**
    a. It requires fewer resources on the server.
    b. It is simpler for a client to use.
    c. It allows clients to selectively delete messages on the server before downloading them.
    d. It can be more easily integrated into environments with multiple SMTP servers.

## 2.5 Define the purpose, function and/or use of the following protocols within TCP/IP (continued):

### HTTP AND HTTPS

### UNDERSTANDING THE OBJECTIVE

HTTP and HTTPS are Application layer protocols in the TCP/IP suite that translate information from Web servers into a user-friendly format. The main difference between HTTP and HTTPS is that HTTPS uses measures to secure information in transit.

### WHAT YOU REALLY NEED TO KNOW

◆ **Hypertext Transport Protocol (HTTP)**, an Application layer protocol, is the language that Web clients and servers use to exchange commands and control information.

◆ When a Web user types the Uniform Resource Locator (URL) or IP address of a Web page in the Web browser's address field, HTTP transports the information about the request to the Web server and returns the Web server's information in **Hypertext Markup Language (HTML)**, the Web document formatting language.

◆ HTTP is also the mechanism that displays a Web page after a user clicks a link.

◆ The original version of HTTP, HTTP/0.9, was released in 1990. This version provided only the simplest means of transferring data over the Internet. Since then, HTTP has been improved to make Web client/server connections more efficient, reliable, and secure.

◆ Simple HTTP information is not secured in transit. To make the HTTP exchange secure, a version of HTTP called S (Secure)-HTTP must be used. Alternately, regular HTTP can be used with an encryption program, such as SSL (Secure Sockets Layer).

◆ When Web page URLs begin with the prefix **HTTPS**, they are requiring that their data be transferred from server to client and vice versa using SSL encryption.

◆ HTTPS uses the TCP port number 443, rather than port 80. To indicate that an SSL connection has been established between a Web server and client, the client's browser displays a padlock in the lower-right corner of the screen (this applies to Internet Explorer and Netscape Communicator versions 4.0 and higher).

### OBJECTIVES ON THE JOB

You should understand the differences between HTTP and HTML for troubleshooting purposes. In addition, you should understand the security limitations of HTTP in case your clients are attempting to transmit secure data. You should also understand when using HTTPS is more appropriate. For example, e-commerce sites or other sites that require financial transactions almost always use HTTPS.

# PRACTICE TEST QUESTIONS

1. **To which layer of the OSI Model does HTTPS belong?**
   a. Data Link
   b. Network
   c. Session
   d. Application

2. **Which of the following is a valid HTTP address?**
   a. 205.23.88.71:80
   b. 267.12.11.89
   c. AE:56:0F:C3:88
   d. 12:80:01:CF

3. **In what year was HTTP first released?**
   a. 1989
   b. 1990
   c. 1991
   d. 1993

4. **Which of the following can be interpreted by HTTP (and result in the display of a Web page)? Choose all that apply.**
   a. http://www.whitehouse.gov
   b. html://www.ibm.net
   c. tcp://www.loc.gov
   d. www.microsoft.net

5. **Which of the following is a secure Web site?**
   a. http://www.ebay.com
   b. www.microsoft.net
   c. https://www.schwab.com/login
   d. html://www.secure.ibm.net

6. **What port does HTTPS use?**
   a. 80
   b. 88
   c. 160
   d. 443

7. **What Transport layer protocol does HTTP rely on?**
   a. TCP
   b. IP
   c. UDP
   d. ICMP

## 2.5   Define the purpose, function and/or use of the following protocols within TCP/IP (continued):

### TELNET

### UNDERSTANDING THE OBJECTIVE

Telnet is a popular terminal emulation utility that enables clients to log on to TCP/IP hosts and perform tasks as if the user were sitting at the device's console.

### WHAT YOU REALLY NEED TO KNOW

◆ **Telnet** is a terminal emulation program that facilitates connections between hosts on a TCP/IP network. Prior to the World Wide Web, Telnet provided the primary means of connecting to other hosts over the Internet.

◆ Often, Telnet is used to connect two dissimilar systems. For example, a remote network administrator could use telnet to log in to a UNIX server from her Windows 2000 PC.

◆ Once connected, a user who has telnetted and logged on to a host can perform any authorized function on that host, just as if she were directly connected to the host.

◆ You can initiate a Telnet session simply by typing `telnet` *Y*, where *Y* is the host name or IP address of the remote host. For example, `telnet lib.dartmouth.edu` will connect you to the Dartmouth library system.

◆ Many options can be used in conjunction with Telnet, including an echo function, flow control, and the selection of full- or half-duplex communication.

◆ Connecting to a host through Telnet requires an authorized logon ID and password. Telnet is a common way to send commands to a server or network device. Routers, for example, can be controlled and managed remotely using the telnet command.

◆ Telnet relies on TCP; thus, it is a connection-oriented service and waits for a receiving node to acknowledge that the connection is sound before transmitting data.

◆ The Telnet service uses port 23 by default.

### OBJECTIVES ON THE JOB

Telnet is the primary method of connecting to network devices, such as routers. It is quick and efficient but does not come with a GUI interface. For this reason, if you are charged with managing routers and other devices, you should memorize the Telnet command options and syntax.

## PRACTICE TEST QUESTIONS

1. **Which of the following could not be controlled through the Telnet utility?**
   a. router
   b. workstation
   c. switch
   d. hub

2. **What port does the Telnet utility use by default?**
   a. 20
   b. 21
   c. 22
   d. 23

3. **In what layer of the OSI Model does Telnet reside?**
   a. Application
   b. Session
   c. Transport
   d. Network

4. **Which of the following utilities allow you to view the directory contents on a remote host, given the proper authority? Choose all that apply.**
   a. PING
   b. Tracert
   c. TFTP
   d. Telnet

5. **Which of the following is a good use for Telnet?**
   a. to browse the contents of an online store
   b. to assess network performance between hosts on the Internet
   c. to send commands to a router
   d. to reconfigure a client whose TCP/IP stack has been damaged

6. **Which of the following is an example of proper Telnet command syntax?**
   a. `telnet 134.45.66.78`
   b. `telnet 134.45.66.78:20`
   c. `tlnt 134.45.66.78:21`
   d. `t 134.45.66.78:23`

7. **Which of the following is a potential disadvantage to using Telnet to remotely log in to a router?**
   a. It is not very secure.
   b. It requires a high-bandwidth connection.
   c. It not very efficient.
   d. It is not compatible with all types of router operating systems.

## 2.5 Define the purpose, function and/or use of the following protocols within TCP/IP (continued):

### ICMP, ARP, AND NTP

### UNDERSTANDING THE OBJECTIVE

ICMP is a protocol that ensures packets arrive at their destination. ARP is a utility that can obtain the MAC address of a device on a TCP/IP network based on its IP address. NTP is a protocol that synchronizes the clocks of all computers on a network.

### WHAT YOU REALLY NEED TO KNOW

◆ Whereas IP ensures that packets reach the correct destination, **Internet Control Message Protocol (ICMP)** notifies the sender when something goes wrong in the transmission process and the packets are not delivered.

◆ ICMP sits between IP and TCP in the Internet layer of the TCP/IP model and does not provide error control. It simply reports which networks are unreachable and which packets have been discarded because the allotted time for their delivery expired.

◆ ICMP is used by diagnostic utilities, such as PING and TRACERT.

◆ **Address Resolution Protocol (ARP)** is a TCP/IP protocol that translates IP addresses into MAC (physical) addresses. ARP accomplishes this translation by broadcasting a packet to the entire network. This packet contains the IP address of the host for which the MAC address needs to be known. When the host whose IP address is being broadcast receives the packet, it responds. Other hosts on the network ignore the broadcast.

◆ Hosts often keep a cache of ARP results, which enable them to respond more quickly to ARP requests (this works as long as IP addresses don't often change). This cache is known as an **ARP table**.

◆ ARP can be a valuable troubleshooting tool for discovering the identity of a machine whose IP address you know or for troubleshooting two machines that are trying to use the same IP address.

◆ **NTP**, the **Network Time Protocol**, is used to synchronize the clocks of computers on a network. It is a very simple protocol that belongs to the Application layer of the TCP/IP Model and depends on UDP.

◆ Time synchronization is necessary on a network (particularly one as large as the Internet) because computers may keep time at slightly different rates. Time discrepancies can adversely affect applications that depend on timed responses.

### OBJECTIVES ON THE JOB

ICMP, ARP, and NTP are important protocols within the TCP/IP suite. You should practice using ARP to determine the MAC address of machines whose IP address you already know, as it may prove to be a valuable troubleshooting tool.

# PRACTICE TEST QUESTIONS

1. **Which of the following utilities make use of ICMP? Choose all that apply.**
   a. TRACERT
   b. winipcfg
   c. PING
   d. inetcfg

2. **What kind of information will an ARP command return? Choose all that apply.**
   a. an IP address
   b. a socket address
   c. an IPX address
   d. a MAC address

3. **What do network hosts do to improve the speed of ARP responses?**
   a. hold ARP tables in cache
   b. keep ARP numbers in their TCP/IP configuration
   c. reassign MAC addresses if a response is not received quickly enough
   d. issue multiple broadcasts to ensure prompt responses

4. **Why is it important that the clocks of all computers on a network are synchronized?**
   a. to ensure that data are delivered to the correct recipient
   b. to ensure that time-dependent applications function properly
   c. to ensure that packets arrive at their destination in the proper order
   d. to ensure that access to shared resources is fairly arbitrated

5. **What type of transmission does ARP use to find a host with a specific IP address?**
   a. multicast
   b. unicast
   c. broadcast
   d. loopback

6. **What Transport layer protocol does NTP rely on?**
   a. TCP
   b. IP
   c. UDP
   d. ICMP

7. **Which of the following devices makes use of ARP tables?**
   a. hub
   b. bridge
   c. router
   d. NIC

## 2.6 Define the function of TCP/UDP ports. Identify well-known ports.

### UNDERSTANDING THE OBJECTIVE

Sockets depend on the assignment of port numbers to different processes. When one computer attempts to communicate with another, it alerts the socket address of the desired process on the other computer. The second computer recognizes the request and establishes the virtual circuit between the two computers so that data exchange can begin.

### WHAT YOU REALLY NEED TO KNOW

◆ A **socket** is a logical address assigned to a specific process running on a host computer. It forms a virtual connection between the host and client.

◆ A **port** is a number assigned to a process running on a host. Port numbers can have any value. Some software programs choose their own port numbers by default.

◆ The socket's address is a combination of the host computer's IP address and the port number associated with a process. For example, the Telnet service on a Web server with an IP address of 10.43.3.87 might have a socket address of 10.43.3.87:23, where 23 is the standard port number for the Telnet service.

◆ Port numbers in the range of 0 to 1023 are also called **well-known ports**, because they were long ago assigned by Internet authorities to popular services (for example, FTP and Telnet), and are, therefore, well-known and frequently used.

◆ Some well-known ports are Telnet - 23, HTTP - 80, FTP - 20 (for data transfer), FTP - 21 (for commands), SMTP - 25, and POP3 - 101.

◆ The use of port numbers simplifies TCP/IP communications. When a client requests communications with a server and specifies port 23, for example, the server knows immediately that the client wants a Telnet session. No extra data exchange is necessary to define the session type, and the server can initiate the Telnet service without delay. The server connects to the client's Telnet port, which by default is also port 23, and establishes a virtual circuit.

◆ Port numbers can be configured through software. Most servers maintain a text-based file of port numbers and their associated services, which is editable. Changing a default port number is not usually a good idea, though, because it goes against the standard. However, some network administrators who are preoccupied with security may change their servers' port numbers in an attempt to confuse potential hackers.

### OBJECTIVES ON THE JOB

You most often use port numbers when networking with the Internet. For example, if you install Web server software, you must identify some ports on that server. You can then leave ports at their defaults (for example, port 80 for the HTTP server) or change them to another number not already reserved by a process.

# PRACTICE TEST QUESTIONS

1. **The socket address 204.113.19.80:23 probably belongs to which of the following services?**
    - a. FTP
    - b. HTTP
    - c. Telnet
    - d. SMTP

2. **In which of the following situations does it make sense to use a port number other than the default assigned by the software?**
    - a. when configuring an FTP server for users of freeware to download a patch
    - b. when configuring a Web server that hosts an online clothing store
    - c. when configuring an FTP server for employees within an organization to download their payroll information
    - d. when configuring the SNMP interface on a server inside an organization's firewall

3. **A socket allows two computers to establish what kind of circuit?**
    - a. virtual
    - b. closed
    - c. transitory
    - d. application

4. **Which of the following processes probably uses the socket address 135.67.99.118:80?**
    - a. HTTP
    - b. Telnet
    - c. FTP
    - d. SNMP

5. **How many ports can be assigned on one server?**
    - a. only one
    - b. no more than 10
    - c. no more than 100
    - d. over 65,000

6. **What is the default port for POP3?**
    - a. 10
    - b. 21
    - c. 90
    - d. 101

7. **Port numbers in the range of 0 to 1023 are called**
    - a. default ports.
    - b. well-known ports.
    - c. constrained ports.
    - d. reserved ports.

# OBJECTIVES

## 2.7    Identify the purpose of the following network services:

### DHCP AND BOOTP

### UNDERSTANDING THE OBJECTIVE

DHCP replaced BOOTP as an easier and more accurate method of assigning IP addresses to clients on a network. Both arose from the need to streamline the IP addressing process when networks became large and relied mostly on TCP/IP. DHCP is ubiquitous on modern networks, and because of its popularity, the software that controls DHCP is part of all network operating systems and client software.

### WHAT YOU REALLY NEED TO KNOW

◆ The **Bootstrap Protocol (BOOTP)** uses a central list of IP addresses and their associated devices' MAC addresses to dynamically assign IP addresses to clients.

◆ When a client that relies on BOOTP first connects to the network, it sends a broadcast message to the network asking to be assigned an IP address. This broadcast message includes the MAC address of the client's NIC. The BOOTP server recognizes a BOOTP client's request, looks up the client's MAC address in its BOOTP table, and responds to the client with the client's IP address, the IP address of the server, the host name of the server, and the IP address of a default router.

◆ **Dynamic Host Configuration Protocol (DHCP)** is an automated means of assigning a unique IP address to every device on a network.

◆ DHCP centrally manages IP allocation from a DHCP server on the network. It leases IP addresses to a client when the client requests a DHCP response via UDP broadcast.

◆ DHCP leases last for a time period that the network administrator specifies, from minutes to forever. The IP address assigned to a node will remain in effect (even after rebooting) until the lease has expired.

◆ DHCP leases can be manually forced to expire or renew at any time from either the client's TCP/IP configuration or the server's DHCP configuration. In Windows terms, the act of terminating a DHCP lease is called a **release**.

◆ DHCP reduces the possibility for error in IP assignment. Nodes cannot be assigned invalid addresses, and two nodes will rarely experience addressing conflicts.

◆ DHCP limits the amount of time that networking staff have to spend managing IP addresses. The opposite of DHCP, static addressing, necessitates manually configuring an IP address on each node.

### OBJECTIVES ON THE JOB

Because it can be easily established and managed, DHCP is a popular method of IP address allocation on large and small networks alike. Client and server operating systems make DHCP even easier by making it part of their TCP/IP software. In fact, DHCP is typically selected as the default method of obtaining IP addresses on client machines.

# PRACTICE TEST QUESTIONS

1. **By what means does a newly connected client find the DHCP server?**
   a. It issues a TCP request to which the DHCP server responds.
   b. It issues an ARP request to which the DHCP server responds.
   c. It issues a UDP broadcast to which the DHCP server responds.
   d. It issues a NETSTAT request to which the DHCP server responds.

2. **What older TCP/IP utility does DHCP replace?**
   a. nbtstat
   b. netstat
   c. RARP
   d. BOOTP

3. **What is the best course of action if a Windows 98 client receives a message upon booting up, indicating that another workstation has reserved the IP address it previously leased from the DHCP server?**
   a. Click OK and ignore the error.
   b. Click OK, click Release, and then click Renew in the TCP/IP Properties dialog box.
   c. Write down the MAC address of the other workstation and reboot that workstation before continuing.
   d. Click OK, then select Release All in the TCP/IP Properties dialog box.

4. **Which two of the following are advantages to using DHCP over older IP addressing methods?**
   a. DHCP uses fewer server resources.
   b. DHCP requires less time to manage.
   c. DHCP reduces the possibility for duplicate addresses.
   d. DHCP requires a much shorter host file.

5. **Which of the following is made easier because of DHCP?**
   a. workstation naming
   b. subnetting
   c. cabling
   d. client moves

6. **What is the opposite of DHCP?**
   a. static addressing
   b. limited-term addressing
   c. octet addressing
   d. physical addressing

7. **If it is not manually terminated, how long does a DHCP lease last?**
   a. two days
   b. one week
   c. as long as the network administrator specifies
   d. 24 hours

## 2.7  Identify the purpose of the following network services (continued):

### DNS AND WINS

### UNDERSTANDING THE OBJECTIVE

DNS associates IP addresses with domains on the Internet to allow clients to transfer information more easily. DNS, which replaces the older method of resolving names via a single host file, is a hierarchical system in which multiple servers across the Internet share the burden of finding machines belonging to specific domains.

### WHAT YOU REALLY NEED TO KNOW

◆ In the mid-1980s a hierarchical way of resolving host and domain names with their IP addresses was developed. This system was called the **Domain Name System (DNS)**. The DNS database does not rely on one file or even one server, but is distributed over key computers on the Internet to prevent catastrophic failure if one or a few computers go down.

◆ DNS is a TCP/IP service that belongs to the Application layer of the OSI Model.

◆ A TCP/IP host is typically associated with a **domain**, a group of computers that have part of their IP addresses in common. Often, this group of computers belongs to the same organization.

◆ A domain is identified by its **domain name**. Usually, a domain name is associated with a company or other type of organization, such as a university or military unit. For example, IBM's domain name is ibm.com.

◆ While some organizations use only one name server, large organizations often maintain two or more name servers. When more than one name server exists, a primary name server is the ultimate naming authority on the network.

◆ Each device on the network relies on the name server and, therefore, must be able to find it. The IP address of the client's primary and secondary DNS servers must be specified in the client's TCP/IP properties.

◆ The **Windows Internet Naming Service (WINS)** provides a means of resolving NetBIOS names with IP addresses. WINS provides for the NetBIOS protocol what DNS provides for the TCP/IP protocol.

◆ WINS can be implemented on servers running Windows NT Server version 3.5 or above. The WINS server maintains a database that accepts requests from Windows or DOS clients to register with a particular NetBIOS name.

◆ WINS does not assign names or IP addresses; it only keeps track of NetBIOS names and their addresses.

### OBJECTIVES ON THE JOB

Every client on the network must be able to access a DNS server to resolve host names to addresses.

# PRACTICE TEST QUESTIONS

1. **Which of the following best describes the relationship between IP addresses and domains?**
    a. Each domain is associated with a single IP address.
    b. Each IP address is associated with a single domain.
    c. Each domain is associated with a range of IP addresses.
    d. Each IP address is associated with a group of domains.

2. **To what layer of the OSI Model does DNS belong?**
    a. Application
    b. Presentation
    c. Session
    d. Transport

3. **Which two of the following domain names could belong to a business?**
    a. ferrari.edu
    b. ferrari.mil
    c. ferrari.com
    d. ferrari.it

4. **Where on a client workstation is WINS configured?**
    a. in the network adapter properties
    b. in the modem settings
    c. in the TCP/IP properties
    d. in the Microsoft client settings

5. **Which one of the following is most likely to use WINS?**
    a. a Windows 3.11 workstation
    b. a Linux server
    c. a Novell server
    d. a Windows 2000 workstation

6. **What is a significant difference between the domain name system and local host files?**
    a. DNS is hierarchical, while a host file is flat.
    b. A host file is easier to maintain than DNS.
    c. A host file is more efficient than DNS.
    d. DNS represents a single point of failure while a host file ensures redundancy.

7. **How many different organizations can use the same domain name?**
    a. one
    b. no more than two
    c. no more than two, as long as they are located in the same country
    d. no more than four

## 2.7 Identify the purpose of the following network services (continued):

### NAT/ICS

### UNDERSTANDING THE OBJECTIVE

Network address translation (NAT) is a method of using an IP gateway to associate Internet-recognized IP addresses with a client. Each time the client accesses the Internet, the NAT gateway assigns the client's data a new source IP address.

### WHAT YOU REALLY NEED TO KNOW

◆ IP gateways can be used to "hide" the IP numbers assigned within an organization and keep its devices' IP addresses secret from any public network (such as the Internet). Clients behind the gateway may use any IP addressing scheme, whether or not it is recognized or sanctioned by the Internet authorities. Once those clients need to connect to the Internet, however, they must have an Internet-recognizable IP address in order to exchange data. When the client's transmission reaches the IP gateway, the gateway assigns the client's transmission a publicly recognized IP address. This process is known as **network address translation (NAT)**.

◆ One reason for using NAT is to add a marginal amount of security to a private network when it is connected to a public network (such as the Internet). Because the transmission is assigned a new IP address when it reaches the public sphere, others outside the organization cannot trace the transmission to the client.

◆ NAT also enables a network administrator to develop her own network addressing scheme that does not conform with a scheme dictated by ICANN. This can make network management and troubleshooting easier.

◆ Yet another reason for using NAT is to share a limited number of publicly recognized IP addresses among multiple machines.

◆ **Internet Connection Sharing (ICS)** is a service found on Microsoft Windows PC operating systems, such as Windows 98 and Windows ME, that allows multiple, networked computers to share a single Internet connection and a single IP address.

◆ ICS assigns one computer to process Internet requests from each connected machine. This computer, or the host, issues each of the connected computers an IP address but that address is only for use within the home network. When the host computer accesses the Internet, it uses just the one IP address, its own.

◆ ICS is similar to NAT in that it prevents multiple nodes from having to reveal their IP addresses when connecting to a public network (such as the Internet).

### OBJECTIVES ON THE JOB

Chances are that you will encounter NAT in an environment where IP addresses are scarce or where the IP addresses of clients on a private network need to be protected from outside detection.

# PRACTICE TEST QUESTIONS

1. **Which of the following computers would use ICS?**
    a. a NetWare 5.x server
    b. a Windows 98 workstation
    c. a Macintosh workstation
    d. a Windows NT server

2. **What type of connectivity device manages NAT?**
    a. bridge
    b. hub
    c. switch
    d. gateway

3. **What does "ICS" stand for?**
    a. Internet connection sharing
    b. Internet configuration system
    c. Intermittent communications session
    d. Integrated communication system

4. **Which of the following are reasons for using NAT? Choose all that apply.**
    a. to share a limited number of valid IP addresses among multiple clients
    b. to automatically assign IP addresses to clients when they log on to a LAN
    c. to mask the real IP addresses of clients on a private network
    d. to increase the speed with which Web pages are retrieved from the Internet

5. **Which of the following is a reason for using ICS?**
    a. to allow remote users to securely log in to a private LAN via the Internet
    b. to cache frequently used Web pages so that they can be subsequently accessed faster
    c. to share a single Internet connection among multiple clients
    d. to detect the presence of suspicious files, such as viruses, in Internet downloads

6. **Which of the following is most likely to use ICS?**
    a. a small nonprofit organization that uses the Internet to solicit contributions
    b. a regional insurance company whose salespeople dial into the corporate LAN each night from their homes
    c. an Internet Service Provider that needs to ensure connectivity between multiple data centers and telecommunications carriers
    d. a local architectural firm that sends drawings to and receives drawings from various clients across the nation

7. **How does NAT compare to firewalls, in terms of securing data between public and private networks?**
    a. NAT offers more security for data in transit.
    b. NAT offers more security for resources on a server.
    c. NAT offers less security for data in transit.
    d. NAT offers more security for private client identification.

## 2.7 Identify the purpose of the following network services (continued):

### SNMP

### UNDERSTANDING THE OBJECTIVE

SNMP is the underlying mechanism through which network devices and connections are managed. It can detect whether a device is responding under certain predefined conditions.

### WHAT YOU REALLY NEED TO KNOW

◆ The **Simple Network Management Protocol (SNMP)** collects information (such as up/down status) about computers, including network components, such as servers and routers. Network administrators rely on SNMP to monitor and manage networks.

◆ As its name implies, SNMP is a very simple subprotocol. Its functionality is limited to determining whether a device is responding under specified conditions.

◆ SNMP is a subprotocol of the TCP/IP suite that resides in the Application layer of the OSI Model.

◆ SNMP relies on the Transport layer subprotocol UDP; therefore, it does not verify that a connection has been established before it attempts to discover information about a device.

◆ Information gathered via SNMP is stored in a **Management Information Base (MIB)** by a network management system. MIBs are then interpreted by sophisticated network management software packages, such as HP OpenView.

◆ In order for devices to submit information to a MIB, they must be SNMP-compliant. Most modern routers, switches, bridges, and managed hubs have this capability.

◆ One drawback to SNMP is that it may generate a large volume of potentially superfluous information along with useful information (for example, it may report each time a NIC is disconnected from the network).

### OBJECTIVES ON THE JOB

Network administrators often use SNMP to determine the health of the network. For example, a Web server's HTTP port can be monitored through SNMP to determine if it is responding. If SNMP doesn't detect a response, a program can use that information to alert the network administrator that the Web page is down. Thanks to SNMP, problems can be detected and addressed quickly.

# PRACTICE TEST QUESTIONS

1. **On which of the following Transport layer subprotocols does SNMP rely?**
   a. TCP
   b. IP
   c. UDP
   d. ICMP

2. **What stores information collected by the SNMP protocol?**
   a. MIP
   b. MIB
   c. SMIP
   d. SMB

3. **Which of the following programs could be considered a network management system?**
   a. Netscape Navigator
   b. Microsoft SQL Server
   c. Microsoft Exchange Server
   d. HP OpenView

4. **In addition to detecting whether a device is running, what other two functions can SNMP help provide? Choose all that apply.**
   a. LAN topology mapping
   b. traffic route optimization
   c. broadcast transmission filtering
   d. notification of network problems

5. **At what layer of the OSI Model does SNMP operate?**
   a. Application
   b. Session
   c. Transport
   d. Data Link

6. **Which of the following network components are likely to issue SNMP data? Choose all that apply.**
   a. server
   b. repeater
   c. router
   d. tape backup drive

7. **Which of the following conditions would SNMP be able to report?**
   a. A Web server is responding to requests at half of its normal speed.
   b. Half of the ports on a switch are not accepting data.
   c. A NIC is issuing broadcast error messages to the rest of the nodes on its segment.
   d. A user is prevented from logging in to the network because he has entered an invalid password three times.

## 2.8  Identify IP addresses (IPv4 and IPv6) and their default subnet masks.

### UNDERSTANDING THE OBJECTIVE

IPv4 is the version of TCP/IP addressing used on most hosts today. Addresses in this scheme are represented by four eight-bit bytes (for a total of 32 bits) separated by periods. In IPv6, the new addressing scheme, addresses are composed of eight 16-bit fields and total 128 bits.

### WHAT YOU REALLY NEED TO KNOW

◆ The current version of IP addressing used by most of the Internet, as well as most private networks, is **IP version 4 (IPv4)**.

◆ In the IPv4 convention, each IP address is a unique 32-bit number, divided into four **octets**, or 8-bit bytes, that are separated by periods. An example of a valid IP address is 144.92.43.178.

◆ Valid octet numbers range from 0 to 255 and represent a binary address. For example, an octet with the value of 68 equals 01 00 01 00 in an 8-bit binary pattern.

◆ In the IPv4 convention, each IP address contains two types of information: network and host. The first octet identifies the network class: A, B, or C.

◆ All nodes on a Class A network share the first octet of their IP numbers, a number between 1 and 126. Nodes on a Class B network share the first two octets, and their IP addresses begin with a number between 128 and 191. Class C network IP numbers share the first three octets, with their first octet being a number between 192 and 223.

◆ Because only 126 Class A networks are available on the Internet, most Class A networks have already been reserved by large corporations, educational institutions, or governments.

◆ To respond to a demand for more IP addresses, a new addressing scheme has been developed, called **IP version 6 (IPv6)**.

◆ IPv6 addresses are composed of eight 16-bit fields and total 128 bits. The added fields and the larger address size results in an increase of $2^{128}$ (or 4 billion times 4 billion times 4 billion) available IP addresses in the IPv6 addressing scheme.

◆ While each octet in an IPv4 address contains binary numbers separated by a period, each field in an IPv6 address contains hexadecimal numbers separated by a colon. An example of a valid IPv6 address is F:F:0:0:0:0:3012:0CE3.

◆ Because many IPv6 addresses will contain multiple fields that have values of 0, shorthand for representing these fields has been established. This shorthand substitutes "::" for any number of adjacent multiple zero-value fields.

### OBJECTIVES ON THE JOB

Even if your network uses DHCP to automatically assign IP addresses to network nodes, you still need to be able to identify, interpret, and manually assign both IP addresses and subnet masks.

# PRACTICE TEST QUESTIONS

1. **What is one of the primary reasons for switching from the IPv4 to the IPv6 addressing scheme?**
   a. IPv6 offers many more IP addresses than IPv4.
   b. IPv6 is more universally accepted and used than IPv4.
   c. IPv6 is more compatible with newer networking hardware and software.
   d. IPv6 offers a simpler management solution to assigning IP addresses.

2. **Which of the following best describes the convention for representing IPv4 addresses?**
   a. eight 16-bit fields separated by periods
   b. 16 eight-bit fields separated by colons
   c. four 8-bit fields separated by periods
   d. four 16-bit fields separated by colons

3. **Which of the following types of IPv4 networks has the most available networks (assuming that subnetting is not in use)?**
   a. Class A
   b. Class B
   c. Class C
   d. They all have the same number of available networks.

4. **Which of the following is a valid IPv6 address?**
   a. AE::00::DC
   b. 124.55.89.112:80
   c. 177.9.3.58
   d. AE:03:FF:00:16:CE:C6:00E2

5. **Which of the following IPv4 addressing techniques is rendered obsolete by IPv6?**
   a. NAT
   b. IPSec
   c. RAS
   d. WINS

6. **On a Class A network in the IPv4 addressing scheme, all nodes have which octet(s) in common?**
   a. the first only
   b. the first and second
   c. the second only
   d. the second and third

7. **To which class of network does the following IPv4 address belong (assuming subnetting is not in use): 198.34.61.207?**
   a. A
   b. B
   c. C
   d. D

## 2.9   Identify the purpose of subnetting and default gateways.

### UNDERSTANDING THE OBJECTIVE

To efficiently use a limited number of IP addresses, the concept of subnetting was devised in the 1980s. Subnetting separates networks into smaller subnets that can use more IP addresses, as long as a subnet mask is specified. On TCP/IP networks, the gateways that connect subnets are called default IP gateways. These gateways are usually interfaces on routers.

### WHAT YOU REALLY NEED TO KNOW

- ◆ **Subnetting** is the process of subdividing a single class of network into multiple, smaller networks. It results in a more efficient use of limited IP addresses.

- ◆ In subnetting, one of the address's octets is used to indicate how the network is subdivided. Rather than consisting simply of network and host information, a subnetted address consists of network, subnet, and host information.

- ◆ Devices in a subnetted network are assigned a **subnet mask**, a special 32-bit number that, combined with a device's IP address, tells the rest of the network the network class to which the device is attached.

- ◆ If a subnet mask is not specified, the default subnet mask for a Class A network is 255.0.0.0. For a Class B network, the default subnet mask is 255.255.0.0, and for a Class C network, the default subnet mask is 255.255.255.0.

- ◆ Every device on a TCP/IP network that connects to other networks has a **default gateway**, the gateway that first interprets its outbound requests to other subnets and last interprets its inbound requests from other subnets.

- ◆ In the TCP/IP configuration of every device, the address of a default gateway has to be specified before the device can communicate with devices on other TCP/IP networks.

- ◆ Each default gateway is assigned its own IP address. Typically, the IP address of a default gateway contains only the number "1" in its last octet.

- ◆ Default gateways may connect more than one internal network or connect an internal network with external networks, such as WANs or the Internet.

### OBJECTIVES ON THE JOB

You should suspect an IP gateway problem when TCP/IP traffic travels properly within a subnet but not outside the subnet. Conversely, if traffic travels beyond the subnet (but has problems elsewhere), you can assume that the problem lies outside the IP default gateway.

## PRACTICE TEST QUESTIONS

1. **Which of the following IP addresses probably belongs to an IP default gateway?**
   a. 161.57.89.110
   b. 161.57.89.10
   c. 161.57.89.0
   d. 161.57.89.1

2. **What is the default subnet mask for a Class B network?**
   a. 0.0.0.0
   b. 255.0.0.0
   c. 255.255.0.0
   d. 255.255.255.255

3. **In which of the following situations would an IP default gateway be necessary (assuming default subnet masks are in use)?**
   a. A printer with an IP address of 159.45.22.144 receives a print job from a server with an IP address of 159.45.22.39.
   b. A client with an IP address of 144.92.104.82 sends an e-mail message to a client with an IP address of 144.92.39.82.
   c. A client with an IP address of 144.92.104.56 downloads a Web page from an HTTP server with an IP address of 10.12.10.13.
   d. A client with an IP address of 144.92.104.56 retrieves a file from a Windows 2000 server with an IP address of 144.92.104.20.

4. **What is the main purpose for subnetting a network?**
   a. to create a more systematic way of tracking addresses on the network
   b. to more equitably allocate addresses to all devices on a network
   c. to make more efficient use of a limited number of addresses
   d. to make TCP/IP client and server configuration easier

5. **What types of information are contained in the IP address of a device on a network that has not been subnetted?**
   a. host, subnet, and network
   b. host, server, and network
   c. protocol and network
   d. host and network

6. **To what type of network does the default subnet mask 255.255.255.0 belong?**
   a. Class A
   b. Class B
   c. Class C
   d. Class D

7. **How many gateways are required to transfer information across the Internet from a client with the IP address 122.09.83.67 to a client with the IP address 155.67.28.30?**
   a. at least one
   b. at least four
   c. at least six
   d. at least eight

## 2.10 Identify the differences between public vs. private networks.

### UNDERSTANDING THE OBJECTIVE

Public networks are accessible to multiple users and can be accessed without credentials. Data traveling over public networks is often susceptible to eavesdropping and, therefore, should be protected. Private networks are accessible only to authorized users.

### WHAT YOU REALLY NEED TO KNOW

◆ A **public network** is one that allows access from any node that has the capability to connect to it. Certain resources of a public network may be restricted but access to the network is not.

◆ Most public networks rely at least in part on public transmission systems, such as the PSTN.

◆ Because they rely on public transmission methods, public networks are more susceptible to eavesdropping. Data transmitted over a public network should be protected through encryption or another technique to secure data.

◆ The Internet is the largest and most familiar example of a public network.

◆ A **private network** is one that allows only authorized users to connect to it and access its resources. Examples of private networks are corporate LANs and WANs.

◆ Private networks use private transmission systems, such as wiring inside a corporation's building, or a T-1 line leased from a telecommunications carrier that is solely dedicated to carrying one organization's network traffic.

◆ When private networks connect to public networks (for example, a corporate LAN that allows its users to connect to the Internet), measures must be taken to protect the private network from public access. NAT, data encryption (such as IPSec), and the use of firewalls can protect a private network and its data from public access.

◆ **Virtual private networks (VPNs)** are secured tunnels that protect data in transit. VPNs are often used to create private WANs over over public transmission systems.

◆ When created across public transmission systems, VPNs serve an organization's users but isolate that organization's traffic from other users of the same public lines. They provide a way of constructing a private WAN from less-expensive public transmission systems.

### OBJECTIVES ON THE JOB

Chances are you will work on a private network that connects to the Internet (a public network) at some point in your career. You should be aware of current techniques for preventing unauthorized users from accessing your private network through the public network. Because these techniques change frequently, a large organization may dedicate an employee or a whole team of people to managing security between the private and public networks.

## PRACTICE TEST QUESTIONS

1. **Which of the following is an example of a public network?**
   - a. PSTN
   - b. VPN
   - c. VLAN
   - d. SONET ring

2. **What kind of private WAN uses a public network's transmission systems?**
   - a. PSTN
   - b. VPN
   - c. VLAN
   - d. SONET ring

3. **On which of the following networks would the security of data in transit be of the greatest concern?**
   - a. a MAN that connects two buildings on a corporate campus via fiber-optic cable
   - b. a WAN that connects 25 buildings of an insurance company through dedicated T-1 lines in a partial mesh topology
   - c. a LAN that connects 56 customer service representatives at a company's headquarters and allows access to the Internet through a gateway and firewall
   - d. a WAN that allows its 250 salespeople to access their company's server over the Internet from hotel rooms around the country

4. **Which of the following is a good way of encrypting data in transit?**
   - a. NAT
   - b. firewalls
   - c. IPSec
   - d. HTTP

5. **Which one of the following networks would be the most expensive to install?**
   - a. a MAN that connects two office buildings on a corporate campus via fiber optic cable
   - b. a WAN that connects 25 buildings of an insurance company through dedicated T-1 lines in a partial mesh topology
   - c. a LAN that connects 56 customer service representatives at a catalog company's headquarters and allows employees to access the Internet through a gateway and firewall
   - d. a WAN that allows its 250 salespeople who work for a pharmaceutical company to dial in to a remote access server from their hotel rooms around the country

6. **Which of the following is characteristic of private networks but not public networks?**
   - a. restricted access to resources
   - b. the use of routers to interconnect dissimilar network types
   - c. the use of gateways
   - d. the use of leased WAN lines

7. **The Internet is an example of a public network. True or false?**

# OBJECTIVES

## 2.11 Identify the basic characteristics (e.g., speed, capacity, media) of the following WAN technologies:

### PACKET SWITCHING VS. CIRCUIT SWITCHING

### UNDERSTANDING THE OBJECTIVE

Circuit switching is a transmission technology used by the PSTN and by T-carriers. In circuit switching, a channel is dedicated to a certain transmission until the transmission is completed. In packet switching, which is used by Ethernet and FDDI, data are divided into packets. The packets may then take any route to their destination, where they are reassembled in their original order.

### WHAT YOU REALLY NEED TO KNOW

- In **circuit switching**, a connection is established between two network nodes before they begin transmitting data. Bandwidth is dedicated to this connection and remains available until the users terminate communication between the two nodes. While the nodes remain connected, all data follow the same path initially selected by the switch.
- The PSTN uses circuit switching. When you place a telephone call, your call goes through a circuit-switched connection. Similarly, when you connect your home PC via modem to your ISP's access server, that connection uses circuit switching.
- Because circuit switching monopolizes its allotted bandwidth while the two stations remain connected (even when no actual communication is taking place), it is not an economical technology.
- Some network applications that cannot tolerate the time delay it takes to reorganize data packets, such as live audio or video conferencing, benefit from circuit switching's dedicated path.
- Some WAN technologies, such as ISDN and T-1 service, also use circuit switching.
- **Packet switching** breaks data into packets before they are transported. Packets can travel any path on the network to their destinations, because each packet contains the destination address and sequencing information. Consequently, packets can attempt to find the fastest circuit available at any instant. They need not follow each other along the same path, nor must they arrive at their destination in the same sequence they left the transmitting node.
- The destination node on a packet-switched network reassembles the packets based on the packets' control information. Because of the time it takes to reassemble the packets into a message, packet switching is not suited to live audio or video transmission. Nevertheless, it is a fast and efficient mechanism for transporting typical network data, such as word-processing or spreadsheet files.
- Examples of packet-switched networks include Ethernet and FDDI.

### OBJECTIVES ON THE JOB

If you work on packet-switched LANs, such as those that use the Ethernet network access method, you must understand how the disassembly, sequencing, and reassembly of packets works.

# PRACTICE TEST QUESTIONS

1. **Which of the following is characteristic of a packet-switched network, but not a circuit-switched network?**
   - a. sequencing
   - b. transceivers
   - c. star topology
   - d. shared channels

2. **Which of the following technologies uses packet switching?**
   - a. PSTN
   - b. Ethernet
   - c. T-1
   - d. ISDN

3. **Which of the following best describes a packet?**
   - a. a collection of data discarded by a router
   - b. a discreet unit of data
   - c. a means to translate packet-switched data into circuit-switched data
   - d. a continuous stream of data

4. **Which of the following is best suited for video conferencing over the network?**
   - a. packet switching
   - b. circuit switching
   - c. Ethernet
   - d. Token Ring

5. **Which of the following networks would certainly use a combination of packet switching and circuit switching?**
   - a. a MAN that connects two office buildings using 100BaseFX
   - b. a WAN that connects 25 buildings of an insurance regional company through dedicated T-1s
   - c. a LAN that connects 200 users within a large bank
   - d. a WAN that connects multiple office buildings using FDDI and allows remote employees to connect by dialing their ISP and logging on to a VPN

6. **What is the single greatest disadvantage to using packet switching?**
   - a. It is expensive.
   - b. It is not highly scalable.
   - c. Its standards are not stable.
   - d. It is ill suited to time-sensitive transmissions.

7. **Which of the following best describes circuit switching?**
   - a. A dedicated connection is established between two network nodes and remains available until the users terminate communication.
   - b. A connection is established between two network nodes and may allow other nodes to use and share the same channel while the first two nodes communicate.
   - c. No dedicated connection is established between two network nodes, but a best path between them is dynamically discovered as they begin transmitting data.
   - d. No connection is established between two network nodes, but data are separated into units that may follow separate paths.

## 2.11 Identify the basic characteristics (e.g., speed, capacity, media) of the following WAN technologies (continued):

### ISDN

### UNDERSTANDING THE OBJECTIVE

ISDN was developed in the mid-1980s to send digital data over public transmission lines. ISDN can be a dial-up connection or dedicated solution. It has been a popular choice for individuals and small businesses who want a faster and more secure connection than the PSTN can offer.

### WHAT YOU REALLY NEED TO KNOW

- ◆ **Integrated Services Digital Network (ISDN)** is a standard established by the International Telecommunications Union (ITU) for transmitting data over digital lines.

- ◆ ISDN is a circuit-switched technology that uses the telephone carrier's lines and dial-up connections, like PSTN. Unlike PSTN, ISDN travels exclusively over digital connections and can carry data and voice simultaneously.

- ◆ All ISDN connections are based on two types of channels: B channels and D channels.

- ◆ The **B channel**, which is the bearer channel, uses circuit-switching techniques to carry voice, video, audio, and data over the ISDN connection. A single B channel has a maximum throughput of 64 Kbps, although it is sometimes limited to 56 Kbps by the ISDN provider. The number of B channels in an ISDN connection can vary.

- ◆ The **D channel** is the data channel that uses packet-switching techniques to carry information about the call, such as session initiation and termination signals, caller identity, call forwarding, and conference calling signals.

- ◆ A single D channel has a maximum throughput of 16 Kbps.

- ◆ North American users commonly use two types of ISDN connections: Basic Rate Interface (BRI) or Primary Rate Interface (PRI).

- ◆ **BRI** uses two B channels and one D channel, as summarized by this notation: 2B+D. The two B channels are treated as separate connections and can carry voice and data or two data streams simultaneously and separately.

- ◆ Through a process called **bonding**, two 64-Kbps B channels can be combined to achieve an effective throughput of 128 Kbps, the maximum throughput for BRI.

- ◆ **PRI** uses 23 B channels and one 64-Kbps D channel, which, when combined, can offer 1.54 Mbps throughput. PRI is less commonly used by individual subscribers than BRI but can be used by organizations needing more throughput.

### OBJECTIVES ON THE JOB

ISDN lines have been a popular choice for small businesses for moderately fast connections to the Internet. Due to their ability to transmit voice and data simultaneously, ISDN lines can also eliminate the need to pay for separate phone lines to support faxes, modems, and voice.

# PRACTICE TEST QUESTIONS

1. **How much throughput is optimally available through BRI?**
   a. 1.455 Mbps
   b. 56 Kbps
   c. 128 Kbps
   d. 768 Kbps

2. **Which of the following is an advantage of ISDN over PSTN?**
   a. It's less expensive.
   b. It provides greater throughput.
   c. It is easier to configure.
   d. It doesn't depend on public transmission lines.

3. **Which of the following is an advantage of DSL over BRI?**
   a. It provides greater throughput.
   b. It's easier to configure.
   c. It doesn't require any special hardware.
   d. It doesn't depend on public transmission lines.

4. **In the context of ISDN services, what does "2B+D" stand for?**
   a. two basic and one denominator
   b. basic, broadband, and digital
   c. two bearer and one data
   d. bearer, broadband, and digital

5. **What is the maximum throughput of one B channel?**
   a. 8 Kbps
   b. 16 Kbps
   c. 64 Kbps
   d. 128 Kbps

6. **What is the Physical layer difference between PSTN and ISDN?**
   a. ISDN uses all digital lines, while PSTN may use analog lines.
   b. ISDN can encapsulate IP packets, while PSTN cannot.
   c. ISDN uses Ethernet NICs, while PSTN uses Token Ring NICs.
   d. ISDN lines can handle 128 Kbps while, PSTN lines can handle only 56 Kbps.

7. **In which of the following situations might ISDN be the best selection?**
   a. for a small nonprofit organization that needs a connection to the Internet to pick up mail every other day
   b. for a multinational insurance company that expects its salespeople to dial in each night from their hotel rooms
   c. for a large software development company that needs to transmit and receive programs all day and all night
   d. for a small, rural architectural firm that needs to pick up e-mail frequently and occasionally send and receive drawings

# OBJECTIVES

## 2.11 Identify the basic characteristics (e.g., speed, capacity, media) of the following WAN technologies (continued):

### FDDI AND ATM

## UNDERSTANDING THE OBJECTIVE

FDDI and ATM are technologies whose network access methods differ from Ethernet and Token Ring. FDDI relies on a double ring of fiber-optic cable, making it very reliable. ATM relies on fixed-size packets called cells and virtual circuits to make it fast and well suited to time-sensitive data.

## WHAT YOU REALLY NEED TO KNOW

- ◆ FDDI (Fiber Distributed Data Interface) is a logical topology that uses a double ring of multimode or single-mode fiber to transmit data at speeds of 100 Mbps.

- ◆ FDDI was the first network transport system to reach the 100 Mbps threshold. For this reason, you will frequently find it supporting network backbones that were installed in the late 1980s and early 1990s.

- ◆ FDDI's double-ring topology makes it especially reliable. Normally, data circulate on the primary ring, but if the primary ring is severed, data are carried by the secondary ring.

- ◆ **ATM (Asynchronous Transfer Mode)** is a circuit-switched logical topology that relies on a fixed packet size to achieve data transfer rates up to 9953 Mbps.

- ◆ ATM may run over specific types of fiber or copper networks, such as SONET or T-carriers. It is typically used on WANs, particularly by large data carriers, such as telephone companies and Internet Service Providers.

- ◆ What sets ATM apart from Token Ring and Ethernet is its fixed packet size. The fixed packet in ATM, which is called a **cell**, consists of 48 bytes of data plus a 5-byte header. This fixed packet size allows ATM to provide predictable traffic patterns and better control over bandwidth utilization.

- ◆ ATM's smaller packet size decreases its potential throughput, but the efficiency of using cells compensates for that loss. ATM has a maximum throughput of 9953 Mbps.

- ◆ ATM relies on virtual circuits. **Virtual circuits** are connections between network nodes that, while based on potentially disparate physical links, logically appear to be direct, dedicated links between those nodes.

- ◆ The significant benefit to using circuit switching is that it allows ATM to guarantee a specific **quality of service (QoS)**. QoS is a standard that specifies that data will be delivered within a certain period of time after their transmission.

## OBJECTIVES ON THE JOB

You may work with ATM on networks that carry audio or video data over fiber media. Because ATM is significantly different from the more popular Ethernet, be certain to understand its use of cells and how that technique affects the media and other components on the network.

# PRACTICE TEST QUESTIONS

1. **What is the maximum throughput of an ATM network?**
   - a. 9.95 Mbps
   - b. 99.5 Mbps
   - c. 995 Mbps
   - d. 9.95 Gbps

2. **What is one primary difference between ATM and Ethernet?**
   - a. ATM uses the token passing network access method, while Ethernet uses CSMA/CD.
   - b. ATM uses fixed-sized packets, while Ethernet uses variable-sized packets
   - c. ATM relies on connection-oriented protocols, while Ethernet relies on connectionless protocols.
   - d. ATM uses permanent virtual circuits, while Ethernet uses temporary virtual circuits.

3. **What kind of switching does ATM use?**
   - a. packet switching
   - b. circuit switching
   - c. message switching
   - d. terminal switching

4. **What is the maximum throughput of a FDDI network?**
   - a. 1 Mbps
   - b. 10 Mbps
   - c. 100 Mbps
   - d. 1 Gbps

5. **What type of connector might be found on a FDDI network?**
   - a. RJ-11
   - b. RJ-45
   - c. SC
   - d. BNC

6. **What does QoS stand for?**
   - a. quality of service
   - b. quantity of sessions
   - c. quick online status
   - d. question or solution

7. **What medium does FDDI require?**
   - a. coaxial cable
   - b. UTP
   - c. single-mode fiber
   - d. multimode fiber

# OBJECTIVES

## 2.11 Identify the basic characteristics (e.g., speed, capacity, media) of the following WAN technologies (continued):

### FRAME RELAY

## UNDERSTANDING THE OBJECTIVE

Frame Relay is a packet-switched technology capable of transmitting data at 1.544 or 45 Mbps throughput using public transmission systems.

## WHAT YOU REALLY NEED TO KNOW

◆ **Frame Relay** is a digital, packet-switched WAN technology. The name is derived from the fact that data is separated into frames which are then relayed from one node to another without any verification or processing.

◆ Frame Relay offers a maximum of either 1.544 Mbps or 45 Mbps throughput. It is similar to X.25 packet switching technology, but because it does not perform the same error checking routines, it is faster.

◆ Frame Relay was standardized in 1984 and became popular in the United States and Canada for reliable long-distance WAN connections. However, now Frame Relay is being replaced by newer, faster technologies.

◆ On networking diagrams, packet-switched networks, such as X.25 and Frame Relay, are depicted as clouds because of the indeterminate nature of their traffic patterns. Because the early version of the Internet relied on such technologies, the Internet is still depicted as a cloud on networking diagrams.

◆ Both X.25 and Frame Relay may be configured as switched virtual circuits (SVCs) or more often, as permanent virtual circuits (PVCs).

◆ **SVCs** are connections that are established when parties need to transmit. They are dismantled once the transmission is complete.

◆ **PVCs** are connections that are established before data needs to be transmitted and maintained after the transmission is complete. Note that in a PVC, the connection is established only between the two points (the sender and receiver); the connection does not specify the exact route the data will travel. Thus, in a PVC, data may follow any number of different paths to move from point A to point B

◆ When you lease an X.25 or Frame Relay circuit from your local carrier, your contract reflects the endpoints you specify and the amount of bandwidth you require between those endpoints. The service provider guarantees a minimum amount of bandwidth, called the **committed information rate (CIR)**.

## OBJECTIVES ON THE JOB

Frame Relay is usually found on WANs as an alternative to T-carrier services. Because Frame Relay is not dedicated, and data may follow any path from point A to point B, it is less expensive than (dedicated) T-carrier lines that offer comparable throughput.

## PRACTICE TEST QUESTIONS

1. **How is a Frame Relay network depicted on a networking diagram?**
    a. as a full-mesh
    b. as a cloud
    c. as a single bus
    d. as a star

2. **What does "CIR" stand for?**
    a. communications inter-relay
    b. connection interface register
    c. communicating internal repeater
    d. committed information rate

3. **Frame Relay is most similar to which of the following types of WAN technologies?**
    a. T-carrier
    b. FDDI
    c. SONET
    d. cable modem technology

4. **What type of switching does a Frame Relay network use?**
    a. circuit switching
    b. packet switching
    c. message switching
    d. terminal switching

5. **What is the difference between an SVC and a PVC?**
    a. An SVC can accept only data cells, while a PVC can accept both frames and cells.
    b. An SVC remains even after a transmission is complete, while a PVC exists only for the duration of a transmission
    c. An SVC can accept only data frames, while a PVC can accept both frames and cells.
    d. An SVC exists only for the duration of a transmission, while a PVC remains in existence even after a transmission is complete.

6. **In what year was the Frame Relay standard established?**
    a. 1975
    b. 1980
    c. 1984
    d. 1991

7. **Frame Relay can reach a maximum throughput of 45 Mbps. True or false?**

## 2.11 Identify the basic characteristics (e.g., speed, capacity, media) of the following WAN technologies (continued):

### SONET/SDH AND OCX

### UNDERSTANDING THE OBJECTIVE

SONET is a fast, highly reliable WAN technology that relies on a double fiber-optic ring topology, similar to FDDI. It can provide data transfer rates as high as 39.8 Gbps.

### WHAT YOU REALLY NEED TO KNOW

◆ **SONET (Synchronous Optical Network)** is a WAN technology that depends on fiber-optic transmission media to achieve its extraordinary quality of service and throughput. It was developed in the 1980s to link phone systems around the world.

◆ SONET can provide data transfer rates from 64 Kbps to 39.8 Gbps using the same TDM technique used by T-carriers. Like T-carriers, it also uses multiplexers and terminal equipment to connect at the customer's end.

◆ A typical SONET network takes the form of a ring topology, similar to FDDI, in which one ring acts as the primary route for data and the other ring acts as a backup. If, for example, a backhoe operator severs one of the rings, SONET technology would automatically reroute traffic along the backup ring. This characteristic, known as **self-healing**, makes SONET very reliable.

◆ Companies can lease an entire SONET ring from their local or long distance carrier, or they can lease part of a SONET, a circuit that offers T1 throughput, to take advantage of SONET's reliability.

◆ SONET has emerged as the best choice for linking WANs between North America, Europe, and Asia, because it can work directly with the different standards used in different countries.

◆ Internationally, SONET is known as **SDH (Synchronous Digital Hierarchy)**.

◆ SONET integrates well with T-carriers, making it a good choice for connecting WANs and LANs over long distances (even within the same country). In fact, SONET is often used to aggregate multiple T1s or T3s. SONET is also used as the underlying technology for ATM transmission.

◆ The data rate of a particular SONET ring is indicated by its **Optical Carrier (OC) level**, a rating that is internationally recognized by networking professionals and standards organizations. For example, **OC1** provides 51.84 Mbps throughput.

### OBJECTIVES ON THE JOB

SONET technology is used by large global companies, long distance companies linking metropolitan areas and countries, or ISPs that want to guarantee fast, reliable access to the Internet.

# PRACTICE TEST QUESTIONS

1. **Which of the following media does SONET require?**
   a. coaxial cable
   b. UTP
   c. STP
   d. fiber-optic cable

2. **What does "SONET" stand for?**
   a. self-organizing network
   b. system originating network
   c. synchronous optical network
   d. session overlay network

3. **What is the European equivalent of SONET?**
   a. SNT
   b. SON
   c. SNS
   d. SDH

4. **What technique does SONET use to increase the throughput it can sustain over a medium?**
   a. time division multiplexing
   b. frequency division multiplexing
   c. wave division multiplexing
   d. amplitude modulation

5. **How are OC levels related to SONET technology?**
   a. They describe SONET's quality of service levels.
   b. They indicate SONET's data rate.
   c. They represent SONET's maximum distance.
   d. They describe SONET's type of path between nodes.

6. **What was the original reason for developing SONET technology?**
   a. to provide the U.S. Defense Department with a secure, national network
   b. to provide U.S. individuals and businesses with a low-cost method of Internet access
   c. to link phone systems around the world
   d. to link international military bases

7. **Which of the following environments would SONET best suit?**
   a. a small nonprofit organization that uses the Internet to solicit contributions
   b. a regional insurance company whose salespeople dial into the corporate LAN each night from their homes to upload sales figures
   c. an Internet Service Provider that needs to ensure connectivity between multiple data centers and telecommunications carriers
   d. an architectural firm that sends and receives drawings from various clients across the nation

## 2.11 Identify the basic characteristics (e.g., speed, capacity, media) of the following WAN technologies (continued):

### T1/E1 AND T3/E3

### UNDERSTANDING THE OBJECTIVE

T1s and T3s (known as E1s and E3s in Europe) use time division multiplexing to achieve high throughput over public transmission systems. A T1 has a maximum throughput of 1.544 Mbps, while a T3 has a maximum throughput of 44.736 Mbps (or 45 Mbps).

### WHAT YOU REALLY NEED TO KNOW

◆ T1s, fractional T1s, and T3s are collectively known as **T-carriers**.

◆ T-carrier transmission uses time division multiplexing over two wire pairs (one for transmitting and one for receiving) to divide a single channel into multiple channels. Multiplexing enables a single T1 circuit to carry 24 channels, each capable of 64 Kbps throughput. Each channel may contain data, voice, or video signals.

◆ AT&T developed T-carrier technology in 1957 in an effort to digitize voice signals, thereby enabling such signals to travel long distances. In the 1970s, many businesses installed T1s to obtain more voice throughput per line.

◆ The most common T-carrier implementations are T1 and T3.

◆ A **T1** circuit can carry the equivalent of 24 voice or data channels, giving a maximum data throughput of 1.544 Mbps.

◆ A **T3** can carry the equivalent of 672 voice or data channels, giving a maximum data throughput of 44.736 Mbps (its throughput is typically rounded up to 45 Mbps for the purposes of discussion).

◆ The speed of a T-carrier depends on its signal level. The **signal level** refers to the T-carrier's Physical layer electrical signaling characteristics as defined by ANSI standards in the early 1980s. **DS0** (which stands for "Data Signals 0") is the equivalent of one data or voice channel. All other signal levels are multiples of DS0.

◆ Technically, T1 is the North American implementation of the international DS1 standard. In Europe, the DS1 standard is implemented as **E1** and offers a slightly higher throughput than T1, while the DS3 standard is implemented as **E3**.

### OBJECTIVES ON THE JOB

As a networking professional, you are most likely to work with T1 or T3 lines. In addition to knowing their capacity, you should be familiar with their costs and uses. T1s are commonly used by businesses to connect branch offices or to connect to a carrier, such as an ISP. Telephone companies also use T1s to connect their smaller central offices. ISPs may use one or more T1s or T3s to connect to their Internet carriers.

# PRACTICE TEST QUESTIONS

1. **How many data channels does a T1 carry?**
   - a. 1
   - b. 16
   - c. 24
   - d. 45

2. **How do E1s and E3s achieve high throughput?**
   - a. time division multiplexing
   - b. frequency division multiplexing
   - c. wave division multiplexing
   - d. amplitude modulation

3. **What is the difference between an E1 and a T1?**
   - a. An E1 has 10 times the capacity of a T1.
   - b. An E1 is the European equivalent of the American T1.
   - c. An E1 offers better quality of service than a T1.
   - d. An E1 uses circuit switching, while a T1 uses packet switching.

4. **What type of device is used to terminate a T-carrier?**
   - a. modem
   - b. CSU/DSU
   - c. bridge
   - d. hub

5. **What is the maximum throughput of a T3?**
   - a. 1.5 Mbps
   - b. 22.5 Mbps
   - c. 45 Mbps
   - d. 99 Mbps

6. **What company developed T-carrier technology?**
   - a. AT&T
   - b. Microsoft
   - c. IBM
   - d. Cisco

7. **What is the capacity of each channel in a T-carrier?**
   - a. 64 Kbps
   - b. 128 Kbps
   - c. 64 Mbps
   - d. 128 Mbps

## 2.12 Define the function of the following remote access protocols and services:

### RAS AND ICA

### UNDERSTANDING THE OBJECTIVE

Microsoft's RAS (Remote Access Service) and Citrix System, Inc.'s ICA (Independent Computing Architecture) client are two methods of remotely accessing private networks.

### WHAT YOU REALLY NEED TO KNOW

◆ The most common type of remote access involves dial-up networking. **Dial-up networking (DUN)** typically refers to a modem connection to a server through the PSTN. It is also the name of the utility that Microsoft provides with its operating systems to achieve this type of connectivity.

◆ A **remote access server** is a combination of software and hardware that provides a central access point for multiple users to dial in to a LAN or WAN.

◆ Once connected to the remote access server, the LAN treats the direct-dial remote client like any other client on the LAN. The computer dialing into the LAN becomes a **remote node** on the network.

◆ Many different software and hardware combinations can provide remote connectivity.

◆ A simple dial-in solution is provided by Microsoft Windows NT and Windows 2000. The software that allows remote clients to dial into these access servers is known as **Remote Access Service (RAS)**.

◆ Another method for remotely accessing LANs by using Citrix System, Inc.'s **ICA (Independent Computing Architecture)** client to connect to a remote access server.

◆ Once installed on a remote user's workstation, the client can connect to a Citrix server via any type of connection, public or private. The ICA client supplies the user with a standard desktop, then exchanges only keystrokes, mouse clicks, and screen updates with the server.

◆ Because all of the processing burden is placed on the server, this type of remote access is well suited to slower connections, such as dial-up PSTN connections.

◆ Citrix's ICA client can work with virtually any operating system or application. Its ease of use and broad compatibility has made the ICA client one of the most popular methods for supplying widespread remote access across an organization.

◆ In order to function properly, the ICA requires Citrix's remote access software running on the access server. Potential drawbacks to this method include cost of Citrix's products and the complex nature of its server software configuration.

### OBJECTIVES ON THE JOB

Remote access is a particular concern for mobile users, such as telecommuters and employees who frequently travel. Companies that purchase remote access servers must carefully evaluate the server options for cost, ease of installation, ease of maintenance, and ease of client use.

# PRACTICE TEST QUESTIONS

1. **In order for a Windows 9x machine to exchange data with a Windows 2000 server via DUN, to which of the following should the DUN software be bound? Choose all that apply.**
   a. TCP/IP
   b. IPX/SPX
   c. Client for Novell Networks
   d. Client for Microsoft Networks

2. **What does RAS stand for?**
   a. remote authentication service
   b. remote access server
   c. remote accounting service
   d. remote addressing server

3. **What transmission media does DUN typically use?**
   a. PSTN
   b. ISDN
   c. T1
   d. T3

4. **What company developed ICA?**
   a. Microsoft
   b. Citrix Systems
   c. IBM
   d. Cisco

5. **Which of the following best describes the type of data transmission that occurs while a user works on a spreadsheet via an ICA connection?**
   a. The server issues a copy of the program to the client's RAM, then the client workstation is responsible for processing program functions.
   b. The server issues pieces of the program to the client's RAM as they are needed, while the client workstation is responsible for processing program functions.
   c. The server issues screenshots of the program to the client, while the client workstation is responsible for processing program functions.
   d. The server issues screenshots of the program to the client, while the client workstation issues keystroke commands to run the program on the server.

6. **What is the maximum throughput of a typical DUN connection?**
   a. 53 Kbps
   b. 1 Mbps
   c. 1.544 Mbps
   d. 10 Mbps

7. **ICA provides encryption for sensitive data in transit. True or false?**

## 2.12 Define the function of the following remote access protocols and services (continued):

### PPP AND PPTP

### UNDERSTANDING THE OBJECTIVE

PPP and PPTP are communications protocols that enable remote access servers and remote clients to network via a dial-up connection.

### WHAT YOU REALLY NEED TO KNOW

♦ **Point-to-Point Protocol (PPP)** is a communications protocol that enables a workstation to connect to a server using a serial connection (in the case of dial-up networking, "serial connection" refers to a modem). Once connected via PPP, a remote workstation can act as a client on the local LAN, with its modem and serial port serving the purpose of a NIC.

♦ Such protocols are necessary to transport Network layer traffic over serial interfaces, which belong to the Data Link layer of the OSI Model. PPP encapsulates higher-layer networking protocols in its lower-layer data frames.

♦ PPP can carry many different types of Network layer packets, such as IPX or AppleTalk.

♦ PPP can support both asynchronous and synchronous transmission.

♦ **Asynchronous** refers to a communications method in which data being transmitted and received by nodes do not have to conform to any timing scheme. In asynchronous communications, a node can transmit at any time and the destination node has to accept the transmission as it comes.

♦ **Synchronous** refers to a communications method in which data being transmitted and received by nodes must conform to a timing scheme.

♦ **Point-to-Point Tunneling Protocol (PPTP)** provides a secure tunnel for data by encapsulating PPP, so any type of PPP data can traverse the Internet masked as pure IP transmissions.

♦ PPTP supports the encryption, authentication, and LAN access services provided by RASs (remote access servers).

♦ Users typically establish a dial-up networking connection with their ISP using PPP. Once that connection is established, they make a PPTP connection (that relies on the PPP connection) to their organization's LAN.

♦ The process of encapsulating one protocol to make it appear as another type of protocol is known as **tunneling**. Tunneling secures data in transit and makes a protocol fit a type of network that the protocol wouldn't normally accommodate.

### OBJECTIVES ON THE JOB

If you are supporting remote clients, you should be familiar with how your access server handles PPP and PPTP connections so that you can assist users in configuring their dial-up software.

# PRACTICE TEST QUESTIONS

1. **By what mechanism does PPP enable Network layer data transmission over a serial interface?**
   a. segmentation
   b. padding
   c. flow control
   d. encapsulation

2. **Which of the following can support IPX transmission? Choose all that apply.**
   a. PPP
   b. SLIP
   c. PPTP
   d. DLC

3. **On a Windows 9x workstation, what options would you choose to select PPP as the remote networking communication protocol?**
   a. Control Panel, Modems, General
   b. Control Panel, Network, Adapter
   c. Dial-Up Networking, Connection Properties, Server Type
   d. Control Panel, System Properties, Device Manager

4. **What type of operating system can be used to supply a PPTP server?**
   a. Banyan VINES
   b. Novell NetWare 3.12 or higher
   c. Windows NT Server 4.0 or higher
   d. Novell NetWare 4.11 or higher

5. **What is the main difference between PPP and PPTP?**
   a. PPP can handle only asynchronous transmission, while PPTP can handle both asynchronous and synchronous transmission.
   b. PPP encapsulates traffic according to its original Network layer protocol, while PPTP encapsulates PPP traffic as IP-based data.
   c. PPP cannot carry Network layer protocols other than TCP/IP, while PPTP can carry any Network layer protocol.
   d. PPP is compatible with only NetWare servers, while PPTP is compatible with both NetWare and Windows NT/2000 servers.

6. **In the context of remote access, what does the term "serial connection" refer to?**
   a. modem
   b. NIC
   c. ISDN adapter
   d. router

7. **What does the "T" in "PPTP" stand for?**
   a. transmission
   b. telecommunications
   c. traffic
   d. tunneling

## 2.13 Identify the following security protocols and describe their purpose and function:

### IPSEC AND L2TP

### UNDERSTANDING THE OBJECTIVE

IPSec and L2TP are two ways of encrypting data in transit between clients and servers. Both are useful for virtual private networks (VPNs).

### WHAT YOU REALLY NEED TO KNOW

◆ The **IPSec (Internet Protocol Security)** protocol defines encryption, authentication, and key management for TCP/IP transmissions.

◆ IPSec is an enhancement to IPv4 and is native to the newer, IPv6 standard.

◆ IPSec is somewhat different from other methods of securing data in transit. Rather than applying encryption to a stream of data, IPSec actually encrypts data by adding security information to the header of all IP packets. In effect, IPSec transforms the data packets. To do so, IPSec operates at the Network layer of the OSI Model.

◆ IPSec accomplishes authentication in two phases. The first phase is key management, and the second phase is encryption. **Key management** refers to how two nodes agree on common parameters for the keys they will use. IPSec relies on **Internet Key Exchange (IKE)** for its key management. A **key** is a series of characters that is combined with a block of data during that data's encryption. IKE is a service that runs on UDP port 500. Once IKE has established the rules for the type of keys two nodes will use, IPSec invokes its second phase, encryption. In this phase two types of encryption may be used: **authentication header (AH)** and **encapsulation security payload (ESP)**.

◆ IPSec can be used with any type of TCP/IP transmission. However, it most commonly runs on routers or other connectivity devices in the context of VPNs. Because VPNs are used to transmit private data over public networks, they require strict encryption and authentication to ensure that data are not compromised.

◆ **Layer 2 Tunneling Protocol (L2TP)** was developed by a number of industry consortia. L2TP is a remote access protocol that supports encryption and can encapsulate multiple Network layer protocols.

◆ L2TP will likely replace PPTP as the protocol of choice for remote access services.

### OBJECTIVES ON THE JOB

If you work on VPNs, you should understand how to install, maintain, and troubleshoot the type of encryption your network requires. IPSec is the latest type of VPN encryption, and it is more sophisticated than L2TP.

# PRACTICE TEST QUESTIONS

1. **IPSec is native to what version of IP?**
    a. 2
    b. 4
    c. 6
    d. 8

2. **Which of the following environments would be best suited to L2TP?**
    a. a small nonprofit organization that uses the Internet to solicit contributions
    b. a regional insurance company whose salespeople dial into the corporate LAN each night from their homes to upload sales figures
    c. an Internet Service Provider that needs to ensure connectivity between multiple data centers and telecommunications carriers
    d. an architectural firm that sends drawings to and receives drawings from various clients across the nation

3. **At what layer of the OSI Model does IPSec operate?**
    a. Physical
    b. Data Link
    c. Network
    d. Transport

4. **How does IPSec achieve encryption?**
    a. by scrambling the payload of packets between the source and destination
    b. by inserting false CRC fields into each packet
    c. by appending security information to the header of each packet
    d. by breaking packets into multiple, smaller packets and scrambling the payload of each smaller packet

5. **In the term "L2TP," what does the "2" represent?**
    a. layer 2 of the OSI Model
    b. the use of two encapsulation techniques
    c. a maximum of two channels within a tunnel
    d. the second generation of this type of encryption

6. **What organization developed L2TP?**
    a. Cisco
    b. Microsoft
    c. Xerox
    d. an industry consortium

7. **What type of device applies IPSec encryption to data?**
    a. router
    b. modem
    c. multiplexer
    d. laser

## 2.13 Identify the following security protocols and describe their purpose and function (continued):

**SSL**

### UNDERSTANDING THE OBJECTIVE

SSL is an alternative to interpreting Web-based information via HTTP. In SSL, data exchanged between the client and the Web server are encrypted to protect their privacy.

### WHAT YOU REALLY NEED TO KNOW

◆ **SSL (Secure Sockets Layer)** is a method of encrypting TCP/IP transmissions—including Web pages and data entered into Web forms—en route between the client and server using public key encryption technology.

◆ SSL is popular in part because it is widely accepted. The most recent versions of Web browsers, such as Netscape Communicator and Internet Explorer, include SSL client support in their software.

◆ Web page URLs that begin with the prefix **HTTPS** require that data be transferred from server to client and vice versa using SSL encryption. HTTPS uses the TCP port number 443, rather than port 80.

◆ Once an SSL connection has been established between a Web server and client, the client's browser displays a padlock in the lower-right corner of the screen (this applies to Internet Explorer and Netscape Communicator versions 4.0 and higher).

◆ Each time a client and server establish an SSL connection, they also establish a unique **SSL session**, or an association between the client and server defined by an agreement on a specific set of encryption techniques.

◆ An SSL session allows the client and server to continue to exchange data securely as long as the client is still connected to the server.

◆ SSL was originally developed by Netscape. Since that time, the Internet Engineering Task Force (IETF) has attempted to standardize SSL in a protocol called **TLS (transport layer security)**.

◆ Besides standardizing SSL for use with software from multiple vendors, IETF also aims to create a version of SSL that will encrypt UDP, as well as TCP transmissions. TLS, which will likely be supported by new Web browsers, uses slightly different encryption algorithms than SSL but otherwise is very similar to the most recent version of SSL.

### OBJECTIVES ON THE JOB

If you are the administrator for an e-commerce Web site, you will most likely use SSL to transmit customer order and payment information. Before specializing in SSL, be certain to understand the concepts behind public key cryptography.

# PRACTICE TEST QUESTIONS

1. **What port does HTTPS use?**
   a. 8
   b. 80
   c. 43
   d. 443

2. **What type of cryptography does SSL use?**
   a. private key
   b. public key
   c. pretty good privacy
   d. PHP

3. **What company developed SSL?**
   a. Microsoft
   b. Symantec
   c. Netscape
   d. Cisco

4. **How can a user tell whether her Web transmissions are using SSL?**
   a. Her browser displays a padlock in the lower-right corner of the screen.
   b. Her browser displays a window indicating that SSL is in use before displaying the SSL-based screen.
   c. The title bar on her browser displays an "SSL" prefix.
   d. There is no sure way to tell.

5. **Which of the following Web sites would probably use SSL?**
   a. a portal site that allows users to obtain stock quotes for free
   b. a family genealogy site that allows users to view pictures of relatives
   c. an art museum site that allows users to view current exhibitions
   d. a travel agency site that allows users to book flight reservations online

6. **What Transport layer protocol does HTTPS rely on?**
   a. TCP
   b. IP
   c. UDP
   d. ICMP

7. **Which of the following software programs interprets HTTPS data?**
   a. Microsoft Excel
   b. Lotus Notes
   c. Netscape Communicator
   d. Apple Quicktime

## 2.13 Identify the following security protocols and describe their purpose and function (continued):

### KERBEROS

### UNDERSTANDING THE OBJECTIVE

Kerberos is a private key encryption service that requires clients to verify their credentials for each service they request from a server. Kerberos also encrypts information exchanged between client and server.

### WHAT YOU REALLY NEED TO KNOW

◆ **Kerberos** is a cross-platform authentication protocol that uses key encryption to verify the identity of clients to servers (and vice versa) and to provide secure information exchange once a client logs on to a system.

◆ Kerberos is an example of **private key encryption**, a type of key encryption in which the sender and receiver have private keys, that only they know.

◆ Kerberos provides significant security advantages over simple network operating system authentication. During a typical client/server logon, the NOS assumes that the client is using a rightfully assigned username and only verifies the user's name against the password in the NOS database. By contrast, Kerberos does not automatically trust the client. Instead, it requires the client to prove its identity through a third party. In addition, it requires the server to provide its identity to the client.

◆ In addition to checking the validity of clients and servers, Kerberos communications are encrypted and unlikely to be deciphered by any device on the network other than the client.

◆ In Kerberos terminology, the server that issues keys to clients during initial client authentication is known as the **key distribution center (KDC)**. In order to authenticate a client, the KDC runs an **authentication service (AS)**. An AS issues a **ticket**, which is a temporary set of credentials that a client uses to prove that its identity has been validated (note that a ticket is not the same as a key, which is used to initially validate its identity). A Kerberos client, or user, is known as a principal.

◆ Kerberos, which is named after the three-headed dog in Greek mythology who guarded the gates of Hades, was designed at Massachusetts Institute of Technology (MIT). MIT still provides free copies of the Kerberos code. In addition, many software vendors have developed their own versions of Kerberos.

### OBJECTIVES ON THE JOB

Kerberos may be found on large private networks where security is a prime concern. For example, a government agency may use Kerberos to ensure that users accessing its research databases are authorized to view the information.

# PRACTICE TEST QUESTIONS

1. **What type of cryptography does Kerberos use?**
   a. private key
   b. public key
   c. pretty good privacy
   d. PHP

2. **With which of the following network operating systems could Kerberos be used? Choose all that apply.**
   a. NetWare
   b. Windows
   c. UNIX
   d. MS-DOS

3. **What does Kerberos use to verify the validity of a client?**
   a. L2TP
   b. IPSec
   c. SSL
   d. tickets

4. **With what type of client software could Kerberos be used? Choose all that apply.**
   a. Novell NetWare
   b. Novell Client 32
   c. Microsoft Windows 98
   d. Apple Macintosh

5. **Which of the following environments is most likely to use Kerberos?**
   a. an online retailer
   b. a local animal shelter with 6 permanent employees and 18 volunteers
   c. a research university with 30,000 students and 2300 faculty
   d. a home network

6. **What characteristic do all key encryption schemes share?**
   a. The more steps required to encrypt data using the key, the easier the key is to discover.
   b. The longer the key, the more difficult the encryption will be to crack.
   c. The more routers a key-encrypted packet must traverse, the more difficult the encryption will be to crack.
   d. The shorter the key, the more difficult the encryption will be to crack.

7. **At what layer of the OSI Model does Kerberos primarily operate?**
   a. Physical
   b. Data Link
   c. Transport
   d. Presentation

## 3.1 Identify the basic capabilities (i.e., client support, interoperability, authentication, file and print services, application support, and security) of the following server operating systems:

### UNIX/LINUX

### UNDERSTANDING THE OBJECTIVE

The term "UNIX" refers to a group of network operating systems that share similar kernels, directory structures, commands, and processing characteristics. UNIX comes in two varieties: proprietary and open source. Linux is the most popular open source version of UNIX.

### WHAT YOU REALLY NEED TO KNOW

◆ A **network operating system (NOS)** is a software package that enables one machine to act as a server in a client-server network.

◆ NOSs differ in many ways, but all perform file- and print-sharing functions, plus provide mail, remote connectivity, security, network management, and Internet services.

◆ UNIX was developed in the 1960s concurrently with the TCP/IP protocol and was used on the first Internet host machines. UNIX still relies on the TCP/IP protocol.

◆ **UNIX** is a general term for a group of network operating systems that share similar kernels, directory structures, commands, and processing characteristics.

◆ UNIX versions may be proprietary (such as IBM's AIX or Sun's Solaris) or open source software. **Linux** is the most popular open source software version of UNIX.

◆ The advantage to using a proprietary version of UNIX is its stability and vendor support. However, open source versions are becoming more standard and more easily supported.

◆ UNIX uses a hierarchical file system, in which the uppermost level is called the root. Standard directories under the root include home, dev, usr, bin, var, and lib.

◆ UNIX software relies on a kernel, which contains the core set of instructions for the operating system.

◆ The creators of UNIX introduced techniques for multiprocessing; thus, UNIX supports multiple processors, as well as multiple NICs and virtual memory.

◆ UNIX servers can access FAT, NTFS, and HPFS file systems, as well as shared drives on Windows or NetWare servers.

◆ A UNIX server can support multiple types of clients, including Microsoft and Novell network clients, because it is based on the standard TCP/IP protocol stack.

### OBJECTIVES ON THE JOB

As the oldest and arguably still the most efficient NOS, some form of UNIX is found in virtually every organization. Often, UNIX is used for HTTP, Telnet, FTP, DNS, or other Internet-related services, as well as robust database servers. While some UNIX systems have GUI interfaces, most network administrators still use the command-line interface, forcing administrators to memorize commands.

# PRACTICE TEST QUESTIONS

1. **Which of the following is true about open source UNIX?**
   a. Open source versions of UNIX typically do not supply as many Internet services as proprietary versions of the software.
   b. Open source versions of UNIX are less accepted in the marketplace for use with robust applications.
   c. Open source versions of UNIX use a different file system than proprietary versions of the software.
   d. Open source versions of UNIX typically do not come with the same amount of vendor support as proprietary versions.

2. **What will typing `man ls` and pressing Enter at the command line of a UNIX server do?**
   a. display the help text for the file list command
   b. display the server's error log
   c. display a list of users currently logged on to the system
   d. display a list of available printers

3. **What is the uppermost level of a UNIX file system called?**
   a. branch
   b. leaf
   c. root
   d. tree

4. **What protocol is native to the UNIX environment?**
   a. IPX/SPX
   b. NetBEUI
   c. TCP/IP
   d. SNA

5. **Which of the following is a popular use for a UNIX server, even in an environment dominated by Windows 2000 or NetWare?**
   a. print server
   b. graphics server
   c. remote access server
   d. HTTP server

6. **Which of the following is a popular version of open source UNIX?**
   a. Linux
   b. VINES
   c. AIX
   d. AnyLAN

7. **What is IBM's proprietary version of UNIX called?**
   a. IBX
   b. AIX
   c. SNAX
   d. INOS

# OBJECTIVES

## 3.1 Identify the basic capabilities (i.e., client support, interoperability, authentication, file and print services, application support, and security) of the following server operating systems (continued):

### NETWARE

### UNDERSTANDING THE OBJECTIVE

In 1983, Novell introduced its NetWare network operating system. NetWare quickly became the standard operating system for LANs and WANs, providing reliable file- and print-sharing services for millions of users. Since then, Novell has refined NetWare to include support for TCP/IP, intranet services, a graphical user interface, and better integration with other operating systems.

### WHAT YOU REALLY NEED TO KNOW

◆ The original version of Novell NetWare was based on the IPX/SPX protocol. Novell has expanded its compatibility with other protocols. NetWare 5.x is based on the TCP/IP protocol.

◆ Versions 4.x and higher of NetWare support multiple processors, multiple NICs, 32-bit addressing, and can use both physical and virtual memory.

◆ NetWare's kernel oversees all critical server functions. The program SERVER.EXE runs the kernel from a DOS prompt and is run from the server's AUTOEXEC.BAT file.

◆ NetWare uses **NetWare Loadable Modules (NLMs)** to load necessary functions or applications (such as the printer console) into memory on the server.

◆ In NetWare versions 4.x and lower, the **server console**, a text-based menu system, is the network administrator's main interface with the server. In NetWare 5.x, administrators may use a GUI interface called **ConsoleOne**.

◆ In NetWare versions 4.x and higher, the NetWare Directory System (NDS) describes how a network's volumes, resources, users, and groups are arranged. The terms "root," "tree," and "leaf" are used to describe different elements of NDS. **NWAdmin** is used to create and administer the NDS.

◆ A NetWare server can accept many different types of clients, including UNIX, Macintosh, Windows 9x, 2000, and NT, MS-DOS, and OS/2.

◆ The NDS for NT tool enables Windows 2000 domains to appear as container objects in NWAdmin. In Novell's terminology, NDS **eDirectory** extends the schema to include Windows 2000 resources. Windows 2000 servers appear as server objects, and groups and users from Windows 2000 domains appear as NDS group and user objects, respectively.

### OBJECTIVES ON THE JOB

The NetWare NOS is favored by many veteran network administrators. To succeed as a network technician or administrator in a NetWare shop, you must be especially familiar with the concepts of NDS, NWAdmin, protocols, and interconnecting with other NOSs.

## PRACTICE TEST QUESTIONS

1. **What does NDS stand for?**
   - a. NetWare Direct System
   - b. NetWare Distributed System
   - c. NetWare Digital Services
   - d. NetWare Directory Services

2. **From what file on a NetWare server is the SERVER.EXE program launched?**
   - a. CONFIG.SYS
   - b. AUTOEXEC.BAT
   - c. SERVER.BAT
   - d. NLM.BAT

3. **On which protocol was the first version of NetWare based?**
   - a. TCP/IP
   - b. NetBEUI
   - c. SNA
   - d. IPX/SPX

4. **What program is used to administer NDS?**
   - a. GSNW
   - b. NWAdmin
   - c. NTFS
   - d. NWConsole

5. **A user is an example of what type of NDS object?**
   - a. root
   - b. branch
   - c. leaf
   - d. stem

6. **What is the main purpose of NLMs?**
   - a. to load applications or services into memory on the server
   - b. to install the NetWare operating system on the server
   - c. to connect NetWare servers with Windows NT servers
   - d. to optimize memory usage on the server

7. **What volume does NetWare create by default upon installation?**
   - a. SYS
   - b. VOL1
   - c. USERS
   - d. DATA

# OBJECTIVES

**3.1 Identify the basic capabilities (i.e., client support, interoperability, authentication, file and print services, application support, and security) of the following server operating systems (continued):**

## WINDOWS

### UNDERSTANDING THE OBJECTIVE

Some of the most popular network operating systems are Microsoft's Windows NT and Windows 2000. Microsoft's NOSs have grown in popularity due to their simple-to-use graphical user interface and their similarity to the Windows desktop operating systems.

### WHAT YOU REALLY NEED TO KNOW

◆ Windows 2000 Server relies on a **graphical user interface (GUI)**, a pictorial representation of computer functions that makes it easy for the network administrator to manage files, users, groups, security, printers, and so on.

◆ Windows 2000 Server uses 32-bit addressing, which helps to process instructions twice as fast as 16-bit addressing and assigns each application its own 32-bit memory area.

◆ Windows 2000 Server can use multiple processors, multiple NICs, and both physical and virtual memory. In order to determine what components can be used in a Windows 2000 server, refer to Microsoft's **Hardware Compatibility List (HCL)**. The HCL lists all the computer components proven to be compatible with Windows 2000 Server.

◆ Windows 2000 uses **Active Directory**, its directory service, for organizing and managing objects on the network.

◆ Windows 2000 can support the following file systems: CDFS, FAT, FAT32, and NTFS. Microsoft developed the **New Technology File System (NTFS)** expressly for Windows NT, the precursor to Windows 2000. NTFS integrates reliability, compression, speed, and the ability to handle large files. The main benefit to NTFS, however, is its superior security. NTFS is the preferred file system for servers running Windows 2000.

◆ A Windows 2000 server can communicate with almost any kind of client. Often, a network dominated by Windows 2000 servers uses Windows 9x, NT, or 2000 workstations.

◆ To communicate with a NetWare server running IPX/SPX, a Windows 2000 server must have the Gateway Services for NetWare (GSNW) installed in addition to the IPX/SPX protocols. To communicate with a UNIX server, a Windows 2000 server need only have the TCP/IP protocols and services installed.

### OBJECTIVES ON THE JOB

Many organizations run the Windows 2000 Server network operating system, even if their network is dominated by other NOSs. Windows 2000 Server is a popular system for Web services (those running Internet Information Server), as well as file and print services.

# PRACTICE TEST QUESTIONS

1. **What server resource does the Windows 2000 NOS use for virtual memory?**
   a. hard disk
   b. RAM
   c. CPU
   d. system board

2. **What protocol must be installed for a Windows 2000 server to communicate with a UNIX server?**
   a. NetBEUI
   b. IPX/SPX
   c. TCP/IP
   d. SNA

3. **What is the name of Windows 2000 Server's directory service?**
   a. Windows Directory Service
   b. Active Directory
   c. Hierarchical Directories
   d. Managed Directory Service

4. **What is the main advantage of assigning each application its own 32-bit memory area?**
   a. The application is less likely to freeze up.
   b. The application is less likely to interfere with other applications.
   c. The application executes with priority over other applications.
   d. The application can be executed from multiple workstations.

5. **Which of the following file systems must be present on a Windows 2000 server so it can communicate with Macintosh workstations?**
   a. NTFS
   b. CDFS
   c. HPFS
   d. FAT

6. **What resource can you use to determine whether your server's NIC works with the Windows 2000 Server NOS?**
   a. the server resource kit
   b. the hardware compatibility list
   c. the Microsoft NT users forum
   d. the emergency repair disk

7. **Which of the following must a Windows 2000 Server have installed in order to communicate with a NetWare server running IPX/SPX?**
   a. IntraNetWare
   b. eDirectory
   c. NDS for 2000
   d. Gateway Services for NetWare

# OBJECTIVES

## 3.1 Identify the basic capabilities (i.e., client support, interoperability, authentication, file and print services, application support, and security) of the following server operating systems (continued):

### MACINTOSH

### UNDERSTANDING THE OBJECTIVE

Macintosh is an operating system developed by Apple Computer, Inc. While it is used as a network operating system in small, limited environments, it is still a popular desktop operating system and can be connected to most any type of network.

### WHAT YOU REALLY NEED TO KNOW

◆ The Macintosh operating system was developed by Apple Computer, Inc. as an intuitive, graphical interface for personal computers. Businesses and institutions involved in art or education, such as advertising agencies, elementary schools, and graphic designers, often use Apple Macintosh computers.

◆ AppleTalk is the protocol suite used to interconnect Macintosh computers. Although it was originally designed to support peer-to-peer networking among Macintoshes, it can now be routed between network segments and integrated with NetWare or Windows networks.

◆ Although Apple has improved AppleTalk's ability to use different network models and span network segments, it remains unsuited to large LANs or WANs. Even Apple has begun supporting the TCP/IP protocol to integrate Macintoshes with other networks, including the Internet.

◆ **LocalTalk** is a network access method designed by Apple Computer, Inc. specifically for networking Macintosh computers. It was included with the Macintosh operating system since 1984, and it provided a simple, cost-effective way of interconnecting Macintosh devices.

◆ However, LocalTalk is only capable of 230 Kbps maximum throughput—much less than the 10 Mbps or 100 Mbps throughput of an Ethernet network.

◆ LocalTalk is not easily supported by non-Macintosh devices. Since Macintosh computers are capable of using Ethernet as a network access method, Ethernet is usually preferred over LocalTalk.

◆ LocalTalk uses a transmission method called **Carrier Sense Multiple Access/Collision Avoidance (CSMA/CA)**. It is similar to the CSMA/CD used in Ethernet networks, except a node on a LocalTalk network signals its intent to transmit before it actually does so. In this way, collisions and the need for data retransmittals are (mostly) avoided.

### OBJECTIVES ON THE JOB

Chances are good that you will never need to build a LocalTalk network, though occasionally you may need to troubleshoot one. LocalTalk might still be appropriate for a home network that requires simple configuration and does not require high throughput.

# PRACTICE TEST QUESTIONS

1. **With which of the following network operating systems can a Macintosh computer act as a client? Choose all that apply.**
   a. MS-DOS
   b. NetWare
   c. Macintosh
   d. Windows

2. **What type of network access method does a Macintosh-based network use?**
   a. CSMA/CD
   b. CSMA/CA
   c. token-passing
   d. demand priority

3. **What logical topology does AppleTalk rely on?**
   a. LocalTalk
   b. AppleNet
   c. Ethernet
   d. Token Ring

4. **Which of the following environments is most likely to use a Macintosh-based network?**
   a. an online retailer
   b. a regional insurance company with 7 locations and 4500 employees
   c. a research university with 30,000 students and 2300 faculty
   d. a home network

5. **AppleTalk is a routable protocol. True or false?**

6. **What is the default protocol used by Macintosh clients on a network?**
   a. AppleTalk
   b. NetBEUI
   c. TCP/IP
   d. IPX/SPX

7. **What is the maximum throughput of a LocalTalk network?**
   a. 56 Kbps
   b. 230 Kbps
   c. 560 Kbps
   d. 1 Mbps

## 3.2  Identify the basic capabilities (i.e., client connectivity, local security mechanisms, and authentication) of the following clients:

### UNIX/LINUX

### UNDERSTANDING THE OBJECTIVE

A UNIX or Linux client is very similar to a UNIX or Linux server. Both rely on the TCP/IP protocol, both require username and password authentication to log on, and both assign read, write, or execute permissions according to files and groups.

### WHAT YOU REALLY NEED TO KNOW

- ◆ UNIX systems may be implemented as clients or as servers. Unlike Windows 2000, in which the server and client operating systems vary considerably, the difference between a UNIX server and a UNIX client lies only in the set of optional packages included during installation. A UNIX system configured as a server has the necessary software to enable sharing of resources such as print queues, file systems, and processor time. A UNIX client typically does not have these resource sharing services installed.

- ◆ UNIX systems rely on the TCP/IP protocol. If necessary, they can also run other protocols such as IPX/SPX or AppleTalk.

- ◆ UNIX clients require users to log on with a username and password. UNIX clients use 56-bit DES encrypted passwords.

- ◆ During installation, you must supply a root password. Once installation has completed, you will be prompted to log onto the system as root, using the password you specified.

- ◆ Files and directories on a UNIX client are available only to those users who are logged on to the client and who have sufficient rights to access those files.

- ◆ Each file and directory on a UNIX client can be assigned read, write, and execute rights. Such rights can be associated with individual users, groups, or all users.

- ◆ **Samba** is a software program that runs on UNIX-based systems and allows it to supply file and printer sharing services to Windows-based clients. Samba is freely available under the same license as the Linux operating system.

### OBJECTIVES ON THE JOB

It is important to have a plan for securing resources on clients and servers before beginning to configure the systems. For instance, on shared UNIX workstations, you may create separate data directories for each user's files and assign permissions so that only the directory's owner can access the directory's contents.

## PRACTICE TEST QUESTIONS

1. **After you install a UNIX client according to the operating system's default options, what protocol will the client attempt to use to connect to the network?**
   a. NetBEUI
   b. TCP/IP
   c. SAMBA
   d. SNA

2. **What command would you use to add a new user called "morton" to a Linux client?**
   a. `chmod -a morton`
   b. `usadd morton`
   c. `useradd morton`
   d. `chmod +add morton`

3. **What command will enable you to view all the users currently logged onto a UNIX system?**
   a. `nslookup`
   b. `who`
   c. `whois`
   d. `ifconfig`

4. **Assuming you have rights to read the contents of a UNIX client's directory, what command would you use to do so?**
   a. `hup files`
   b. `list files`
   c. `listdir`
   d. `ls`

5. **If you wanted to learn more about the command that allows you to change the file and directory privileges on a UNIX client, what would you type at the shell prompt?**
   a. `help config`
   b. `mkdir /?`
   c. `chdir -?`
   d. `man chmod`

6. **What is one primary difference between the UNIX client operating system and the UNIX server operating system?**
   a. The server operating system is capable of multiprocessing, while the client operating system is not.
   b. The client operating system typically doesn't have services such as print queue sharing installed.
   c. The server operating system can support multiple users, while the client operating system cannot.
   d. The client operating system installs multiple Network layer protocols by default.

7. **In order to be able to use FTP on a Linux client, you must first install the FTP software. True or false?**

## 3.2  Identify the basic capabilities (i.e., client connectivity, local security mechanisms, and authentication) of the following clients (continued):

### WINDOWS

### UNDERSTANDING THE OBJECTIVE

Windows clients rely on a graphical user interface to supply functionality. They can support many types of protocols, including TCP/IP, NetBEUI, IPX/SPX, and AppleTalk. The Windows NT and Windows 2000 Professional versions require local users to log onto the client, supplying a username and password.

### WHAT YOU REALLY NEED TO KNOW

◆ Windows operating systems vary considerably, not only between different versions of the operating system, but also between client and server software within each version.

◆ By default, Windows 98, NT, and 2000 operating systems rely on the TCP/IP protocol. All of the Windows operating systems can also run other protocols, such as IPX/SPX or AppleTalk.

◆ Windows clients can connect to NetWare and UNIX servers as well as servers running a version of the Windows NOS.

◆ Windows NT Workstation and Windows 2000 Professional clients provide more local file security than Windows 3.1, 9x, or ME clients. Windows NT and 2000 Professional clients require users to log onto the system with a username and password.

◆ During installation of the Windows NT Workstation and 2000 Professional client operating systems, you must supply an Administrator password. Once installation has completed, you will be prompted to log onto the system as Administrator, using the password you specified.

◆ Local access to files and directories on Windows NT Workstation and Windows 2000 Professional clients is available only to those users who are logged on to the client and who have sufficient rights to access those files.

◆ Each file and directory on such clients can be assigned full control, modify, read & execute, list folder contents, read, or write rights. Such rights can be associated with individual users, groups, or all users.

◆ Files and directories on Windows 3.1, Windows 9x, and Windows ME clients are not secured by assigning rights to users and groups. Other means (such as encryption) must be used to secure files on these versions of the Windows client operating system.

### OBJECTIVES ON THE JOB

Windows clients are popular choices for many organizations because they are well-supported and well-understood. When working with Windows clients, be certain to understand the significant differences between multiple versions, including Windows 3.1, 95, 98, NT, 2000, and ME.

# PRACTICE TEST QUESTIONS

1. **On which of the following Windows clients are you most likely to use NetBEUI?**
   a. Windows 2000 Professional
   b. Windows NT Workstation 4.0
   c. Windows 3.1
   d. Windows 98

2. **What is the name of the account that is created when you install Windows 2000 Professional on a workstation?**
   a. Root
   b. admin
   c. Master
   d. Administrator

3. **In order for a Windows 98 client to log onto a NetWare 4.11 server running IPX/SPX, which of the following must be installed on the client? Choose all that apply.**
   a. NWLink IPX/SPX protocol
   b. Client for NetWare Networks
   c. TCP/IP
   d. NDS eDirectory

4. **Which of the following is the most secure client operating system?**
   a. Windows ME
   b. Windows 95
   c. Windows 98
   d. Windows NT Workstation

5. **What would be the best way to secure files on your Windows 98 workstation so that only you could read them?**
   a. Modify the local file sharing properties so that only your user account has access to the files.
   b. Encrypt the files.
   c. Assign file scan rights only to those files.
   d. Compress the files and put them in an unnamed folder.

6. **Which of the following would a Windows 98 computer require in order to log onto a UNIX server?**
   a. TCP/IP
   b. IPX/SPX
   c. NetBEUI
   d. SAMBA

7. **What options would you choose to enable clients on a peer-to-peer network to read from your Windows 2000 Professional workstation's C:\MyPrograms directory?**
   a. My Computer, Folder properties, File Sharing tab
   b. Network Neighborhood, Network Properties, Security tab
   c. My Network Places, Network Properties, Access tab
   d. My Network Places, Users and Groups, Access tab

## 3.2  Identify the basic capabilities (i.e., client connectivity, local security mechanisms, and authentication) of the following clients (continued):

### MACINTOSH

### UNDERSTANDING THE OBJECTIVE

Macintosh clients can connect to Windows, NetWare, UNIX/Linux, or Macintosh clients, using AppleTalk or TCP/IP protocols.

### WHAT YOU REALLY NEED TO KNOW

◆ Network connections for a Macintosh client can be viewed and enabled by selecting the Chooser option from the Apple menu.

◆ Older Macintosh clients used LocalTalk on AppleTalk networks. However, most modern Macintosh clients rely on TCP/IP to connect to a network, whether they are directly connected to a LAN or dial in to a remote access server.

◆ The original version of TCP/IP used on Macintosh clients is called **MacTCP**. However, since System 7.5.2, Apple has used newer TCP/IP version for Macintosh clients called **Open Transport**.

◆ Open Transport provides support for DHCP, IP Multicast, and the use of multiple simultaneous TCP connections, among other features.

◆ The current implementation of Open Transport has two components, AppleTalk and TCP/IP, each managed and configured through a separate Control Panel. Once the software is installed, you need to configure AppleTalk and TCP/IP services through their respective Control Panels.

◆ In the TCP/IP Control Panel, you can specify whether or not the client uses DHCP. You can also specify the client's host and domain name, subnet mask, IP address (if static addressing is used), name server, and the gateway (or router) address. Using the "Connect via" drop-down list in the TCP/IP Control Panel, you can choose whether the client will connect to the network via Ethernet or AppleTalk.

◆ If you choose AppleTalk as the network type, you will be prompted to indicate what zone your Macintosh client belongs to.

◆ Using TCP/IP, Macintosh clients can connect to Windows, NetWare, UNIX/Linux, and Macintosh servers.

◆ The latest Macintosh operating system, OS X, supports multiple encryption techniques, including Kerberos and SSL. It also supports file-based permissions (similar to those on a UNIX client) that can be tailored according to user or group. Further, OS X allows users to fully encrypt all or part of their Macintosh hard disks.

### OBJECTIVES ON THE JOB

Macintosh clients are popular among educational and creative organizations (such as advertising agencies). Their TCP/IP configuration is similar to that of a Windows or UNIX client.

## PRACTICE TEST QUESTIONS

1. **What version of TCP/IP was standard on Macintosh clients prior to System 7.5?**
   a. AppleTalk
   b. MacTCP
   c. Open Transport
   d. NWLink

2. **What option would you choose to configure your Macintosh workstation to use DHCP rather than static IP addressing?**
   a. Apple, TCP/IP Control Panel, Configure "Using DHCP"
   b. Apple, Chooser, Network Properties, TCP/IP Controls, DHCP
   c. Apple, Chooser, Networks, Protocols, TCP/IP, Use DHCP
   d. Apple, TCP/IP Control Panel, IP Addressing tab, Use DHCP

3. **What network type would you probably choose for a Macintosh client that is connecting to a NetWare 5.0 server?**
   a. AppleTalk
   b. LocalTalk
   c. Ethernet
   d. Token Ring

4. **The router address prompt in the Macintosh TCP/IP Control Panel refers to what?**
   a. the client's core Internet router
   b. the client's IP gateway
   c. the client's closest router
   d. the client's closest connectivity device of any type

5. **What is one advantage of Open Transport over MacTCP?**
   a. It can connect to Windows servers as well as UNIX and Macintosh servers.
   b. It uses less temporary memory.
   c. It offers the option of running over LocalTalk or Ethernet.
   d. It supports DHCP.

6. **Setting file and directory permissions on a Macintosh client running the new OS X would be very similar to setting file and directory permissions on what other OS?**
   a. Windows 2000 Professional
   b. Windows 2000 Server
   c. NetWare 5.1
   d. UNIX

7. **If you didn't want anyone to read the contents of your Macintosh hard disk, even if they sat down at your computer, what type of security technique should you use?**
   a. Kerberos
   b. SSL
   c. IPSec
   d. encrypt the hard disk data

## 3.3   Identify the main characteristics of VLANs.

### UNDERSTANDING THE OBJECTIVE

A virtual local area network (VLAN) is a network of nodes logically created by configuring ports on a switch or multiple switches. VLANs are useful for isolating traffic, either with the aim of improving performance or increasing data privacy.

### WHAT YOU REALLY NEED TO KNOW

- A **virtual local area network (VLAN)** is a logically separate network within a network.
- To create a VLAN, you use a switch (or switches) to group a number of ports into a broadcast domain. The ports do not have to reside on the same switch or even on the same network segment.
- A **broadcast domain** (also known as a **collision domain**) is a combination of ports that make up a Layer 2 segment and must be connected by a Layer 3 device, such as a router or Layer 3 switch.
- A VLAN can include servers, workstations, printers, routers, or any other network device you can connect to a switch.
- One great advantage of VLANs is their ability to link geographically distant users and create small workgroups from large LANs.
- VLANs are also helpful if you are interested in keeping one workgroup's network traffic separate from another workgroup's network traffic for improved security or performance.
- To create a VLAN, you must configure the switch properly. In addition to identifying the ports that belong to each logical network, you can specify security parameters, filtering instructions (if the switch should not forward any frames from a certain segment, for example), performance requirements for certain users, and network management options.
- In setting up a VLAN, you are not merely including a certain group of nodes—you are also excluding another group. As a result, you can potentially cut a group off from the rest of the network. VLAN implementation requires careful planning to ensure that all the groups of users who need to communicate can do so after the VLAN is in operation.

### OBJECTIVES ON THE JOB

If you are charged with designing a network or installing switches, you should research VLANs further. Some trade publications (and many switch manufacturers) have touted VLANs as the most advanced approach to networking—and the wave of the future.

# PRACTICE TEST QUESTIONS

1. **What connectivity device is responsible for creating VLANs?**
   a. hub
   b. router
   c. switch
   d. gateway

2. **Why couldn't bridges be used to create a VLAN?**
   a. because they cannot interpret Layer 3 information
   b. because they do not contain multiple ports
   c. because they do not work with the Ethernet network access method
   d. because they cannot determine the MAC addresses of connected nodes

3. **Which of the following parameters can you specify for a VLAN when configuring a switch? Choose all that apply.**
   a. performance requirements for certain nodes
   b. the method of signaling required by certain nodes
   c. security parameters
   d. filtering instructions based on segment

4. **What is one potential pitfall when creating VLANs?**
   a. You could inadvertently forget to assign a port to a node, thus disabling all traffic on that node's segment.
   b. You could inadvertently assign one node to more than one port, thus disabling traffic to and from that node.
   c. You could inadvertently connect a segment to itself, thus causing a loop in traffic.
   d. You could inadvertently cut off network access to some nodes.

5. **Which of the following nodes could belong to a single broadcast domain? Choose all that apply.**
   a. workstation
   b. router
   c. server
   d. printer

6. **In order for two workstations to belong to the same VLAN, they must connect to the same switch. True or false?**

7. **In which of the following situations would a VLAN be most useful and appropriate?**
   a. an office of eight users connected via a peer-to-peer LAN for file and printer sharing
   b. a startup company of 18 computer scientists using a Gigabit Ethernet LAN to share data and programs
   c. a university WAN dedicated to offering long distance education to all students
   d. a pharmaceutical company's headquarters with 530 employees from various departments connected to a Fast Ethernet LAN

## 3.4   Identify the main characteristics of network attached storage.

### UNDERSTANDING THE OBJECTIVE

Network attached storage (NAS) is a highly fault-tolerant method of storing shared data and programs on a network. Because NAS devices use their own file system and server hardware, they can access and transmit data to clients very quickly.

### WHAT YOU REALLY NEED TO KNOW

◆ **Network attached storage (NAS)** is a specialized storage device or group of storage devices that provides centralized fault-tolerant data storage for a network.

◆ NAS differs from RAID in that it maintains its own interface to the LAN rather than relying on a separate server to connect it to the network and control its functions.

◆ The advantage to NAS as compared to a typical file server is that a NAS device contains its own file system that is optimized to read and write files (as opposed to also running a full-service operating system, managing printing, authenticating logon IDs, and so on). Because of this optimization, NAS reads and writes from its disk significantly faster than other types of servers could.

◆ Another advantage to using NAS is that it can easily be expanded without interrupting service. For instance, if you purchased a NAS device with 40 GB of disk space, then six months later realized you need three times as much storage space, you could add the new 80 GB to the NAS device without requiring users to log off the network or taking down the NAS device. After physically installing the new disk space, the NAS device would recognize the added storage and add it to its pool of available disk space.

◆ Although NAS is a separate device with its own file system, it still cannot communicate directly with clients on the network. When using NAS, the client requests a file from its usual file server (such as a Windows, UNIX/Linux, or NetWare server) over the LAN. The server then requests the file from the NAS device on the network. In response, the NAS device retrieves the file and transmits it to the server, which transmits it to the client.

◆ NAS is appropriate for small or medium sized enterprises that require fault tolerance, and fast access to data. Since NAS devices can store and retrieve data for any type of client (providing it can run TCP/IP), NAS is also appropriate for organizations that use a mix of different operating systems on their desktops.

### OBJECTIVES ON THE JOB

If your organization relies on data or programs that must always be available, network attached storage might be an excellent way to store and serve these resources. If you work with NAS, remember that it uses its own software and hardware. Thus, installing, configuring, and maintaining NAS can be quite different from installing, configuring, and maintaining off-the-shelf servers using the Windows, NetWare or UNIX/Linux operating systems.

## PRACTICE TEST QUESTIONS

1. **What is one advantage of using NAS compared to using a Windows 2000 server running RAID level 3?**
   a. It is directly attached to the file server.
   b. It can read and write data faster.
   c. It is easier to configure.
   d. It is less expensive.

2. **What type of operating system do NAS devices use?**
   a. Linux
   b. NetWare
   c. Windows 2000 Server
   d. a unique, proprietary O/S that depends on the NAS vendor

3. **On a 100BaseTX network, what type of access method would a group of NAS devices use?**
   a. demand priority
   b. CSMA/CA
   c. CSMA/CD
   d. token passing

4. **What is one advantage of NAS devices compared to a Pentium file server running NetWare 5.x?**
   a. They are easier to install and maintain.
   b. They are capable of multiprocessing.
   c. They can accept new hard disks without interruption of service.
   d. They can provide Internet services, remote access services, and management services, as well as file and print sharing services.

5. **NAS devices cannot communicate directly with clients on the same network. True or false?**

6. **Which of the following protocols do the majority of NAS devices use?**
   a. TCP/IP
   b. NetBEUI
   c. NetBIOS
   d. IPX/SPX

7. **Which of the following clients would be compatible with NAS? Choose all that apply.**
   a. MS-DOS
   b. Macintosh
   c. Windows 95
   d. Windows 98

## 3.5   Identify the purpose and characteristics of fault tolerance.

### UNDERSTANDING THE OBJECTIVE

Fault tolerance is the capacity for a system to withstand faults. On a network, many techniques, including redundancy, backups, mirroring, clustering, and disk striping can ensure fault tolerance.

### WHAT YOU REALLY NEED TO KNOW

◆ **Fault tolerance** is the capacity for a system to continue performing despite an unexpected hardware or software malfunction. A **fault** is the malfunction of one component of a system. A fault can result in a **failure**, or a deviation from a specified level of system performance for a given period of time.

◆ The aim of fault tolerance is to employ as many techniques as is prudent to prevent faults from becoming failures. Most of these techniques address single points of failure, or places in the network where one fault could immobilize the entire network.

◆ **Redundancy** is the use of duplicate components or machines on a network. The aim of redundancy is to eliminate single points of failure. Networks often include redundant power sources, cabling, server hard disks, NICs, and data links.

◆ **Server mirroring** is a fault-tolerance technique in which one server duplicates the transactions and data storage of another. The servers must be identical machines.

◆ Another fault-tolerance technique is **disk mirroring**, in which data are simultaneously written to two (usually) identical disks attached to a computer.

◆ A simple implementation of disk mirroring on a server is also known as **redundant array of inexpensive disks (RAID) level 1**.

◆ **RAID level 0** is the simplest implementation of disk striping. In RAID level 0, data is written in 64K blocks equally across all disks (or partitions) in the array.

◆ Disk striping alone does not ensure availability because if one of the disks fails, its data will be inaccessible. Thus, RAID level 0 does not provide true redundancy.

◆ **RAID level 3** involves disk striping with a special type of ECC (error correction code) known as parity error correction code. It writes parity information to a single disk.

◆ **RAID level 5** is the most common, highly fault-tolerant technique for data storage. In RAID level 5, data are written in small blocks across several disks. At the same time, parity error checking information is also distributed among the disks.

### OBJECTIVES ON THE JOB

Of all fault tolerance techniques, RAID level 5 is most common on modern networks. You should understand how your server handles RAID and what kind of hardware it requires. Consider having RAID components installed by the manufacturer. That way, you are certain to get RAID components that are compatible with your hardware.

# PRACTICE TEST QUESTIONS

1. **Which of the following is the least expensive method of ensuring availability on a network of 100 nodes?**
   a. using redundant NICs on all servers
   b. using redundant fiber links to the ISP
   c. using a SONET ring to connect to the local telecommunications facility
   d. leasing off-site facilities for data backup storage

2. **Which of the following will definitely render a network unusable?**
   a. failure
   b. fault
   c. redundancy
   d. security breach

3. **Which of the following components should be redundant in a fault-tolerant network?**
   a. the servers' NICs
   b. the root password
   c. the NOS software installation
   d. the SYS volume

4. **What is the aim of fault tolerance?**
   a. to eliminate faults
   b. to ensure that faults don't result in failures
   c. to address the least severe faults
   d. to create potential faults for testing purposes

5. **Which of the following could be a single point of failure for an entire network? Choose all that apply.**
   a. a server
   b. a router
   c. a hub
   d. a workstation

6. **Which of the following statements is true about mirroring?**
   a. Mirrored servers must connect to the network at the same speed.
   b. Mirrored servers must have identical NICs.
   c. Mirrored servers must be in the same computer room.
   d. Mirrored servers must use the same backup scheme.

7. **Which of the following is most likely to be implemented on a modern network?**
   a. RAID level 0
   b. RAID level 1
   c. RAID level 3
   d. RAID level 5

## 3.6 Identify the purpose and characteristics of disaster recovery.

### UNDERSTANDING THE OBJECTIVE

Disaster recovery will allow your organization and, in particular, its computer systems to regain functionality after a disaster (such as a tornado, flood, or terrorist attack) affects you.

### WHAT YOU REALLY NEED TO KNOW

◆ **Disaster recovery** is the process of restoring critical functionality and data after an enterprise-wide outage that affects more than a single system or a limited group of users.

◆ When planning for disaster recovery, you must take into account the possible extremes, rather than considering only relatively minor outages, failures, security breaches, or data corruption. In a disaster recovery plan, you should consider the worst-case scenarios, from a catastrophic hurricane to a terrorist attack.

◆ Disaster recovery should also address what might happen if your typical networking staff isn't available. The plan should outline multiple contingencies, in case your best options don't pan out. It should also specify alternate sites that can be used to supply temporary functionality.

◆ Every organization should have a disaster recovery team (with an appointed coordinator) and a disaster recovery plan. This plan should address not only computer systems, but also power, telephony, and paper-based files.

◆ The computer systems part of a disaster recovery plan should address the following issues:

- Contact names for emergency coordinators who will execute the disaster recovery response, as well as roles and responsibilities of other staff.

- Details on which data and servers are backed up, how frequently backups occur, where backups are kept (off-site), and, most importantly, how backed-up data can be recovered in full.

- Details on network topology, redundancy, and agreements with national service carriers, in case vendors fall prey to the same disaster.

- Strategies for regularly testing the disaster recovery plan.

- A plan for managing the crisis, including regular communications with employees and customers. Consider the possibility that regular communications modes (such as phone lines) might be unavailable.

### OBJECTIVES ON THE JOB

Having a comprehensive disaster recovery plan not only lessens the risk of losing critical data in case of extreme situations, but also makes potential customers and your insurance providers look more favorably on your organization.

## PRACTICE TEST QUESTIONS

1. **Which of the following details should be recorded in a disaster recovery plan? Choose all that apply.**
   a. where backup tapes are kept
   b. home telephone number of the network administrator
   c. what type of disaster might occur
   d. how the plan will be tested

2. **Which of the following are disasters that would be addressed by a disaster recovery plan?**
   a. a vendor going out of business
   b. a hurricane demolishing the organization's headquarters
   c. a riot in a nearby city
   d. a hacker gaining access to your Web server

3. **Which of the following would be the person most likely to coordinate an organization's computer systems disaster recovery effort?**
   a. help desk technician
   b. company CFO
   c. database programmer
   d. IT manager

4. **Besides computer systems, what other resources must be addressed by a disaster recovery plan? Choose all that apply.**
   a. paper files
   b. power
   c. IP address reservations with ICANN
   d. employees' cars

5. **Why would it be necessary to include details about an organization's service agreements with telecommunications carriers in a disaster recovery plan?**
   a. They will have to supply the organization with new equipment.
   b. The carriers may also be affected by the disaster and may owe the organization compensation for downtime.
   c. The agreements may change as a result of the disaster.
   d. The carriers may decide to void their agreement after the disaster.

6. **The computer systems part of a good disaster recovery plan should assign duties to the IT department personnel only. True or false?**

7. **A disaster recovery plan should contain several different approaches for recovering from a disaster. True or false?**

# OBJECTIVES

## 3.7   Given a remote connectivity scenario (e.g., IP, IPX, dial-up, PPPoE, authentication, physical connectivity, etc.), configure the connection.

### UNDERSTANDING THE OBJECTIVE

Many utilities, software programs, protocols, and hardware combinations are used to establish a remote connection. The modem on the client must be properly installed and configured. For Windows clients, the dial-up networking (DUN) software must be configured; then the DUN software and the TCP/IP protocol must be bound to both TCP/IP and the Client for Microsoft Networks.

### WHAT YOU REALLY NEED TO KNOW

◆ The most common type of remote access involves dial-up networking. **Dial-up networking (DUN)** typically refers to a modem connection to a server through the PSTN. It is also the name of the utility that Microsoft provides with its operating systems to achieve this type of connectivity. To use dial-up networking, the modem and the networking client software must be properly installed and configured.

◆ Nearly all dial-up networking connections rely on TCP/IP network protocols. Most Windows-based clients use the PPP protocol.

◆ To connect to a Windows-based remote access server from a Windows workstation, the Client for Microsoft Networks and the TCP/IP protocol must be installed. Also, the dial-up networking utility must be installed and bound to TCP/IP and the Client for Microsoft Networks.

◆ Settings you can identify through the DUN connection properties include the server type, network and remote access protocols that will be transmitted, whether data must be encrypted, IP address, and default gateway. Most modern dial-up connections rely on DHCP to assign IP addresses.

◆ If incomplete or incorrect information is entered into this configuration, a session can be established, but the client might be unable to send or receive data. If the client is dialing into an ISP's server, the ISP must provide client configuration information.

◆ A remote access server is a combination of software and hardware that provides a central access point for multiple users to dial into a LAN or WAN.

◆ Different software and hardware combinations can provide remote connectivity. One example is the Windows 2000 Server's **Routing and Remote Access Service (RRAS)**.

### OBJECTIVES ON THE JOB

Knowing how to establish and troubleshoot a dial-up networking connection is a basic skill related to knowing how to establish and troubleshoot any other connection to the LAN. Be sure to verify that a proper Physical layer connection exists, that appropriate protocols and clients have been correctly bound to the hardware, and that dial-up networking software and address settings are correct.

# PRACTICE TEST QUESTIONS

1. **Which of the following must be specified by an ISP for its clients to establish DUN connections to its remote access server?**
   a. default gateway address
   b. TCP/IP version
   c. maximum modem port speed
   d. modem IRQ

2. **In order for a Windows 9x machine to send and receive data via DUN to a Windows 2000 Server running RRAS and TCP/IP, to which of the following should the DUN software be bound? Choose all that apply.**
   a. TCP/IP
   b. IPX/SPX
   c. Client for NetWare Networks
   d. Client for Microsoft Networks

3. **What option would you choose to create a DUN connection on a Windows 2000 Professional workstation?**
   a. Network and Dial-up Connections, Make New Connection
   b. Control Panel, Modems, General
   c. Dial-Up Networking, Make New Connection
   d. Dial-Up Networking, Properties

4. **What does RAS stand for?**
   a. remote authentication service
   b. remote access service
   c. remote accounting service
   d. remote addressing server

5. **After you have created a Dial-up Networking connection on a Windows 2000 workstation, how would you indicate that PPP should be used?**
   a. Network Neighborhood, Connection properties, Network, Protocol Type
   b. Network and Dial-up Connections, Dial-up Connection Properties, Network, Type of dial-up server I am calling
   c. Network and Dial-up Connections, Options, Security, Protocol
   d. Network Neighborhood, Dial-up networking, Server type

6. **Which of the following transmission systems are commonly used for dial-up networking? Choose all that apply.**
   a. ISDN
   b. PSTN
   c. T-1
   d. SONET

7. **Which two of the following can be supported through the Windows DUN connection?**
   a. SNA
   b. IPX
   c. IP
   d. DLC

## 3.8   Identify the purpose, benefits, and characteristics of using a firewall.

### UNDERSTANDING THE OBJECTIVE

Firewalls are combinations of hardware and software that operate at the Network and Transport layers of the OSI model to filter traffic coming in and going out of a network. Firewalls most often run on router hardware, though they can also work on PCs.

### WHAT YOU REALLY NEED TO KNOW

◆ A **firewall** is a specialized device (typically a router, but possibly only a PC running special software) that selectively filters or blocks traffic between networks.

◆ A firewall typically involves a combination of hardware (for example, a router) and software (for example, the router's operating system and configuration). It can be placed between two interconnected private networks or between a private network and a public network.

◆ The simplest and most common form of a firewall is a **packet filtering firewall**, which is a router that operates at the Network and Transport layers of the OSI model, examining the data headers to determine whether each packet is authorized to continue to its destination. Packet filtering firewalls are also called **screening firewalls**.

◆ You must customize a packet filtering firewall to make it effective. Specifically, you must configure the firewall to accept or deny certain types of traffic. Some of the criteria a firewall can use to accept or deny data include: source and destination IP addresses; source and destination ports (such as ports that supply TCP/UDP connections, FTP, Telnet, SNMP, and RealAudio); TCP, UDP, or ICMP protocol; whether a packet is the first packet in a new data stream or a subsequent packet; whether the packet is inbound or outbound to or from a private network; whether the packet came from or is destined for an application on your private network.

◆ Because firewalls must be tailored to your network's needs, you cannot simply purchase a firewall and install it between your private LAN and the Internet and expect it to offer much security.

◆ Packet filtering routers cannot distinguish which user is trying to get through the firewall, nor can they determine whether that user is authorized to do so.

### OBJECTIVES ON THE JOB

It can take weeks to configure a firewall properly so that it is not so strict that it prevents authorized users from transmitting and receiving necessary data, and not so lenient that you risk security breaches. Also plan to create exceptions to the rules.

# PRACTICE TEST QUESTIONS

1. **On which two of the following devices could a firewall run?**
   a. server
   b. printer
   c. hub
   d. router

2. **At what layers of the OSI model do firewalls operate?**
   a. Application and Session
   b. Data Link and Physical
   c. Transport and Network
   d. Presentation and Session

3. **Which two of the following criteria could be used to filter traffic on a firewall?**
   a. IP address
   b. login ID
   c. password
   d. destination port

4. **Which of the following types of networks necessarily uses more than one firewall?**
   a. WAN
   b. VPN
   c. LAN
   d. MAN

5. **Which of the following protocols can be interpreted by a firewall?**
   a. SNA
   b. DLC
   c. TCP/IP
   d. NetBEUI

6. **Before a firewall can effectively filter unwanted traffic anywhere on a network, it must be**
   a. placed between a private and public network.
   b. configured according to an organization's security needs.
   c. combined with a proxy server.
   d. attached to switch on the internal LAN.

7. **A type of firewall that masks the IP addresses of internal devices by replacing them with its own is called a**
   a. gateway.
   b. proxy.
   c. packet filtering firewall.
   d. screening firewall.

## 3.9  Identify the purpose, benefits, and characteristics of using a proxy.

### UNDERSTANDING THE OBJECTIVE

A proxy service is one that acts on behalf of another service. Typically, a proxy server is used in networking at the border between an internal LAN and an outside WAN (such as the Internet). A proxy server can filter outgoing and incoming requests for data, cache frequently used Web pages, and obscure the specific IP addresses of devices on an internal LAN. Proxy servers are typically used in conjunction with a firewall.

### WHAT YOU REALLY NEED TO KNOW

- ◆ In networking, the term **proxy** means a device or service that acts on behalf of another device or service.

- ◆ Using a proxy for a server or network device can improve security and the performance of servers, or simplify addressing on a local network.

- ◆ Proxy servers situated between internal LAN clients and the Internet can improve performance by caching requests and saving them on local disks for future retrieval. This saves subsequent clients who request the same data from having to connect to a remote host on the Internet, thus expediting the retrieval.

- ◆ A proxy device may determine what type of traffic can be exchanged between clients on an internal LAN and the Internet. The proxy may filter requests to the Internet, for example, or allow only specific IP addresses to send traffic through while denying transmission attempts from other IP addresses.

- ◆ A proxy server also acts as a way to obscure internal IP addresses. After a client sends its data to the proxy server, the proxy server repackages the data frames that make up the message so that, rather than the workstation's IP address being the source, the proxy server inserts its own IP address as the source.

- ◆ A proxy server may also allow or deny transmission requests depending on the type of protocol. For instance, a proxy server can prevent outside clients from reaching a server's FTP service, but allow outside clients to access its HTTP service.

- ◆ If a network uses a proxy server for Web access, each client's browser must be configured to point to the proxy server. All major Internet browser programs contain a space for the proxy server's IP address in their properties or preferences options.

- ◆ While proxy servers do provide some measure of security, they are usually placed on the network together with a firewall.

### OBJECTIVES ON THE JOB

To use a proxy server, clients must be configured to point to the server. This is accomplished by entering a parameter into the client's Web browser. All network operating systems can supply some type of proxy server software, either as part of their program or as an add-on program.

## PRACTICE TEST QUESTIONS

1. **How does a proxy server improve Web performance for clients on a private LAN?**
   a. It expedites incoming data to clients because it replaces client IP addresses.
   b. It enables incoming requests to bypass the firewall.
   c. It holds Web requests in a cache so that subsequent requests for those pages can be fulfilled locally.
   d. It enables users to save frequently used bookmarks in a shared location.

2. **Which of the following can a proxy server use as criteria to filter incoming traffic? Choose all that apply.**
   a. IP address
   b. MAC address
   c. protocol
   d. TTL

3. **Which of the following IP ranges is most likely to be found on a small, private network that uses a proxy server to share limited IP addresses?**
   a. 10.09.1.1 – 10.10.1.254
   b. 124.89.33.1 – 124.89.33.230
   c. 222.45.112.1 – 222.45.113.1
   d. 188.30.10.1 – 188.30.10.10

4. **Which of the following is a potential disadvantage to Web caching?**
   a. It takes more time to initially retrieve the Web pages for the cache.
   b. It requires clients to configure an additional parameter in their Web browsers.
   c. It does not guarantee that the cached Web pages are the most current.
   d. It is difficult to configure.

5. **If a client on a local LAN uses an IP address of 100.100.10.2 and the LAN's proxy server uses an IP address of 205.66.127.88, what will the remote host regard as the client's IP address when the client connects to a remote host on the Internet?**
   a. 100.100.10.2
   b. 100.100.10.1
   c. 205.66.127.1
   d. 205.66.127.88

6. **What device is usually found near a proxy server on the network?**
   a. modem
   b. firewall
   c. switch
   d. protocol analyzer

7. **Where in Netscape Communicator could you enter the IP address of a proxy server?**
   a. Edit, Preferences, Advanced, Proxies
   b. Tools, Internet Options, Proxy Server
   c. Tools, Internet Options, Connections, Settings
   d. Edit, Preferences, Advanced, Cache

## 3.10    Given a scenario, predict the impact of a particular security implementation on network functionality (e.g., blocking port numbers, encryption, etc.).

### UNDERSTANDING THE OBJECTIVE

Security is a necessary part of network management. However, with each new access restriction, a network administrator risks limiting authorized access to resources and reducing network performance.

### WHAT YOU REALLY NEED TO KNOW

◆ Nearly all data security measures affect network performance and access to network resources. Firewalls add another device through which data must travel, as well as another potential point of failure in the network. Authentication takes a few extra seconds of a user's time. Encryption adds time to the process of assembling and disassembling data frames.

◆ To improve network security, a network administrator could disable—or block—certain well-known ports, such as the FTP ports (20 and 21) in a device's configuration. Blocking ports prevents *any* user from connecting to and completing a transmission through those ports. This technique is useful to further guard against unauthorized access to the network.

◆ One danger of blocking ports is that the administrator may also block communication for authorized users as well. This peril can be avoided by using alternate ports, specifying access restrictions (for example, according to source address) for certain ports, or separating private and public network devices.

◆ **Authentication** is the process of verifying a user's validity and authority on a system; it generally takes place during the login process and, when properly configured, helps keep a network secure. When improperly configured, the authentication process can restrict authorized access. (For example, if you inadvertently limit the time of day an authorized user can log on to the network, the user won't be able to log in.)

◆ **Encryption** is the use of an algorithm to scramble data into a format that can be read only by reversing the algorithm—that is, by decrypting the data. The purpose of encryption is to keep information private. Many forms of encryption exist, with some being more secure than others.

◆ Encryption can limit authorized access if the recipient of encrypted data does not have the proper software, system, credentials, or configuration to decrypt the data.

### OBJECTIVES ON THE JOB

The benefits of security measures must be weighed against their impact on authorized network access and network performance. For example, if you have secured the perimeter of a private LAN from outside access, you may decide that your need for data encryption within the organization is insignificant and forego encryption in favor of faster data transmission.

## PRACTICE TEST QUESTIONS

1. **Which of the following security measures would slow transmissions between two workstations on the same segment? Choose all that apply.**
   a. private key encryption
   b. firewall
   c. NOS authentication
   d. public key encryption

2. **Which of the following would potentially prevent authorized users from accessing their LAN resources while they travel?**
   a. private key encryption
   b. firewall
   c. NOS authentication
   d. public key encryption

3. **What port(s) should you block in order to prevent insecure FTP transmissions from going to or from your Web server? Choose all that apply.**
   a. 20
   b. 21
   c. 22
   d. 23

4. **What is the name of the most highly privileged account on a UNIX or Linux system?**
   a. tree
   b. admin
   c. root
   d. master

5. **When using a firewall to guard a private LAN from Internet-based intrusion, how can you still allow authorized users to access the network from home?**
   a. open access to all the router's ports
   b. allow access to select ports based on incoming IP address
   c. allow some users to bypass the firewall
   d. apply time of day restrictions to some of the firewall's ports

6. **What pieces of information do all modern NOSs require for authentication?**
   a. user name and password
   b. first name, last name, and date of birth
   c. username, IP address, and password
   d. last name, IP address, and location

7. **Ensuring that authorized users have appropriate access to the resources they need is part of an effective security policy. True or false?**

## 3.11  Given a network configuration, select the appropriate NIC and network configuration settings (DHCP, DNS, WINS, protocols, NetBIOS/host name, etc.).

### UNDERSTANDING THE OBJECTIVE

Several elements contribute to the proper configuration of a network interface card and network connection. The manufacturer encodes some configuration information on the NIC. The computer's BIOS, if it is Plug and Play compatible, assigns more information such as the IRQ, DMA channel, and I/O address, which can be later changed through the operating system. Network protocols and services are also specified through the O/S.

### WHAT YOU REALLY NEED TO KNOW

◆ **Plug and Play (PnP)** technology automatically attempts to configure newly inserted devices such as NICs, monitors, sound cards, etc. In order for PnP to work, the BIOS, hardware, and operating system must all be PnP compatible.

◆ Plug and Play technology can assign IRQ addresses, DMA channels, and I/O addresses. However, even if PnP is used, **device drivers**, the software unique to each component that allows it to communicate with the operating system, must be installed and configured properly through the O/S.

◆ Before a node on a TCP/IP network can exchange data with another node, it must have an IP address, client software, and TCP/IP services bound to its network interface.

◆ **WINS (Windows Internet Naming Service)** translates NetBIOS names into IP addresses, and is only used on NetBIOS networks. If WINS is used, the IP address of the WINS server must be specified in the clients' TCP/IP configuration.

◆ **Dynamic Host Configuration Protocol (DHCP)** automatically assigns IP addresses to clients on a TCP/IP network. Once the DHCP service is specified in an interface's TCP/IP properties, no individual TCP/IP addresses or servers must be specified.

◆ A **host name** is the unique name of a TCP/IP node that adheres to DNS naming conventions. **DNS (Domain Name System)** is a hierarchical way of identifying IP addresses with easily readable names. You can specify DNS server names as well as the node's host name in a client's TCP/IP configuration.

◆ A **domain name** is the name assigned to a group of hosts. A client's domain name should also be specified in that client's TCP/IP properties.

◆ If a client uses NetBIOS, that client will also require a NetBIOS name to uniquely identify it on the network.

### OBJECTIVES ON THE JOB

Modifying a network interface's settings, from protocols to host names to services, is one of the most common tasks a network technician performs. It should become second nature.

# PRACTICE TEST QUESTIONS

1. Which of the following will allow a networked workstation to obtain an IP address automatically once it logs onto the network?
   a. DNS
   b. WINS
   c. NetBIOS
   d. DHCP

2. What service allows a Windows computer to automatically recognize newly added hardware?
   a. SNMP
   b. PnP
   c. DHCP
   d. WINS

3. What service associates NetBIOS names with IP addresses?
   a. DNS
   b. WINS
   c. NetBIOS
   d. DHCP

4. Which of the following do not have to be specified if a workstation uses DHCP? Choose all that apply.
   a. subnet mask
   b. host name
   c. frame type
   d. IP address

5. What options would you select to configure the TCP/IP protocol on a Windows 2000 server?
   a. Local Area Connection Properties, Network Interface, Internet Protocol (TCP/IP) Properties
   b. Network Neighborhood, Properties, General, TCP/IP
   c. Network Neighborhood, Local Area Connection Properties, TCP/IP protocol Properties
   d. Network and Dial-up Connections, Local Area Connection, Properties, Protocol (TCP/IP)

6. DHCP is selected by default when you install the Windows 2000 Professional operating system. True or false?

7. Which of the following might allow a workstation to exchange data within a private, TCP/IP-based LAN, but prevent it from exchanging data with the Internet?
   a. Its TCP/IP protocol is not bound to its NIC.
   b. Its DHCP settings are incorrect.
   c. Its DNS settings are incorrect.
   d. Its WINS settings are incorrect.

# OBJECTIVES

## 4.1   Given a troubleshooting scenario, select the appropriate TCP/IP utility from among the following:

### TRACERT, NETSTAT, AND NBTSTAT

### UNDERSTANDING THE OBJECTIVE

Tracert is a utility that sends a packet to a specified host and retrieves information on the path the packet took to reach the host. netstat is a similar utility, but provides information about all connected TCP/IP hosts, including the connections' port numbers and status. Nbtstat is a utility that reveals the NetBIOS names and status of connected devices running NetBIOS over TCP/IP (NBT).

### WHAT YOU REALLY NEED TO KNOW

◆ **Tracert** (or traceroute on UNIX systems) is a TCP/IP utility that traces the path of a packet from the originating host to another host. In its simplest form, it displays the number of router hops the packet traverses, those routers' addresses, and how long the packet took to go from one router to the next.

◆ Tracert is most useful for determining where network bottlenecks are occurring. It also indicates whether a host is unreachable.

◆ The most commonly used expression of the tracert command is `tracert Y`, where Y is the IP address or host name of a system.

◆ **Netstat** is a utility that displays specifics about active inbound and outbound TCP/IP connections on a host. When used in its most basic form, netstat displays the address (or host name) of connected systems, and the connected port, the type of Transport layer protocol in use, and the connection status.

◆ Netstat can be used with numerous parameters that supply more information about a host's connections, including statistics for network interfaces and routing tables for active connections.

◆ **Nbtstat** displays information about connected devices running NetBIOS over TCP/IP (NBT). Thus, nbtstat is useful only on Windows-based networks.

◆ Nbtstat can be used with several parameters to discover, for example, the workgroup and domain to which the NetBIOS machine belongs, MAC addresses, IP addresses, and sessions with connected hosts.

◆ Nbtstat is most commonly used with the following syntax to determine the NetBIOS name of a machine: `nbtstat -a X` (where X is the machine's IP address)

### OBJECTIVES ON THE JOB

Nbtstat, netstat, and tracert are important utilities included with the TCP/IP software provided with every modern operating system. Although many software developers have created updated versions of these utilities, they are so easy to use that many network administrators don't bother with newer, modified versions.

# PRACTICE TEST QUESTIONS

1. **Which of the following can reveal the time it takes a packet to reach a host? Choose all that apply.**
   a. Telnet
   b. PING
   c. tracert
   d. netstat

2. **Which of the following can reveal hackers connected to a TCP/IP host?**
   a. PING
   b. Telnet
   c. tracert
   d. netstat

3. **Which of the following can reveal the number of router hops a packet has taken on its way to a remote host?**
   a. netstat
   b. PING
   c. tracert
   d. Telnet

4. **If you are working on the help desk when a user calls and complains about slow connection times to a particular Web site, what utility would you recommend using to locate the performance problem?**
   a. SNMP
   b. netstat
   c. nbtstat
   d. tracert

5. **What parameter should be used with the nbtstat command when attempting to determine the NetBIOS name of a machine whose IP address you know?**
   a. -a
   b. -s
   c. -i
   d. -I

6. **Suppose you are logged on to the Internet and have accessed the www.yahoo.com Web site. What utility would you use to determine which port on your machine is being used to connect to the Web site?**
   a. nbtstat
   b. netstat
   c. Telnet
   d. tracert

7. **The nbtstat utility can easily show whether an IP gateway to the Internet is down. True or false?**

## 4.1   Given a troubleshooting scenario, select the appropriate TCP/IP utility from among the following (continued):

### PING

### UNDERSTANDING THE OBJECTIVE

The PING command is one of the most commonly used troubleshooting tools. PING sends at least one packet to the specified host and waits for a response. If there is no response, you can assume that the device or its TCP/IP stack is not functioning properly. If there is a response, information about the packets' return, such as the time it took the packets to reach the host, helps in discovering network performance problems.

### WHAT YOU REALLY NEED TO KNOW

- ◆ **Packet Internet Groper (PING)** is a TCP/IP utility that sends at least one packet to a specified address and waits for a response.

- ◆ PING is a powerful troubleshooting tool. It is primarily used to help determine whether a node on a TCP/IP-based network is connected and responding.

- ◆ PING assigns a sequence number and time stamp on the packets it sends. Thus, if the response from the device is positive, PING can also detect how long the packets took to return and whether any were damaged in transmission. This can be helpful in troubleshooting network performance problems.

- ◆ PING is often the first troubleshooting tool used when a client cannot communicate with a server or vice versa.

- ◆ The syntax of a simple PING command is `ping X`, where X is the IP address or host name of the device. If the host responds, the output contains the following message: `reply from X: bytes=32 time=100 ms TTL=252`, where X is the IP address or host name. The other numbers may vary.

- ◆ One of the first PING commands to try is `ping 127.0.0.1`. This IP address is reserved for the **loopback address**. Use this command to attempt to contact your own device's TCP/IP stack. If this command results in a negative response, chances are your TCP/IP protocol is corrupted or improperly installed.

- ◆ If the loopback PING test results in a positive response, the next devices to ping include another local host, the default IP gateway, the DNS server, or other critical devices on the network. Pinging different devices can uncover a network bottleneck.

### OBJECTIVES ON THE JOB

PING is perhaps the most useful and frequently used utility in the network technician's troubleshooting repertoire. In a situation where a client cannot access a server, PING can help determine where the problem is occurring. In most cases, sufficient information about a downed node or bottleneck can be obtained from the simple PING command. However, in some cases, using one of the many PING parameters provides a necessary troubleshooting clue.

# PRACTICE TEST QUESTIONS

1. **What Application layer TCP/IP protocol does PING use to request responses from devices?**
   a. SNMP
   b. SMTP
   c. ICMP
   d. RARP

2. **Which of the following is the loopback address in the IP version 4 addressing scheme?**
   a. 100.100.100.100
   b. 01.01.01.01
   c. 122.0.0.7
   d. 127.0.0.1

3. **What does TTL stand for?**
   a. time to live
   b. time to link
   c. transfer time load
   d. transfer time lost

4. **Which of the following can a PING test indicate? Choose all that apply.**
   a. what type of device is being contacted
   b. whether a packet has been damaged in transit
   c. how many routers a packet has to traverse on its way to a host
   d. how long it takes for a packet to reach a host

5. **In a response to a PING command, which of the following might point to a network congestion problem?**
   a. widely fluctuating TTL values
   b. excessive damaged packets
   c. a hostname listed as the responding node, rather than the IP address you typed
   d. a different host name than that listed in the original PING command

6. **Suppose that a client on a private LAN is connected to the Internet but cannot reach the www.microsoft.com Web page. However, the client's loopback PING test is positive, and the client can reach www.netscape.com. What should you ping next?**
   a. the LAN's gateway router
   b. the nearest core Internet gateway
   c. the ISP's DNS server
   d. www.microsoft.com

7. **What Transport layer protocol does PING rely on?**
   a. TCP
   b. UDP
   c. ARP
   d. FTP

## 4.1 Given a troubleshooting scenario, select the appropriate TCP/IP utility from among the following (continued):

### ARP AND NSLOOKUP

### UNDERSTANDING THE OBJECTIVE

ARP can be used as a diagnostic utility to provide information about a computer's ARP table. Nslookup provides information about a network's DNS database.

### WHAT YOU REALLY NEED TO KNOW

◆ The ARP utility provides a way of manipulating and obtaining information from a device's ARP table. It can be a valuable troubleshooting tool for discovering the identity of a machine whose IP address you know, or for solving the problem of two machines trying to use the same IP address.

◆ Typing the ARP command alone from a Windows system will display the proper syntax and list of switches available for this command. To return useful data, the ARP command requires at least one switch. For example, typing arp -a provides the entire ARP table for your host. Following is a list of the most popular ARP switches:

-a   Displays the ARP table for the host from which you issue the command.

-d   Removes an entry from the ARP table; this switch must be followed by the hostname corresponding to the ARP entry that you wish to remove.

-s   Adds an entry to the ARP table—in other words, creates a static ARP table entry. This switch must be followed by the hostname and MAC address of the device you wish to add.

◆ The **nslookup** utility allows you to query the DNS database from any computer on the network. Using nslookup, you can find the DNS host name of a device by specifying its IP address, or vice versa. This ability is useful for verifying that a host is configured correctly or for troubleshooting DNS resolution problems.

◆ The nslookup command returns not only the host's IP address, but also provides the primary DNS server name and address that holds the record for this name. To find the host name of a device whose IP address you know, type nslookup *ip_address* and press Enter.

◆ Many other nslookup options exist, and as with other UNIX-based commands, you can find the complete list of them in the nslookup man pages.

◆ The nslookup utility is available on UNIX and Windows 2000 systems.

### OBJECTIVES ON THE JOB

Nslookup is a particularly useful tool for determining the IP address of a computer or network whose DNS information you already know.

## PRACTICE TEST QUESTIONS

1. **Which of the following commands would you use to add an entry to a computer's ARP table?**
   a. `arp -a`
   b. `arp -d`
   c. `arp -s`
   d. `arp -n`

2. **On which of the following computers could you successfully use the nslookup command to determine the IP address of a host? Choose all that apply.**
   a. a Windows 98 workstation
   b. a Linux workstation
   c. a Windows 2000 Professional workstation
   d. a Macintosh workstation

3. **What command would you type to find out more about the nslookup command on a UNIX server?**
   a. `man nslookup`
   b. `help nslookup`
   c. `nslookup /?`
   d. `type nslookup`

4. **Which of the following pieces of information would you obtain from a simple nslookup command? Choose all that apply.**
   a. the host's IP address
   b. the host's location on the network
   c. the host's primary DNS server
   d. the last time the host successfully responded to an nslookup command

5. **Which of the following commands would display the ARP table for a Windows 2000 server?**
   a. `arp -a`
   b. `arp -d`
   c. `arp -s`
   d. arp -n

6. **What type of output will you receive if you type the ARP command alone at a Windows 2000 command prompt?**
   a. the computer's complete ARP table
   b. information on proper syntax for the ARP command
   c. information on the computer's ARP configuration
   d. nothing

7. **You would type the command `arp student1.class.com` to view the ARP table entry for a computer whose hostname was student1.class.com. True or false?**

## 4.1   Given a troubleshooting scenario, select the appropriate TCP/IP utility from among the following (continued):

### IPCONFIG AND WINIPCFG

### UNDERSTANDING THE OBJECTIVE

When run from the command prompt on a Windows 2000 computer, ipconfig displays the IP address, subnet mask, and default gateway address. When run from the command prompt on a Windows 9x machine, winipcfg displays the workstation's MAC address, IP address, subnet mask, and default gateway in the IP Configuration dialog box.

### WHAT YOU REALLY NEED TO KNOW

◆ **Ipconfig** is a utility that comes with the Windows NT and Windows 2000 operating systems. When run from a machine's command prompt, it displays the TCP/IP configuration information.

◆ In its simplest form, ipconfig displays only the IP address, subnet mask, and default gateway for each adapter bound to TCP/IP.

◆ To display all the current TCP/IP configuration values, including the IP address, subnet mask, default gateway, and WINS and DNS configuration, use the following command: `ipconfig /all`.

◆ The command `ipconfig /?` displays a help message describing the ipconfig utility.

◆ On systems that use DHCP, you can use the `/release` or `/renew` options with ipconfig to release or renew the IP address of a network adapter.

◆ **Winipcfg** utility, when run from the command prompt, displays TCP/IP settings on Windows 9x workstations.

◆ In its simplest form, winipcfg displays the workstation's MAC address, IP address, subnet mask, and default gateway in the IP Configuration dialog box.

◆ Winipcfg can be used with many different switches to reveal more information about a workstation's TCP/IP settings.

◆ The command `winipcfg /?` displays a help message describing the use of the winipcfg utility.

◆ For more information about TCP/IP settings on a Windows 9x workstation, click the More Info button in the lower-right corner of the IP Configuration dialog box. Other settings you can view include DHCP server IP address, node type, and NetBIOS ID.

◆ On systems that use DHCP, you can use the `/release` or `/renew` options with winipcfg to release or renew the IP address of a network adapter.

### OBJECTIVES ON THE JOB

Ipconfig and winipcfg should be familiar to network technicians and even end users. When a user is having connectivity problems, a help desk analyst will often ask the user to type one of these commands to determine basic TCP/IP information.

# PRACTICE TEST QUESTIONS

1. Which two of the following can be displayed by typing `ipconfig` at the command prompt of a Windows 2000 Professional workstation?
   a. subnet mask
   b. NIC MAC address
   c. DHCP server address
   d. default gateway address

2. Which command displays the DHCP server address on a Windows 98 computer?
   a. `ipconfig /all`
   b. `ipconfig /?`
   c. `winipcfg /all`
   d. `winipcfg`

3. A user calls and complains of receiving the following error message after trying unsuccessfully to log into the network: "This address in use by station AC:05:20:41:CC:2D." Once you find the Windows 2000 workstation with this MAC address, what do you do to determine its IP address?
   a. Type `ipconfig /release` at the command prompt.
   b. Type `ipconfig /all` at the command prompt.
   c. Type `winipcfg /renew` at the command prompt.
   d. Type `winipcfg /all` at the command prompt.

4. What command would you use to discover the NetBIOS ID of a Windows 98 workstation?
   a. `ipconfig /all`
   b. `winipcfg /all`
   c. `ipconfig /NB`
   d. `winipcfg /NB`

5. How can you determine if a Windows 98 workstation is using DHCP?
   a. Type the `winipcfg` command at the command prompt.
   b. Start, Settings, Control Panel, Network, TCP/IP, DHCP Settings tab.
   c. Start, Settings, Control Panel, Network, TCP/IP, IP Address tab.
   d. Type the `ipconfig /all` command at the command prompt.

6. What is the fastest way to view the IP address of a Windows 2000 workstation?
   a. Type `winipcfg` at the command prompt.
   b. Type `ping 127.0.0.1` at the command prompt.
   c. Type `ipconfig` at the command prompt.
   d. Type `winipcfg /all` at the command prompt.

7. If a Windows NT server has two NICs bound to the TCP/IP protocol, how many subnet masks will be displayed when you type the `ipconfig /all` command?
   a. one
   b. two
   c. three
   d. none

## 4.1  Given a troubleshooting scenario, select the appropriate TCP/IP utility from among the following (continued):

### IFCONFIG

### UNDERSTANDING THE OBJECTIVE

Ifconfig is the utility used to reveal and modify TCP/IP properties on a UNIX or Linux computer.

### WHAT YOU REALLY NEED TO KNOW

◆ **Ifconfig** is the TCP/IP configuration and management utility used on UNIX systems.

◆ As with ipconfig on Windows 2000 systems and winipcfg on Windows 9x systems, ifconfig enables you to modify TCP/IP settings for a network interface, release and renew DHCP-assigned addresses, or simply check the status of your machine's TCP/IP settings.

◆ Ifconfig also runs when a UNIX system starts in order to establish the TCP/IP configuration for that system.

◆ As with the other operating systems' TCP/IP configuration utilities, ifconfig can be used alone, or it can be used with switches to reveal more customized information. For example, if you wanted to view the TCP/IP information associated with every interface on a device, you could type: `ifconfig -a`. Notice that the syntax of the `ifconfig` command uses a hyphen (-) before some of the switches and no preceding character for other switches.

◆ The following list describes some of the popular switches you may use with ifconfig. To view a complete list of options, you can read the ifconfig man pages:

   `-a`  Applies the command to all interfaces on a device

   `auto-dhcp`  Automatically obtains an IP address from a DHCP server for an interface (as a shortcut, you can type simply `dhcp`).

   `auto-dhcp release`  Releases the DHCP-assigned address from an interface.

   `auto-dhcp status`  Displays the status of an interface's DHCP configuration.

   `down`  Marks the interface as unavailable to the network.

   `up`  Reinitializes the interface after it has been "taken down," so that it is once again available to the network.

### OBJECTIVES ON THE JOB

If you work with UNIX or Linux-based servers or clients, you will need to be familiar with the ifconfig command, not only to view the computer's TCP/IP settings, but also to modify them.

## PRACTICE TEST QUESTIONS

1. Which of the following commands would list the TCP/IP settings for all network interfaces on a UNIX server?
   a. `ifconfig /all`
   b. `ifconfig_renew`
   c. `ifconfig -a`
   d. `ifconfig -?`

2. Which of the following commands makes a UNIX or Linux computer's network interface unavailable to the rest of the network?
   a. `ifconfig down`
   b. `ifconfig_release`
   c. `ifconfig -stop`
   d. `ifconfig -disable`

3. In addition to its use for reporting TCP/IP information, ifconfig also
   a. initializes TCP/IP services when a UNIX or Linux computer boots up.
   b. releases all DHCP-assigned IP addresses for a UNIX or Linux computer's network interfaces.
   c. responds to BOOTP requests from clients attached to the same segment.
   d. updates the local ARP cache.

4. Which of the following pieces of information would the `ifconfig-a` command reveal? Choose all that apply.
   a. subnet mask
   b. MAC address
   c. DHCP server address
   d. username

5. What is the name of the Windows 2000 utility that provides the same type of information that the UNIX/Linux ifconfig utility provides?
   a. winipcfg
   b. ifconfig
   c. ipconfig
   d. netipcfg

6. Which of the following commands would re-enable a network interface on a Linux server after it has been disabled?
   a. `ifconfig on`
   b. `ifconfig_renew`
   c. `ifconfig -start`
   d. `ifconfig up`

7. To find out more about using ifconfig, you could type `help ifconfig` at the UNIX shell prompt. True or false?

**4.2  Given a troubleshooting scenario involving a small office/home office network failure (e.g., xDSL, cable, home satellite, wireless, POTS), identify the cause of the failure.**

## UNDERSTANDING THE OBJECTIVE

Many connectivity options exist for home or small office users, including DSL, ISDN, POTS, cable modem, and home satellite. Each has different throughput and security characteristics and requires different connectivity equipment.

## WHAT YOU REALLY NEED TO KNOW

- ◆ **PSTN**, which stands for **Public Switched Telephone Network**, refers to the network of typical telephone lines and carrier equipment that service most homes. PSTN may also be called **plain old telephone service (POTS)**.

- ◆ PSTN was originally composed of analog lines and developed to handle voice-based traffic. Now, however, most of the PSTN uses digital transmission through fiber-optic and copper twisted-pair cable, microwave, and satellite connections.

- ◆ The term **xDSL** refers to all DSL varieties, of which at least eight currently exist. The types of DSL vary in terms of their capacity and maximum line length.

- ◆ Once inside the customer's office or home, the DSL line must pass through a **DSL modem**, a device that demodulates the signal, extracting the information and passing it on to the computer. The DSL modem may also contain a splitter to separate the line into multiple channels for voice and data signals. The DSL modem may be external to the computer and connect to a computer's Ethernet NIC via UTP cable or to the computer's USB port. Newer DSL modems come in the form of PCI expansion boards. If the DSL bandwidth is to be shared on a LAN, the DSL modem could connect to a connectivity device, such as a hub or router, rather than just one computer.

- ◆ Cable technology relies on the coaxial cable wiring used for TV signals, which could transmit as much as 36 Mbps downstream and as much as 10 Mbps upstream.

- ◆ Cable connections require a special **cable modem**, a device that modulates and demodulates signals for transmission and reception via cable wiring. The cable modem then connects to a customer's PC via its USB port or through a UTP cable to a (typically Ethernet) NIC. Alternatively, the cable modem could connect to a connectivity device, such as a hub or router, to supply bandwidth to a LAN rather than just one computer. Before customers can subscribe to cable modem service, their local cable company must have the necessary infrastructure.

## OBJECTIVES ON THE JOB

If you are troubleshooting a home or small office connection, be certain to understand the type of service to which the user has subscribed and the carrier's policies on equipment and maintenance.

# PRACTICE TEST QUESTIONS

1. **If you subscribed to cable modem service and wanted to connect three PCs to your cable data line, which of the following would you require?**
   a. hub
   b. multiplexer
   c. time domain reflectometer
   d. CSU/DSU

2. **Which of the following offers the lowest throughput for a home office Internet connection?**
   a. ADSL
   b. cable modem
   c. POTS
   d. ISDN

3. **A technology in which the downstream throughput is greater than the upstream throughput is known as:**
   a. symmetrical
   b. asymmetrical
   c. high voltage
   d. frequency modulated

4. **What technique do DSL providers use to achieve extraordinary throughput over typical POTS lines?**
   a. time division multiplexing
   b. frequency division multiplexing
   c. wave division multiplexing
   d. data modulation

5. **Why do cable TV providers have to upgrade their infrastructure before they can provide Internet connectivity to their customers?**
   a. because cable TV infrastructure is not available everywhere
   b. because cable TV infrastructure is not typically capable of bi-directional signaling
   c. because cable TV infrastructure relies at least in part on the PSTN
   d. because cable TV infrastructure is subject to short distance limitations between the customer and the cable company's POP

6. **Which of the following technologies allow data and voice signals to simultaneously share the same line to a home or business? Choose all that apply.**
   a. xDSL
   b. ISDN
   c. cable modem
   d. POTS

7. **Cable modem technology is asymmetrical. True or false?**

## 4.3  Given a troubleshooting scenario involving a remote connectivity problem (e.g., authentication failure, protocol configuration, physical connectivity), identify the cause of the problem.

### UNDERSTANDING THE OBJECTIVE

Remote connectivity requires proper configuration on both the remote client and remote access server. Connectivity can fail due to incompatible protocols, Physical layer (or line) problems, or improper or insufficient authentication.

### WHAT YOU REALLY NEED TO KNOW

◆ Dial-up networking (DUN) is the most common type of remote access. It typically involves a modem connection to a server through the PSTN.

◆ Because dial-up networking requires configuration on both the server and the client side, and relies on public transmission systems, many opportunities for failed or unsatisfactory connectivity arise.

◆ A dial-up networking connection may fail due to a Physical layer problem such as a faulty modem, missing or faulty lines or terminators, improperly configured Network layer protocols, improperly configured remote access protocols, typing an incorrect username or password, or a hardware or software failure on the server end of the connection.

◆ A dial-up networking connection may suffer poor performance due to a poor quality phone cable connecting the modem to the wall jack (causing crosstalk, for example), loose connections between the modem and the wall jack, the use of Y adapters, splitters, and similar equipment in the path between the modem and the wall jack, or twisted or partially damaged cable. To ensure the fastest connection, configure phone wiring for the most direct path from the computer to the point where the telephone line enters the house. Remove devices from the path to see if something else is causing the problem. Answering machines, Caller ID boxes, cordless phones, and other equipment can create enough interference to impair connectivity.

◆ The following settings must be specified in order to ensure remote access connectivity: server type, network and remote access protocols that will be transmitted, whether data must be encrypted, IP address, and default gateway. Most modern dial-up connections rely on DHCP to assign IP addresses.

◆ If incomplete or incorrect configuration information is supplied, a session may be established, but the client might be unable to send or receive data.

### OBJECTIVES ON THE JOB

If you work on the help desk of a large corporation, chances are you will be asked to help remote users dial into your network. In order to provide the best support, have the specific dial-in configuration parameters for your network close at hand.

# PRACTICE TEST QUESTIONS

1. **Which of the following can prevent a dial-up user from connecting to a remote access server? Choose all that apply.**
   a. using a different operating system from the remote access server's operating system
   b. the incorrect hostname specified in the client's TCP/IP properties
   c. a damaged phone line
   d. improper modem configuration

2. **Which of the following remote access protocols is most likely to be used by a Windows 98 client connecting to a Windows NT remote access server?**
   a. L2TP
   b. PPP
   c. PPTP
   d. EIGRP

3. **If you attempt to initiate a dial-up connection from your Windows 2000 Professional workstation and you receive an error saying "There is no dial tone," what should you check?**
   a. the connection between the modem and the wall jack
   b. the quality of the cabling between the carrier's access point to your home and your wall jack
   c. the remote access protocol configuration in your dial-up software
   d. the DHCP server specification in your TCP/IP settings

4. **What is the function of a modem?**
   a. to negotiate the Session layer protocols necessary to establish a connection between a dial-up client and a remote access server
   b. to separate data into frames as it is transmitted from the computer to the PSTN, then strip data from frames as it is received from the PSTN
   c. to encrypt data as it is transmitted from the computer to the PSTN, then decrypt data as it is received from the PSTN
   d. to convert a source computer's digital pulses into analog signals for the PSTN, then convert analog signals back into digital pulses for the destination computer

5. **Why is the maximum capability of a 56 Kbps telephone line never achieved when dialing into a network over the PSTN?**
   a. The PSTN is a shared network, and therefore no single user can reserve its entire bandwidth.
   b. Every telecommunications carrier throttles the amount of bandwidth it will allow consumers, after meeting its own bandwidth needs first.
   c. The FCC limits the use of PSTN lines to 53 Kbps in order to reduce the effects of crosstalk.
   d. At that speed the client and server would not have enough time to complete the authentication process.

6. **If you did not specify your workstation's IP address in your TCP/IP configuration when dialing into your Internet Service Provider, you could not complete a connection. True or false?**

7. **A dial-VPN is a private network that relies on the PSTN. True or false?**

## 4.4 Given specific parameters, configure a client to connect to the following servers:

### UNIX/LINUX, NETWARE, WINDOWS, AND MACINTOSH

### UNDERSTANDING THE OBJECTIVE

Each client must have Physical layer components, protocols, and client software appropriate for the network and server that they're logging onto.

### WHAT YOU REALLY NEED TO KNOW

◆ Most modern servers, including UNIX, Linux, NetWare 5.x, Windows NT and Windows 2000 Server, and Macintosh support and prefer the use of the IP as a Network layer protocol for client connections.

◆ In order to connect to a UNIX or Linux server, clients must have a NIC compatible with the network type, the TCP/IP protocol installed, a physical connection to the LAN where the server is located, plus a username and password valid on the server.

◆ In order to connect to a Windows 2000 server, clients must have the TCP/IP protocol installed and bound to the network interface, client software (such as Client for Microsoft Networks) appropriate for the server's network operating system, a physical connection to the LAN where the server is located, the appropriate domain controller specified, plus a username and password valid on the server.

◆ In order to connect to a NetWare 4.x or 5.x server, clients must have the TCP/IP or IPX/SPX protocol installed and bound to the network interface, client software (such as Novell's Client for NetWare Networks) appropriate for the server's NOS, a physical connection to the LAN, the appropriate NDS context specified, plus a username and password that are valid on the server.

◆ Most clients on modern networks run some form of the Windows operating system. If a client runs Windows 9x, the network parameters can be specified by choosing Start/ /Settings/Control Panel/Network. The Network Properties dialog box appears.

◆ If a client runs Windows 2000 Professional, the network parameters can be specified by choosing Start/Settings/Network and Dial-up Connections/Local Area Connection Properties. The Local Area Connection Properties dialog box appears.

◆ If a client runs the Macintosh operating system, the type of network it uses can be specified by selecting Chooser through the Apple menu.

◆ On a UNIX client, network interface and TCP/IP parameters are specified through use of the ifconfig command. A UNIX client logs onto a server from the shell prompt using the `login` command.

### OBJECTIVES ON THE JOB

Both novice and experienced networking professionals have to configure clients frequently. Be certain to understand all the configuration requirements for your network, as well as any exceptions to those configurations (for example, settings for older clients).

# PRACTICE TEST QUESTIONS

1. Which of the following would be required for a Windows 2000 Professional workstation to connect to a NetWare 5.1 server? Choose all that apply.
   - a. TCP/IP
   - b. IPX/SPX
   - c. Client for NetWare Networks
   - d. Client for Microsoft Networks

2. What type of NIC would a Windows 2000 Professional workstation require to connect to a NetWare 5.1 server?
   - a. 10Base2
   - b. 10BaseT
   - c. 100BaseT
   - d. NIC type depends on the network access method and speed, not the server NOS.

3. When logging onto a Windows 2000 server, what, besides username and password, must the user supply?
   - a. NDS context
   - b. domain
   - c. workgroup
   - d. segment

4. When logging on to a NetWare 5.1 server, what, besides username and password, must the user supply?
   - a. NDS context
   - b. domain
   - c. workgroup
   - d. segment

5. What networking component is responsible for prompting the user for his username and password, then communicating this information to a server?
   - a. Network layer protocols
   - b. NIC driver
   - c. client software
   - d. NOS

6. What menu options would you choose on a Macintosh client to modify its IP address?
   - a. Apple, TCP/IP Control Panel, IP Address
   - b. Apple, Network Properties, IP Address
   - c. Apple, Chooser, TCP/IP Services, IP Address
   - d. Apple, Chooser, Network Properties, TCP/IP Address

7. A UNIX server can accept connections from any client that can run TCP/IP. True or false?

# OBJECTIVES

**4.5   Given a wiring task, select the appropriate tool (e.g., wire crimper, media tester/certifier, punch down tool, tone generator, optical tester, etc.).**

## UNDERSTANDING THE OBJECTIVE

In order to ensure connectivity and optimal network performance, cables must be constructed and installed properly. Many tools are available to ensure that these two conditions are met.

## WHAT YOU REALLY NEED TO KNOW

- ◆ It is important to follow both the manufacturer's installation guidelines and the TIA/EIA standards for making and installing cable to ensure proper connectivity.

- ◆ Many network problems can be traced to poor cable installation techniques. For example, if you don't crimp twisted-pair wires in the correct position in an RJ-45 connector, the cable will fail to transmit or receive data (or both).

- ◆ Installing the wrong grade of cable can either cause your network to fail or render it more susceptible to damage (for example, using typical, inexpensive twisted-pair cable in areas that might be susceptible to fire damage).

- ◆ A **crimper** (or crimping tool) is used to terminate wires in a connector, such as an RJ-45 plug.

- ◆ Basic **cable checkers** determine whether your cabling can provide connectivity. To accomplish this task, they apply a small voltage to each conductor at one end of the cable, and then check whether that voltage is detectable at the other end.

- ◆ A **cable tester** performs the same continuity and fault tests as a cable checker, but may also ensure that the cable is not too long, measure the distance to a fault, measure attenuation, resistance, and crosstalk, and issue pass/fail ratings for different cabling standards.

- ◆ A **time domain reflectometer (TDR)** is a high-end instrument for testing wire cable and connector imperfections.

- ◆ **Optical time domain reflectometers (OTDRs)** issue a light-based signal over a fiber-optic cable. Based on the type of return light signal, the OTDR can gauge the length of the fiber, attenuation, and the location of faulty splices, breaks, connectors, or bends.

- ◆ A **tone generator** is a small electronic device that issues a signal on a wire pair. A **tone locator** is a device that emits a tone when it detects electrical activity on a wire pair. By placing the tone generator at one end of a wire and attaching a tone locator to the other end, you can verify the location of the wire's termination.

## OBJECTIVES ON THE JOB

Before leaving the area in which you were working, clean it up. For instance, if you created a new patch cable in a telecommunications room, remove the debris created while splicing the cable.

# PRACTICE TEST QUESTIONS

1. **Which of the following tools could determine the location of a faulty splice in a fiber optic link?**
   - a. cable checker
   - b. multimeter
   - c. TDR
   - d. OTDR

2. **What tool is used to terminate wires in an RJ-11 plug?**
   - a. crimper
   - b. pliers
   - c. wire stripper
   - d. allen wrench

3. **Which of the following tools could issue a pass/fail rating for a Category 5 cable?**
   - a. cable checker
   - b. cable tester
   - c. multimeter
   - d. tone generator

4. **If a patch cable allows a workstation to receive data, but not to transmit data, which of the following could be at fault? Choose all that apply.**
   - a. The cable may not have the proper plenum rating.
   - b. The cable may not have a sufficiently high twist ratio for the network on which it is being used.
   - c. The wires responsible for data transmission may not be properly terminated in one of the patch cable's connectors.
   - d. The transmit wire pair may be physically damaged.

5. **Which of the following can be used to determine the location of a particular wire in a bundle of wires?**
   - a. cable checker
   - b. cable tester
   - c. multimeter
   - d. tone generator

6. **What organization has established standards for structured cabling?**
   - a. IEEE
   - b. TIA/EIA
   - c. IETF
   - d. ISO

7. **Which of the following can test whether a UTP cable is transmitting an electrical signal? Choose all that apply.**
   - a. multimeter
   - b. cable checker
   - c. TDR
   - d. OTDR

# OBJECTIVES

## 4.6 Given a network scenario, interpret visual indicators (e.g., link lights, collision lights, etc.) to determine the nature of the problem.

### UNDERSTANDING THE OBJECTIVE

Without performing sophisticated diagnostics, you can sometimes tell at a glance whether a hub port is faulty or a server is processing incoming data. On hubs, routers, and NICs of every sort, LEDs indicate whether they are live and accepting/sending transmissions, experiencing excessive errors, or receiving no power.

### WHAT YOU REALLY NEED TO KNOW

◆ Viewing the link LEDs on hub ports, NICs, router ports, and other devices can reveal transmission problems.

◆ In general, a steady or blinking green link light (the LED next to a data port) or on a NIC indicates that data is being transmitted to or received from that network interface.

◆ In general, a steady or blinking amber LED next to a port or on a NIC indicates that a problem exists, such as excessive errors.

◆ If an LED next to a port or on a NIC is not lit, the port, NIC, or device is not in use or it is not receiving power.

◆ In general, hubs have another light called the collision LED that will indicate, by blinking, the volume of collisions the hub's (Ethernet) segment is experiencing.

◆ The front of a server or workstation often has a blinking green LED to indicate that data is being written to or read from the hard disk. In addition, another LED indicates in solid green whether the machine is receiving power.

◆ Many types of software, including network operating systems, maintain error logs to indicate whether errors have been generated through the use or attempted use of the software.

◆ While some software programs save error logs as text files, NOSs provide an interface where you can easily view error logs. In Windows 2000 Server, you can display this error log by choosing Event Viewer in the Administrative Tools submenu.

◆ Network operating system logs provide information about attempted security breaches as well as about errors in loading drivers, recognizing hardware, authenticating users, launching applications, and maintenance operations.

### OBJECTIVES ON THE JOB

The LED indicator guidelines above are only generalizations. Many models and types of hardware differ. Be sure to read your manuals and understand the meaning of LED lights for your particular equipment.

# PRACTICE TEST QUESTIONS

1. **How would a NIC indicate that a workstation is properly connecting to the network?**
   a. Its LED is steady amber.
   b. Its LED is blinking green.
   c. Its LED remains unlit.
   d. Its LED is steady blue.

2. **If the LED on the front of a router is not lit, what can you assume about the router?**
   a. It is properly transmitting and receiving data.
   b. It has at least one faulty port.
   c. It is waiting for incoming data.
   d. It is not receiving power.

3. **Viewing your server's resource statistics, you notice a sudden 50% decrease in a server's available hard disk resources. What might be the cause?**
   a. A user has attempted to back up his workstation to the network.
   b. The server's statistics display program has failed.
   c. The server's RAM has failed and it is relying entirely on virtual memory.
   d. The server is caching large requests for data from the Internet.

4. **How could you determine, by looking at a hub, whether an excessive number of collisions is occurring on that hub's segment?**
   a. Its uplink port LED is rapidly blinking amber.
   b. Its collision LED is rapidly blinking red.
   c. Some of its data port LEDs are rapidly blinking green.
   d. Some of its data port LEDs are not lit.

5. **What tool would you use on a Windows 2000 Server to discover trends in the amount of CPU utilization on the server over the last week?**
   a. Event Viewer
   b. Performance Monitor
   c. Account Utility
   d. Volumes Utility

6. **If one of the LEDs on the front of a server is blinking green, which of the following might be occurring?**
   a. The server is experiencing significant data errors.
   b. The server's hard disk is failing.
   c. The server's hard disk is being written to.
   d. The server's NIC is overtaxed.

7. **Which of the following could help you diagnose a server performance problem? Choose all that apply.**
   a. percent of disk space left on the DATA volume
   b. percent of CPU resources utilized
   c. percent of total users currently logged in
   d. ratio of IP traffic to IPX traffic

## 4.7   Given output from a diagnostic utility (e.g., tracert, ping, ipconfig, etc.), identify the utility and interpret the output.

### UNDERSTANDING THE OBJECTIVE

Each diagnostic utility results in different output that is most useful in different situations. Tracert can help determine the path packets take and how much network congestion is present. Ping can determine whether a TCP/IP host is responding. Ipconfig, winipcfg, and ifconfig can reveal TCP/IP settings for a host.

### WHAT YOU REALLY NEED TO KNOW

◆ The simplest form of the `traceroute` command is `traceroute ip_address`. On computers that use the Windows-based operating system, the proper syntax is `tracert ip_address`. This command will include lines similar to following:

10   140 ms   114 ms   129 ms   p1-0.chcgil2-cr1.bbnplanet.net [4.24.7.134]

11   118 ms   131 ms   114 ms   p.xchcgil26-att.bbnplanet.net [4.24.202.6]

◆ The output of a successful ping command resembles the following:

Reply from 216.119.103.72: bytes=32 time=173ms TTL=114

Reply from 216.119.103.72: bytes=32 time=175ms TTL=114

Reply from 216.119.103.72: bytes=32 time=2240ms TTL=114

Reply from 216.119.103.72: bytes=32 time=178ms TTL=114

Ping statistics for 216.119.103.72:

   Packets: Sent = 4, Received = 4, Lost = 0 (0% loss),

Approximate round trip times in milli-seconds:

   Minimum = 173ms, Maximum = 2240ms, Average = 691ms

◆ The output of an unsuccessful ping command resembles the following:

Request timed out.

Request timed out.

Request timed out.

Request timed out.

◆ The `ipconfig` command on a Windows 2000 computer reveals information about that computer's TCP/IP settings. The `winipcfg` command does the same on a Windows 9x computer, while the `Ifconfig` command does the same on a UNIX or Linux computer.

### OBJECTIVES ON THE JOB

In order to properly diagnose network problems using common utilities, you must not only know their syntax, but also be able to interpret their output. For instance, when using a traceroute command, requests between the source and destination may time out, indicating network congestion, but that congestion may be so distant from your network that it is inconsequential.

# PRACTICE TEST QUESTIONS

1. Which of the following would be included in the output of an unsuccessful ping test?
    a. Reply from 127.0.0.1: bytes=32 time=173ms TTL=114
    b. Packets: Sent = 4, Received = 4, Lost = 0 (0% loss)
    c. Request timed out.
    d. Host not responding.

2. What command would reveal the DHCP server address for a Windows 2000 server?
    a. winipcfg /all
    b. ifconfig -a
    c. ifconfig dhcp
    d. ipconfig /all

3. How many packets does a simple `ping` command, when used on a Microsoft Windows 2000 Professional client, issue?
    a. 1
    b. 2
    c. 3
    d. 4

4. What is the maximum number of router hops a simple traceroute command will traverse?
    a. 5
    b. 15
    c. 30
    d. 64

5. Which of the following commands would indicate the number of Ethernet interfaces installed on a UNIX server?
    a. ifconfig
    b. ipconfig /all
    c. ipconfig -a
    d. ipnetcfg -a

6. What does it mean when lines 15 through 20 of a traceroute command's response read, "Request timed out"?
    a. The client's traceroute command is not functioning properly.
    b. The network between the source and destination is experiencing congestion.
    c. The destination host is not connected to the network.
    d. The client used improper traceroute command syntax.

7. How large are the packets issued by the default `ping` command?
    a. 4 bytes
    b. 16 bytes
    c. 32 bytes
    d. 64 bytes

# OBJECTIVES

## 4.8 Given a scenario, predict the impact of modifying, adding, or removing network services (e.g., DHCP, DNS, WINS, etc.) on network resources and users.

### UNDERSTANDING THE OBJECTIVE

Each network requires different services and settings for those services. In order to properly connect to the network, clients must use correct protocol, service, and client software settings.

### WHAT YOU REALLY NEED TO KNOW

◆ On a TCP/IP network, each device is assigned a host name that is associated with its IP address. Together with its domain name, a host name uniquely identifies that device to other devices on the TCP/IP network.

◆ Every TCP/IP network that wants to communicate with the Internet must have a DNS server at its disposal (whether the server is local or remote).

◆ DNS is organized hierarchically for the worldwide Internet. If an organization's DNS server does not know the IP address of a requested host, it queries a higher-level DNS server. If that DNS server also doesn't know the IP address of the host, it queries a higher-level DNS server, and so on.

◆ In order to communicate over the Internet, clients must specify their DNS server address and hostname in their TCP/IP settings.

◆ In order to use the Windows Internet Naming Service (WINS), a client must specify the address or name of its WINS server in its network interface configuration, and the WINS service must be bound to the network interface.

◆ DHCP (Dynamic Host Configuration Protocol) is a service that automatically assigns IP addresses to network nodes, as well as other TCP/IP parameters such as default gateway and DNS server addresses. DHCP runs on a server, which may be a dedicated DHCP server or may also act as another type of server.

### OBJECTIVES ON THE JOB

Before modifying the network or protocol properties on a client, be certain to understand how your changes might affect service. For example, if you change a workstation's TCP/IP settings from using a static IP address to using DHCP, remember that you no longer need to specify that client's default gateway address, for example, because the DHCP server will supply that information.

# PRACTICE TEST QUESTIONS

1. **What options would you choose to configure a Windows 9x client to use DHCP?**
   a. Control Panel, Network, TCP/IP Properties, IP Address tab, Obtain IP address automatically
   b. Network and Dial-up Connections, Local Area Network Properties, Internet Protocol (TCP/IP) Properties
   c. Network Neighborhood Properties, Network Adapter Properties, TCP/IP Properties, DHCP tab
   d. Network and Dial-up Connections, Network Adapter Properties, Internet Protocol (TCP/IP) Properties, DHCP tab

2. **What is the function of a DNS server?**
   a. to supply hosts with a host name when they first log onto the network
   b. to request MAC address information based on a client's IP address
   c. to indicate which hosts are not responding to server requests at any given time
   d. to resolve hostnames with their IP addresses as requested by network nodes

3. **What options would you choose to add an additional DNS server to your Windows 2000 server's DNS settings?**
   a. Start, Settings, Control Panel, Network, TCP/IP Protocol
   b. Network and Dial-up Connections, Local Area Network Properties, Internet Protocol (TCP/IP) Properties, DNS tab
   c. Network and Dial-up Connections, Local Area Network, Properties, Internet Protocol (TCP/IP)
   d. Control Panel, Network, Properties, IP Address tab

4. **On a network that relies on NetWare 5.1 servers, clients need not specify a DNS server address in their TCP/IP configuration. True or false?**

5. **What would probably happen if you removed the binding between the Client for Microsoft Networks and the network adapter on a client that connected to a Windows 2000 server?**
   a. The client would be unable to log onto the network.
   b. The client would be able to log on, but not communicate with the network.
   c. The client would be able to log onto the network and communicate only with nodes running TCP/IP.
   d. The client's network connectivity would not be affected.

6. **What would happen if you uninstalled File and Printer Sharing for Microsoft Networks on a workstation that belonged to a Windows 2000 peer-to-peer network?**
   a. The workstation would not be able to access shared files on any other computer.
   b. Other workstations couldn't access that workstation's shared folders.
   c. No workstations could access another workstation's shared folders.
   d. The workstation would not be able to access its own shared folders.

7. **In addition to the TCP/IP protocol, DHCP services must be bound separately to a client's network interface. True or false?**

**4.9   Given a network problem scenario, select an appropriate course of action based on a general troubleshooting strategy that includes the following steps:**

**ESTABLISH THE SYMPTOMS, IDENTIFY THE AFFECTED AREA, ESTABLISH WHAT HAS CHANGED, AND SELECT THE MOST PROBABLE CAUSE**

### UNDERSTANDING THE OBJECTIVE

Successful troubleshooters proceed logically and methodically. The steps listed below are the first four steps in the process: identify the symptoms, identify the scope of the problem, establish what has changed in the network, and determine the most likely cause of the problem.

### WHAT YOU REALLY NEED TO KNOW

◆ Following a logical progression of steps in troubleshooting can help you solve problems faster and more thoroughly than a haphazard approach.

◆ Steps to troubleshooting network problems include:

- Identify the symptoms. Carefully document what you learn from people or systems that alerted you to the problem and keep that documentation handy.

- Identify the scope of the problem. Is it universal? That is, are all users on the network experiencing the problem at all times? Or is the problem limited to a specific geographic area of the network, to a specific group of users, or to a particular period of time? In other words, is the problem subject to geographic, organizational, or chronological constraints?

- Establish what has changed on the network. Recent hardware or software changes may be causing the symptoms.

- Determine the most probable cause of the problem. This determination may include the following techniques:

  Verify user competency

  Recreate the problem and ensure that you can reproduce it reliably.

  Verify the physical integrity of the network connection (such as cable connections, NIC installations, and power to devices), starting at the affected nodes and moving outward toward the backbone.

  Verify the logical integrity of the network connection (such as addressing, protocol bindings, software installations, and so on).

### OBJECTIVES ON THE JOB

In addition to the organized method of troubleshooting described above, a general rule for troubleshooting is "Pay attention to the obvious!" While some questions sound too simple to bother asking, don't discount them. If a problem is caused by an obvious error, such as a cable being disconnected, you can save yourself a lot of time by checking cable connections first.

# PRACTICE TEST QUESTIONS

1. **You receive a call from a remote user who says the network won't accept her password. How can you determine whether this problem is due to user error or client software?**
   a. Ask her to reboot and try again.
   b. Ask her to change her password.
   c. Try logging in under her user ID from your workstation.
   d. Ask her when the problem began.

2. **Suppose a user can't log on to the network, and you have verified that she is using the right password, that her protocols are correctly installed and bound to the NIC, and that the client software is correctly installed and configured. What should you check next?**
   a. the connection between the hub and the file server
   b. the connection between the workstation's NIC and the wall jack
   c. the connection between the patch panel and the hub
   d. the connection between the hub and the router

3. **A user can retrieve files from the network but cannot print to her usual printer. When you attempt to replicate the problem from a nearby workstation using her login ID, you find that you can print to that printer. What is the most likely cause of her problem?**
   a. The problem is caused by insufficient print server permissions for her user ID.
   b. The problem lies with her workstation's printer drivers.
   c. The problem lies with her workstation's NIC.
   d. The problem lies with her workstation's protocol bindings.

4. **What is a common reason for users typing in an incorrect password?**
   a. They wrote it down wrong.
   b. They have Caps Lock on and the password is case sensitive.
   c. They think they have changed the password when they actually haven't.
   d. They don't believe that it matters what password they enter.

5. **What can testing a problem with a test ID reveal that testing with an administrative ID cannot?**
   a. a problem related to rights
   b. an operator error
   c. a file corruption problem
   d. a network connectivity problem

6. **You try to reproduce a user's inability to launch the MS Excel program from the file server by logging in as the same user on a nearby workstation. Which two of the following could cause misleading results? Choose all that apply.**
   a. The nearby workstation was not identical to the user's workstation.
   b. The nearby workstation was not on the same LAN segment.
   c. The user's profile was different on the nearby workstation.
   d. The nearby workstation did not have an icon for MS Excel on its desktop.

7. **In following the proper series of troubleshooting steps, you should attempt to verify the user's competency before checking his physical and logical connections. True or false?**

## 4.9 Given a network problem scenario, select an appropriate course of action based on a general troubleshooting strategy that includes the following steps (continued):

### IMPLEMENT A SOLUTION, TEST THE RESULT, RECOGNIZE THE POTENTIAL EFFECTS OF THE SOLUTION, AND DOCUMENT THE SOLUTION

### UNDERSTANDING THE OBJECTIVE

The next four steps in troubleshooting are to implement a solution, test the solution, determine whether the solution might cause other problems or repercussions, then document the solution so that you and other staff will have a record of your troubleshooting efforts.

### WHAT YOU REALLY NEED TO KNOW

◆ Once you have followed the first four troubleshooting steps in order to find the cause of a problem, you can follow the next four steps to remedy the problem and help assure that it doesn't happen again or that your solution doesn't cause other problems. These next four troubleshooting steps are listed below.

◆ Implement a solution. The following steps will help you implement a safe and reliable solution:

- Collect all the documentation you have about a problem's symptoms from your investigation and keep it handy while solving the problem.

- If you're reinstalling software, make a backup of the device's existing software installation. If you're changing hardware, keep the old parts handy. If you are changing the configuration of a program or device, take the time to print out the current configuration.

- Perform the change, replacement, move, or addition that you believe will solve the problem. Record your actions in detail.

◆ Test the solution.

◆ Recognize the potential effects of the solution. For example, if you have to reassign IP addresses, how will the change of an IP address on a server affect its clients? Or in another case, if you upgrade the type of client software used on a workstation, how will that affect a user's daily routine?

◆ Document the solution. Make sure that both you and your colleagues understand the cause of the problem and how you solved it. This information should be kept in a centrally available repository.

### OBJECTIVES ON THE JOB

The logical troubleshooting steps provided here are only guidelines. Experience in your network environment may prompt you to follow the steps in a different order or to skip certain steps entirely.

# PRACTICE TEST QUESTIONS

1. **What should you be certain to do as you replace a faulty memory chip on a server?**
   a. Call the server manufacturer to notify your vendor about the faulty chip.
   b. Keep the faulty chip in a safe place in case the solution doesn't work.
   c. Keep the server powered on.
   d. Write the date and the nature of the problem on the chip.

2. **What facts should always be recorded in the documentation of a network problem? Choose all that apply.**
   a. when the problem occurred
   b. the user's password
   c. the user's date of hire
   d. how the problem was resolved

3. **You solved a user's problem by modifying his client's ODBC driver properties. When he asks you to explain why it wasn't working before, how do you respond?**
   a. Tell him that he was missing a driver.
   b. Tell him that he wasn't logging on correctly.
   c. Tell him that it didn't matter because it's fixed now.
   d. Tell him that you had to modify a parameter in his database connection.

4. **While troubleshooting a campus network performance problem, you discover that the Music Hall's wiring consists of largely CAT3 cables. What do you do?**
   a. Tell users that they will always have poor network performance.
   b. Verify the extent of the problem, notify your colleagues that this building contains older wiring, and schedule a time to upgrade it.
   c. Modify all client software to run only at lower transmission rates.
   d. Check the hubs in the building to make sure they are compatible.

5. **What is the name for the type of software that holds information about technical support requests, problems, and solutions?**
   a. network management software
   b. clustering software
   c. call tracking software
   d. network monitoring software

6. **What should you have in hand when trying to reproduce a difficult NIC problem?**
   a. the network operating system CDs
   b. the disaster recovery plan
   c. the backup schedule
   d. the NIC documentation

7. **What should you do just before applying a patch to your NOS software? Choose all that apply.**
   a. backup the current NOS installation
   b. call the NOS manufacturer to ensure that you have the latest patch
   c. evaluate other NOS options
   d. prevent users from logging into the server

# OBJECTIVES

**4.10    Given a troubleshooting scenario involving a network with a particular physical topology (i.e., bus, star/hierarchical, mesh, ring, or wireless) and including a network diagram, identify the network area affected and the cause of the problem.**

## UNDERSTANDING THE OBJECTIVE

Each physical topology has different cabling requirements and access methods, thus presenting different potential failures. Simple bus and ring physical topologies are the least fault tolerant.

## WHAT YOU REALLY NEED TO KNOW

◆ A bus topology consists of a single channel shared by all nodes on the network.

◆ The bus topology is the least fault-tolerant of any topology, because one break in the cable can take down the entire network, and bus topology faults are difficult to find.

◆ In a ring topology each node is connected to the two nearest nodes so that the entire network forms a circle. Data are transmitted in one direction (unidirectionally) around the ring. Each workstation accepts and responds to packets addressed to it, then forwards the other packets to the next workstation in the ring.

◆ A disadvantage of the ring topology is that, as with the bus topology, one defective node can take down the network.

◆ Star topologies are more fault-tolerant and provide better performance than bus or ring topologies. A single cable or node fault will not immobilize a star-wired network.

◆ Full mesh topologies are the most expensive physical topologies because they require the most equipment, connectivity, setup, and maintenance. However, they are also the most fault-tolerant physical topologies.

◆ A less expensive, yet still fault-tolerant alternative to full-mesh topologies is a partial mesh topology, in which only some of the nodes on a network are directly connected to other nodes.

◆ Nodes on a wireless network use special NICs with infrared or radio frequency transmitters to issue signals to a base station.

◆ When a large number of mobile clients are used, or when clients must communicate over a large geographical range, the number of access points must increase.

◆ Broadcast transmission is susceptible to eavesdropping. Thus, security is a concern in wireless networking. Using spread-spectrum radio frequency transmission is one way of improving wireless communications security.

## OBJECTIVES ON THE JOB

Because star-based physical topologies are the most fault tolerant, these form the basis of most modern LANs. When working with such LANs, bear in mind segment and network length restrictions.

# PRACTICE TEST QUESTIONS

1. Which of the following physical topologies is the most fault-tolerant?
   a. bus
   b. ring
   c. wireless
   d. full mesh

2. On which of the following networks could a single node failure disable an entire segment? Choose all that apply.
   a. bus
   b. ring
   c. wireless
   d. full mesh

3. In general, which of the following topologies is most expensive?
   a. bus
   b. ring
   c. wireless
   d. full mesh

4. What type of symptom might indicate that a bus network has not been properly terminated?
   a. Users cannot log onto the network.
   b. Network performance is very slow.
   c. New nodes cannot be added to the network.
   d. Data in shared folders is corrupted.

5. A user on a wireless network complains that he occasionally cannot log onto the network. Which of the following might be at fault?
   a. His laptop is not running the proper protocols.
   b. He is roaming out of range of network access points.
   c. His NIC is not bound to the client services.
   d. He is using an incompatible version of the client software.

6. If all of the workstations in a workgroup on a star network lose connectivity to the network, which of the following is the most likely cause?
   a. The workgroup hub has failed.
   b. The workstation NICs have all failed.
   c. One workstation in the workgroup has failed.
   d. One patch cable in the workgroup has failed.

7. What would happen on a simple ring network if one of the users turned off her workstation?
   a. Only her workstation would lose network connectivity.
   b. None of the workstations would lose network connectivity.
   c. The workstations on either side of hers in the ring would lose network connectivity.
   d. The entire network would fail.

# OBJECTIVES

## 4.11 Given a network troubleshooting scenario involving a client connectivity problem (e.g., incorrect protocol/client software/authentication configuration, or insufficient rights/permissions), identify the cause of the problem.

### UNDERSTANDING THE OBJECTIVE

Client connectivity depends on many factors: a physical connection to the network, proper protocols, proper network interface configuration, logon rights and permissions to resources.

### WHAT YOU REALLY NEED TO KNOW

- ◆ It's important to understand the login process for troubleshooting purposes. Both the client software and the network operating system participate in logging a client on to the server.

- ◆ First, the user launches the client software from his desktop. Then he enters his user name and password and presses the Enter key. At this point a service on the client workstation (called the **redirector**) intercepts the request to determine whether it should be handled by the client or by the server. Once the client's redirector decides that the request is meant for the server, the client transmits this data over the network to the server. At the server, the network operating system receives the client's request and attempts to match the user name to a name in its user database. If it is successful, it then compares the password associated with that user name to the password supplied by the user. If the passwords match, the NOS responds to the client by granting it access to resources on the network, according to limitations specified for this client.

- ◆ Insufficient permissions will result in a client being unable to access certain resources on the server.

- ◆ Account errors will result in a client being unable to log onto the network (for example, if a user's account has been disabled).

- ◆ Physical connection faults, such as a severed cable or missing cable, will result in an inability to connect to the network.

- ◆ NIC configuration errors may manifest as an inability to log onto the network or an inability to exchange data with certain parts of a network.

- ◆ Many client connectivity problems can be traced to user errors. Before changing software or hardware, verify that the user is performing operations correctly.

### OBJECTIVES ON THE JOB

Perhaps one of the most common problems you'll address as a network troubleshooter is an inability to access the network. This problem can be caused by a variety of failures (either hardware or software) and situations (for example, user error or changes in the network infrastructure). Asking the right questions will help you find the problem and solve it faster.

# PRACTICE TEST QUESTIONS

1. **A user complains that she can log onto the network, but cannot retrieve a spreadsheet file in a colleague's data directory. Which of the following might be the cause of the problem?**
   a. The patch cable between her workstation and the wall jack is faulty.
   b. Her user account has been disabled.
   c. She does not have sufficient rights to access the file.
   d. Her network interface's protocol settings are incorrect.

2. **A user complains that suddenly, this morning, he cannot log onto the network at all. Which of the following might be the cause of the problem? Choose all that apply.**
   a. The patch cable between his workstation and the wall jack has been removed.
   b. His user account does not have sufficient privileges.
   c. His protocols have been uninstalled.
   d. His client software is suffering performance problems.

3. **What is the name of the service that determines whether a request should be handled by a client or the server in client/server networking?**
   a. redirector
   b. reflectometer
   c. requestor
   d. reflexor

4. **A user complains that he receives a "password incorrect" message when he attempts to log onto the network. Which of the following might be the cause of the problem? Choose all that apply.**
   a. He is typing his password incorrectly.
   b. He is using an incompatible version of the client software.
   c. His NIC is experiencing intermittent packet loss.
   d. He is attempting to log onto the wrong server.

5. **Using the wrong frame type on an Ethernet network would not prevent a client from logging onto the network. True or false?**

6. **If you are on the phone helping a user with a problem, what should you do to gain more information that will allow you to diagnose her problem?**
   a. ask her to reboot
   b. attempt to replicate the problem at your workstation
   c. ask her to read the error message that appears on her screen
   d. modify her user account properties so that she has increased privileges

7. **If all users within your organization are unable to log onto the network, what can you probably conclude about the scope of the problem?**
   a. It is limited to one network segment.
   b. It affects the entire network.
   c. It is limited to a particular time of day.
   d. It is a result of a regional Internet failure.

# OBJECTIVES

## 4.12 Given a network troubleshooting scenario involving a wiring/infrastructure problem, identify the cause of the problem (e.g., bad media, interference, network hardware).

### UNDERSTANDING THE OBJECTIVE

Wiring and infrastructure problems occur at or below the Physical layer of the OSI Model. Because most LANs are dependent on many different lengths of wiring scattered across a building and installed and maintained by different people, the potential for wiring errors is great.

### WHAT YOU REALLY NEED TO KNOW

◆ If a segment or network length exceeds the IEEE maximum standards for a particular network type, the segment or network will experience an excessive number of late collisions, resulting in difficulty connecting to the network or exchanging data over the network. The solution is to reconfigure the topology so that the network and segment lengths comply with IEEE maximums.

◆ Noise affecting a signal (from EMI or RFI sources, improper grounding, or crosstalk) will result in an excessive number of packet errors such as runts, giants, and damaged frame check sequence fields. Users recognize this problem as intermittent difficulty in connecting to the network or exchanging data over the network. The solution is to remove sources of EMI or RFI from cabling areas, encase cables in conduit, or reroute cabling if necessary. If this is not possible, consider changing cable types to one with better resistance to noise. Ensure proper grounding on coaxial cable networks. Reduce crosstalk on twisted pair networks by using wires with a higher twist ratio and making sure cables are not bundled too tightly.

◆ Damaged cables (for example, crimped, bent, nicked, or partially severed cables) will result in an excessive number of normal collisions or packet errors (such as giants and runts), but few late collisions. Users recognize this problem as frequent difficulty connecting to or exchanging data with the network, very poor network response time, or a complete inability to connect to the network. Replace the faulty cable.

◆ Improper terminations, faulty connectors, loose connectors, or poorly crimped connections result in an excessive number of normal collisions and packet errors (such as giants and runts), but few late collisions. Users will recognize this as frequent problems connecting to or exchanging data with the network, very poor network response time, or a complete inability to connect to the network. Replace the connector with a good connector, reseat the loose connector, or correct the termination error.

### OBJECTIVES ON THE JOB

By some estimates, more than half of all network problems occur at the Physical layer of the OSI Model, which includes cabling, network adapters, repeaters, and hubs. Because Physical layer faults are so common, you should be thoroughly familiar with the symptoms of such problems.

# PRACTICE TEST QUESTIONS

1. **Which of the following symptoms could point to a faulty terminator? Choose all that apply.**
   a. garbled data in a spreadsheet or document file
   b. slow network response to requests for data
   c. an excessive number of late collisions
   d. inability to log onto the network

2. **What is the most practical way to resolve a problem with a network segment that exceeds the IEEE maximum length?**
   a. Move the connectivity devices to different telecommunications closets so the segment length is reduced.
   b. Separate the segment into two shorter segments by adding a connectivity device in between.
   c. Move the nodes on the segment closer to their central connectivity device.
   d. Recable the entire network to make certain no segments exceed the IEEE maximum length.

3. **Which of the following problems could result in excessive number of damaged packets on an Ethernet network?**
   a. excessive network lengths
   b. a severed patch cable
   c. a hub that is not powered on
   d. crosstalk

4. **At what layer of the OSI Model does EMI affect a signal?**
   a. Physical layer
   b. Data Link layer
   c. Network layer
   d. Transport layer

5. **A poorly crimped RJ-45 connector on a workstation's patch cable could result in the inability for a user to log onto the network. True or false?**

6. **What type of tool can help determine at what point in a cable a physical fault has occurred?**
   a. multimeter
   b. cable checker
   c. tone locator
   d. time domain reflectometer

7. **Which of the following is the best way to shield cables from EMI if they cannot be rerouted or replaced?**
   a. wrap them in electrician's tape
   b. encase them in a conduit
   c. erect aluminum shields between the cable runs and the EMI source(s)
   d. increase the temperature of the area through which the cables are routed

## Domain 1.0 Media and Topologies
### Objective 1.1 - Star/hierarchical topology
Practice Questions:
1. a
2. b
3. d
4. c
5. c
6. b
7. d

### Objective 1.1 - Bus topology
Practice Questions:
1. c
2. a
3. c and d
4. d
5. b
6. a
7. c

### Objective 1.1 - Mesh topology
Practice Questions:
1. b
2. b
3. c
4. c and d
5. c
6. b
7. true

### Objective 1.1 - Ring topology
Practice Questions:
1. a and c
2. a
3. d
4. d
5. a
6. c
7. d

# Objective 1.1 - Wireless topology
Practice Questions:
1. d
2. c
3. a
4. d
5. true
6. c
7. d

# Objective 1.2 - 802.2 (LLC) standards
Practice Questions:
1. b
2. d
3. a
4. b and c
5. d
6. false
7. a

# Objective 1.2 - 802.3 (Ethernet) standards
Practice Questions:
1. d
2. a and b
3. c
4. a
5. c
6. a, b, and d
7. d

# Objective 1.2 - 802.5 (Token Ring) standards
Practice Questions:
1. b and d
2. c
3. b, c, and d
4. b
5. d
6. c
7. c

## Objective 1.2 - 802.11b – Wireless standards
Practice Questions:
1. a
2. c
3. a
4. b
5. a
6. b
7. b

## Objective 1.2 - FDDI
Practice Questions:
1. b
2. d
3. d
4. a
5. d
6. a
7. b

## Objective 1.3 - Ethernet (802.3) standards
Practice Questions:
1. a and c
2. d
3. c
4. a and b
5. c and d
6. b
7. c and d

## Objective 1.3 - 10BaseT
Practice Questions:
1. a
2. a and b
3. d
4. c
5. b
6. c
7. b

## Objective 1.3 - 100BaseT and 100BaseTX
Practice Questions:
1. b
2. c
3. c
4. c
5. b
6. a and b
7. b

## Objective 1.3 - 10Base2
Practice Questions:
1. d
2. b
3. c
4. c
5. a
6. a
7. d

## Objective 1.3 - 10Base5
Practice Questions:
1. b
2. d
3. a
4. d
5. a
6. a
7. c

## Objective 1.3 - 100BaseFX
Practice Questions:
1. c
2. d
3. b
4. b
5. d
6. a
7. d

## Objective 1.3 - Gigabit Ethernet
Practice Questions:
1. d
2. b
3. a
4. d
5. d
6. c
7. d

## Objective 1.4 - RJ-11, RJ-45, AUI, and BNC connectors
Practice Questions:
1. b
2. a
3. c
4. b
5. d
6. b
7. a

## Objective 1.4 - SC and ST connectors
Practice Questions:
1. a
2. d
3. b
4. true
5. d
6. b
7. false

## Objective 1.5 - Media type and connectors
Practice Questions:
1. c and d
2. a
3. a
4. b
5. b
6. b
7. b and c

# Objective 1.6 - Hubs
Practice Questions:
1. c
2. c
3. a
4. d
5. a
6. a and d
7. c

# Objective 1.6 - Switches and Bridges
Practice Questions:
1. c
2. a
3. d
4. b
5. a
6. c
7. b

# Objective 1.6 - Routers
Practice Questions:
1. b
2. a
3. d
4. b and d
5. a
6. d
7. a

# Objective 1.6 - Gateways and CSU/DSUs
Practice Questions:
1. b
2. c
3. a and d
4. a and b
5. d
6. b
7. c

### Objective 1.6 - Network Interface Cards/ISDN adapters/system area network cards and wireless access points
Practice Questions:
1. d
2. c
3. b and d
4. a
5. b
6. a
7. a and d

### Objective 1.6 - Modems
Practice Questions:
1. c
2. d
3. c
4. a
5. a
6. c
7. b

## Domain 2.0 Protocols and Standards

### Objective 2.1 - Identify a MAC address
Practice Questions:
1. b
2. c
3. a
4. c
5. b
6. c
7. a

### Objective 2.2 - Layers 1 through 3 of the OSI Model
Practice Questions:
1. a
2. c
3. b
4. c
5. d
6. b
7. a

# Objective 2.2 - Layers 4 through 7 of the OSI model
Practice Questions:
1. b
2. b
3. c
4. a
5. d
6. a
7. c

# Objective 2.3 - TCP/IP
Practice Questions:
1. d
2. c
3. d
4. a
5. b
6. b
7. b

# Objective 2.3 - IPX/SPX
Practice Questions:
1. b
2. c
3. b
4. b
5. b
6. a
7. d

# Objective 2.3 - NetBEUI
Practice Questions:
1. c
2. d
3. d
4. a
5. b
6. a
7. b

## Objective 2.3 - AppleTalk
Practice Questions:
1. b
2. c
3. a
4. a, b, and c
5. d
6. a and b
7. b

## Objective 2.4 - OSI layers for hubs, switches, bridges, routers, network interface cards
Practice Questions:
1. b and c
2. c
3. b
4. d
5. c
6. b
7. a

## Objective 2.5 - IP, TCP, and UDP
Practice Questions:
1. b
2. a
3. d
4. b and c
5. b and d
6. a
7. c

## Objective 2.5 - FTP and TFTP
Practice Questions:
1. d
2. c
3. a
4. a
5. b
6. d
7. d

# Objective 2.5 - SMTP, POP3, and IMAP4

Practice Questions:

1. c
2. c
3. a
4. d
5. a
6. a
7. c

# Objective 2.5 - HTTP and HTTPS

Practice Questions:

1. d
2. a
3. b
4. a and d
5. c
6. d
7. a

# Objective 2.5 - TELNET

Practice Questions:

1. d
2. d
3. a
4. c and d
5. c
6. a
7. a

# Objective 2.5 - ICMP, ARP, and NTP

Practice Questions:

1. a and c
2. a and d
3. a
4. b
5. c
6. c
7. b

## Objective 2.6 - TCP/UDP ports
Practice Questions:
1. c
2. c
3. a
4. a
5. d
6. d
7. b

## Objective 2.7 - DHCP and BOOTP
Practice Questions:
1. c
2. d
3. b
4. b and c
5. d
6. a
7. c

## Objective 2.7 - DNS and WINS
Practice Questions:
1. c
2. a
3. c and d
4. c
5. a
6. a
7. a

## Objective 2.7 - NAT/ICS
Practice Questions:
1. b
2. d
3. a
4. a and c
5. c
6. a
7. d

## Objective 2.7 - SNMP
Practice Questions:
1. c
2. b
3. d
4. a and d
5. a
6. a and c
7. b

## Objective 2.8 - IP addresses and their default subnet masks
Practice Questions:
1. a
2. c
3. c
4. d
5. a
6. a
7. c

## Objective 2.9 - Subnetting and default gateways
Practice Questions:
1. d
2. c
3. c
4. c
5. d
6. c
7. a

## Objective 2.10 - Public vs. private networks
Practice Questions:
1. a
2. b
3. d  (It could be argued that answer c is also correct; however, if the company has a firewall, it is likely that public access is restricted.)
4. c
5. b
6. a
7. true

## Objective 2.11 - Packet switching vs. circuit switching
Practice Questions:
1. a
2. b
3. b
4. b
5. d
6. d
7. a

## Objective 2.11 - ISDN
Practice Questions:
1. c
2. b
3. a
4. c
5. c
6. a
7. d

## Objective 2.11 - FDDI and ATM
Practice Questions:
1. d
2. b
3. b
4. c
5. c
6. a
7. d

## Objective 2.11 - Frame Relay
Practice Questions:
1. b
2. d
3. a
4. b
5. d
6. c
7. true

## Objective 2.11 - SONET/SDH and OCx
Practice Questions:
1. d
2. c
3. d
4. a
5. b
6. c
7. c

## Objective 2.11 - T1/E1 and T3/E3
Practice Questions:
1. c
2. a
3. b
4. b
5. c
6. a
7. a

## Objective 2.12 - RAS and ICA
Practice Questions:
1. a and d
2. b
3. a
4. b
5. d
6. a
7. false

## Objective 2.12 - PPP and PPTP
Practice Questions:
1. d
2. a and c
3. c
4. c
5. b
6. a
7. d

### Objective 2.13 - IPSec and L2TP

Practice Questions:

1. c
2. b
3. c
4. c
5. a
6. d
7. a

### Objective 2.13 - SSL

Practice Questions:

1. d
2. b
3. c
4. a
5. d
6. a
7. c

### Objective 2.13 - Kerberos

Practice Questions:

1. a
2. a, b, and c
3. d
4. b, c, and d
5. c
6. b
7. d

# Domain 3.0 Network Implementation

### Objective 3.1 - UNIX/Linux server operating system

Practice Questions:

1. d
2. a
3. c
4. c
5. d
6. a
7. b

## Objective 3.1 – NetWare server operating system
Practice Questions:
1. d
2. b
3. d
4. b
5. c
6. a
7. a

## Objective 3.1 – Windows server operating systems
Practice Questions:
1. a
2. c
3. b
4. b
5. a
6. b
7. d

## Objective 3.1 – Macintosh server operating systems
Practice Questions:
1. b, c, and d
2. b
3. a
4. d
5. true
6. c
7. b

## Objective 3.2 - UNIX/Linux clients
Practice Questions:
1. b
2. c
3. b
4. d
5. d
6. b
7. false

## Objective 3.2 – Windows clients
Practice Questions:
1. c
2. d
3. a and b
4. d
5. b
6. a
7. a

## Objective 3.2 – Macintosh clients
Practice Questions:
1. b
2. a
3. c
4. b
5. d
6. d
7. d

## Objective 3.3 - VLANs
Practice Questions:
1. c
2. b
3. a, c, and d
4. d
5. a, b ,c and d
6. false
7. d

## Objective 3.4 - Network attached storage
Practice Questions:
1. b
2. d
3. c
4. d
5. true
6. a
7. a, b, c, and d

## Objective 3.5 - Fault tolerance
Practice Questions:
1. a
2. a
3. a
4. b
5. a, b, c, and d
6. b
7. d

## Objective 3.6 - Disaster recovery
Practice Questions:
1. a, b, and d
2. b
3. d
4. a and b
5. b
6. false
7. true

## Objective 3.7 - Configure a remote connectivity connection
Practice Questions:
1. a
2. a and d
3. a
4. b
5. b
6. a and b
7. b and c

## Objective 3.8 - Firewalls
Practice Questions:
1. a and d
2. c
3. a and d
4. a
5. c
6. b
7. b

## Objective 3.9 - Proxies
Practice Questions:
1. c
2. a and b
3. a
4. b
5. d
6. b
7. c

## Objective 3.10 - Impact of a security implementation
Practice Questions:
1. a and d
2. b
3. a and b
4. c
5. b
6. a
7. true

## Objective 3.11 - NIC and network configuration settings
Practice Questions:
1. d
2. b
3. b
4. a and d
5. d
6. true
7. c

# Domain 4.0 Network Support

## Objective 4.1 - Tracert, netstat, and nbtstat
Practice Questions:
1. b and c
2. d
3. c
4. d
5. a
6. b
7. false

## Objective 4.1 - Ping
Practice Questions:
1. c
2. d
3. a
4. b and d
5. a
6. d
7. b

## Objective 4.1 - Arp and nslookup
Practice Questions:
1. c
2. b and c
3. a
4. a and c
5. a
6. b
7. a

## Objective 4.1 - Ipconfig and winipcfg
Practice Questions:
1. a and d
2. c
3. b
4. b
5. c
6. c
7. b

## Objective 4.1 - Ifconfig
Practice Questions:
1. c
2. a
3. a
4. a and b
5. c
6. d
7. false

## Objective 4.2 - Cause of a small office/home office network failure
Practice Questions:
1. a
2. c
3. b
4. d
5. b
6. a, b, and c
7. true

## Objective 4.3 - Cause of a connectivity problem
Practice Questions:
1. c and d
2. b
3. a
4. d
5. c
6. false
7. true

## Objective 4.4 - Configure clients for UNIX/Linux, NetWare, Windows, and Macintosh
Practice Questions:
1. a and c
2. d
3. b
4. a
5. c
6. a
7. true

## Objective 4.5 - Select the appropriate tool
Practice Questions:
1. d
2. a
3. b
4. c and d
5. d
6. b
7. a, b, and c

## Objective 4.6 - Interpret visual indicators
Practice Questions:
1. b
2. d
3. a
4. b
5. b
6. c
7. a, b, and c

## Objective 4.7 - Diagnostic utilities
Practice Questions:
1. c
2. d
3. d
4. c
5. a
6. b
7. c

## Objective 4.8 - Modifying, adding, or removing network services
Practice Questions:
1. a
2. d
3. c
4. false
5. a
6. b
7. false

## Objective 4.9 - Establish a problem's symptoms and affected area, establish what has changed, and select a probable cause
Practice Questions:
1. c
2. b
3. b
4. b
5. a
6. a and b
7. true

## Objective 4.9 - Implement, test, recognize effects of, and document a solution
Practice Questions:
1. b
2. a and d
3. d
4. b
5. c
6. d
7. a and d

## Objective 4.10 - Identify network area affected and cause of the problem
Practice Questions:
1. d
2. a and b
3. d
4. b
5. b
6. a
7. d

## Objective 4.11 - Identify the cause of a connectivity problem

Practice Questions:

1. c
2. a and c
3. a
4. a and d
5. false
6. c
7. b

## Objective 4.12 - Identify the cause of a wiring/infrastructure problem

Practice Questions:

1. b and d
2. b
3. d
4. a
5. true
6. d
7. b

# GLOSSARY

**1 gigabit Ethernet** — An Ethernet standard for networks that achieve 1-Gbps maximum throughput. 1 Gigabit Ethernet runs (preferably) on fiber, but may also run over twisted pair. It is primarily used for network backbones.

**1 gigabit per second (Gbps)** — 1,000,000,000 bits per second.

**1 kilobit per second (Kbps)** — 1000 bits per second.

**1 megabit per second (Mbps)** — 1,000,000 bits per second.

**1 terabit per second (Tbps)** — 1,000,000,000 bits per second.

**10 Gigabit Ethernet** — A standard currently being defined by the IEEE 802.3ae committee. 10 Gigabit Ethernet will allow 10-Gbps throughput and will include full-duplexing and multimode fiber requirements.

**100BaseFX** — A Physical layer standard for networks that specifies baseband transmission, multimode fiber cabling, and 100-Mbps throughput. 100BaseFX networks have a maximum segment length of 400 meters. 100BaseFX may also be called "Fast Ethernet."

**100BaseT** — A Physical layer standard for networks that specifies baseband transmission, twisted-pair cabling, and 100-Mbps throughput. 100BaseT networks have a maximum segment length of 100 meters and use the star topology. 100BaseT is also known as Fast Ethernet.

**100BaseT4** — A type of 100BaseT network that uses all four wire pairs in a twisted-pair cable to achieve its 100-Mbps throughput. 100BaseT4 is not capable of full-duplex transmission and requires CAT3 or higher media.

**100BaseTX** — A type of 100BaseT network that uses two wire pairs in a twisted-pair cable, but uses faster signaling to achieve 100-Mbps throughput. It is capable of full-duplex transmission and requires CAT5 or higher media.

**100BaseVG (100VG-AnyLAN)** — A Physical layer standard for networks that specifies baseband transmission, twisted-pair media, and 100-Mbps throughput. 100BaseVG uses a different and more efficient method than 100BaseT for allowing nodes to transmit data on the media. However, 100BaseVG is rarely used.

**10Base2** — See *Thinnet*.

**10Base5** — See *Thicknet*.

**10BaseF** — A Physical layer standard for networks that specifies baseband transmission, multimode fiber cabling, and 10-Mbps throughput. 10BaseF networks have a maximum segment length of 1000 or 2000 meters, depending on the version, and employ a star topology.

**10BaseT** — A Physical layer standard for networks that specifies baseband transmission, twisted pair media, and 10-Mbps throughput. 10BaseT networks have a maximum segment length of 100 meters and rely on a star topology.

**802.3** — The IEEE standard for Ethernet networking devices and data handling.

**802.4** — The IEEE standard for Token Bus networking devices and data handling.

**802.5** — The IEEE standard for Token Ring networking devices and data handling.

**802.6** — The IEEE standard for Metropolitan Area Network (MAN) networking.

**802.10** — The IEEE standard that describes network access controls, encryption, certification, and other security topics.

**802.11** — The IEEE standard for wireless networking.

## A

**A+** — Professional certification established by CompTIA that verifies knowledge about PC operation, repair, and management.

**access method** — A network's method of controlling how network nodes access the communications channel. CSMA/CD is the access method used by Ethernet networks.

**access server** — See *communications server*.

**account** — A record of a user that contains all of his or her properties, including rights to resources, password, username, and so on.

**acknowledgment (ACK)** — A response generated at the Transport layer of the OSI Model that confirms to a sender that its frame was received.

**Active Directory** — Windows 2000 Server's method for organizing and managing objects associated with the network.

**active monitor** — On a Token Ring network, the workstation that maintains timing for token passing, monitors token and frame transmission, detects lost tokens, and corrects problems when a timing error or other disruption occurs. Only one workstation on the ring can act as the active monitor at any given time.

**active topology** — A topology in which each workstation participates in transmitting data over the network.

**adapter card** — See *expansion board*.

**address** — A number that uniquely identifies each workstation and device on a network. Without unique addresses, computers on the network could not reliably communicate.

**address management** — Centrally administering a finite number of network addresses for an entire LAN. Usually this task can be accomplished without touching the client workstations.

**Address Resolution Protocol (ARP)** — A core protocol in the TCP/IP suite that belongs in the Internet layer. It obtains the MAC (physical) address of a host, or node, and then creates a local database that maps the MAC address to the host's IP (logical) address.

**address resource record** — A type of DNS data record that maps the IP address of an Internet-connected device to its domain name.

**addressing** — The scheme for assigning a unique identifying number to every workstation and device on the network. The type of addressing used on a network depends on its protocols and network operating system.

**Administrator** — A user account that has unlimited privileges to resources and objects managed by a server or domain. The administrator account is created during NOS installation.

**AIX** — IBM's proprietary implementation of the UNIX system.

**alias** — A nickname for a node's host name. Aliases can be specified in a local host file.

**amplifier** — A device that boosts, or strengthens, an analog signal.

**amplitude** — A measure of a signal's strength.

**amplitude modulation (AM)** — A modulation technique in which the amplitude of the carrier signal is modified by the application of a data signal.

**analog** — A signal that uses variable voltage to create continuous waves, resulting in an inexact transmission.

**ANSI (American National Standards Institute)** — An organization composed of more than 1000 representatives from industry and government who together determine standards for the electronics industry in addition to other fields, such as chemical and nuclear engineering, health and safety, and construction.

**anycast address** — A type of address specified in IPv6 that represents a group of interfaces, any one of which (and usually the first available of which) can accept a transmission. At this time, anycast addresses are not designed to be assigned to hosts, such as servers or workstations, but rather to routers.

**AppleTalk** — The protocol suite used to interconnect Macintosh computers. Although AppleTalk was originally designed to support peer-to-peer networking among Macintoshes, it can now be routed between network segments and integrated with NetWare- or Microsoft-based networks.

**AppleTalk network number** — A unique 16-bit number that identifies the network to which an AppleTalk node is connected.

**AppleTalk node ID** — A unique 8-bit or 16-bit (if you are using extended networking, in which a network can have multiple addresses and support multiple zones) number that identifies a computer on an AppleTalk network.

**AppleTalk zone** — Logical groups of computers defined on an AppleTalk network.

**Application layer** — The seventh layer of the OSI Model. The Application layer provides interfaces to the software that enable programs to use network services.

**application programming interface (API)** — A routine (or set of instructions) that allows a program to interact with the operating system. APIs belong to the Application layer of the OSI Model.

**application switch** — Another term for a Layer 3 or Layer 4 switch.

**ARP table** — The database that lists MAC addresses and their associated IP addresses used for ARP queries.

**array** — A group of hard disks.

**asset management** — A system for collecting and storing data on the quantity and types of software and hardware assets in an organization's network.

**asymmetric encryption** — A type of encryption (such as public key encryption) that uses a different key for encoding data than is used for decoding the cipher text.

**asymmetric multiprocessing** — A multiprocessing method that assigns each subtask to a specific processor.

**asymmetrical** — The characteristic of a transmission technology that affords greater bandwidth in one direction (either from the customer to the carrier, or vice versa) than in the other direction.

**asymmetrical DSL** — A variation of DSL that offers more throughput when data travels downstream — downloading from a local carrier's POP to the customer — than when it travels upstream — uploading from the customer to the local carrier's POP.

**asynchronous** — A transmission method in which data being transmitted and received by nodes do not have to conform to any timing scheme. In asynchronous communications, a node can transmit at any time and the destination node must accept the transmission as it comes.

**Asynchronous Transfer Mode (ATM)** — A technology originally conceived in 1983 at Bell Labs, but standardized only in the mid-1990s. It relies on a fixed packet size to achieve data transfer rates up to 9953 Mbps. The fixed packet consists of 48 bytes of data plus a 5-byte header. The fixed packet size allows ATM to provide predictable traffic patterns and better control over bandwidth utilization.

**attenuate** — To lose signal strength as a transmission travels farther away from its source.

**attenuation** — A signal's loss of strength as it travels farther from its source.

**attribute** — A variable property associated with a network object. For example, a restriction on the time of day a user can log on is an attribute associated with that user object.

**AUI (Attachment Unit Interface)** — An Ethernet standard for connecting coaxial cables with transceivers and networked nodes.

**authentication** — The process whereby a network operating system verifies that a client's user name and password are valid and allows the client to log onto the network.

**authentication header (AH)** — In the context of IPSec, a type of encryption that provides authentication of the IP packet's data payload through public key techniques.

**authentication service (AS)** — In Kerberos terminology, the process that runs on a key distribution center (KDC) to initially validate a client who's logging in. The authentication service issues session keys to the client and the service the client wants to access.

**authenticator** — In Kerberos authentication, the user's timestamp encrypted with the session key. The authenticator is used to help the service verify that a user's ticket is valid.

**autosense** — A feature of modern NICs that enables a NIC to automatically sense what types of frames are running on a network and set itself to that specification.

**availability** — How consistently and reliably a file, device, or connection can be accessed by authorized personnel.

# B

**B channel** — In ISDN, the "bearer" channel, so named because it bears traffic from point to point.

**backbone** — The cabling or part of a network that connects separate LAN segments. Backbone wiring provides interconnection between telecommunications closets, equipment rooms, and entrance facilities.

**backleveling** — The process of reverting to a previous version of a software program after attempting to upgrade it.

**back up** — A copy of data or program files created for archiving or safekeeping purposes.

**backup** — The process of copying critical data files to a secure storage area. Often backups are performed according to a formulaic schedule.

**backup rotation scheme** — A plan for when and how often backups occur, and which backups are full, incremental, or differential.

**bandwidth** — A measure of the difference between the highest and lowest frequencies that a medium can transmit.

**base I/O port** — A setting that specifies, in hexadecimal notation, which area of memory will act as a channel for moving data between the network adapter and the CPU. Like its IRQ, a device's base I/O port cannot be used by any other device.

**baseband** — A form of transmission in which digital signals are sent through direct current pulses applied to the wire. This direct current requires exclusive use of the wire's capacity, so baseband systems can transmit only one signal, or one channel, at a time. Every device on a baseband system shares a single channel.

**baseline** — A record of how well the network operates under normal conditions (including its performance, collision rate, utilization rate, and so on). Baselines are used for comparison when conditions change.

**baselining** — The practice of measuring and recording a network's current state of operation.

**bend radius** — The radius of the maximum arc into which you can loop a cable before you will cause data transmission errors. Generally, a twisted-pair cable's bend radius is equal to or greater than four times the diameter of the cable.

**best path** — The most efficient route from one node on a network to another. Under optimal network conditions, the best path is the most direct path between two points.

**binary** — A system founded on using 1s and 0s to encode information.

**binding** — The process of assigning one network component to work with another.

**bio-recognition access** — A method of authentication in which a device scans an individual's unique physical characteristics (such as the color patterns in his or her eye's iris or the geometry of his or her hand) to verify the user's identity.

**BIOS (basic input/output system)** — Firmware attached to the system board that controls the computer's communication with its devices, among other things.

**bit** — Short for binary digit. A bit equals a single pulse in the digital encoding system. It may have only one of two values: 0 or 1.

**blackout** — A complete power loss.

**block** — A unit of disk space and the smallest unit of disk space that can be controlled by the NetWare system. Smaller blocks require more server memory.

**block ID** — The first set of six characters that make up the MAC address and that are unique to a particular vendor.

**block suballocation** — A NetWare technique for using hard disk space more efficiently. Files that don't fit neatly into a whole number of blocks can take up fractions of blocks, leaving the remaining fractions free for use by other data.

**BNC barrel connector** — A connector used on Thinnet networks with two open ends used to connect two Thinnet coaxial cables.

**BNC T-connector** — A connector used on Thinnet networks with three open ends. It attaches to the Ethernet interface card at the base of the "T" and to the Thinnet cable at its two sides so as to allow the signal in and out of the NIC.

**bonding** — The process of combining more than one bearer channel of an ISDN line to increase throughput. For example, BRI's two 64-Kbps B channels are bonded to create an effective throughput of 128 Kbps.

**boot sector virus** — A virus that resides on the boot sector of a floppy disk and is transferred to the partition sector or the DOS boot sector on a hard disk. A boot sector virus can move from a floppy to a hard disk only if the floppy disk is left in the drive when the machine starts up.

**Bootstrap Protocol (BOOTP)** — A service that simplifies IP address management. BOOTP maintains a central list of IP addresses and their associated devices' MAC addresses, and assigns IP addresses to clients when they request it.

**Border Gateway Protocol (BGP)** — The routing protocol of Internet backbones. The router stress created by Internet growth has driven the development of BGP, the most complex of the routing protocols. The developers of BGP had to contend with the prospect of 100,000 routes as well as the goal of routing traffic efficiently and fairly through the hundreds of Internet backbones.

**braiding** — A braided metal shielding used to insulate some types of coaxial cable.

**BRI (Basic Rate Interface)** — A variety of ISDN that uses two 64-Kbps bearer channels and one 16-Kbps data channel, as summarized by the following notation: 2B + D. BRI is the most common form of ISDN employed by home users.

**bridge** — A device that looks like a repeater, in that it has a single input and a single output, but is different from a repeater in that it can interpret the data it retransmits.

**bridge router (brouter)** — A router capable of providing Layer 2 bridging functions.

**broadband** — 1) A form of transmission in which signals are modulated as radiofrequency analog pulses with different frequency ranges. Unlike baseband, broadband technology does not involve binary encoding. The use of multiple frequencies enables a broadband system to operate over several channels and therefore carry much more data than a baseband system. 2) A group of network connection types or transmission technologies that are generally capable of exceeding 1.544 Mbps throughput. Examples of broadband include DSL and SONET.

**broadcast** — A transmission that involves one transmitter and multiple receivers.

**broadcast domain** — In a virtual local area network (VLAN), a combination of ports that make up a Layer 2 segment and must be connected by a Layer 3 device, such as a router or Layer 3 switch.

**brouter** — See *bridge router*.

**brownout** — A momentary decrease in voltage, also known as a *sag*. An overtaxed electrical system may cause brownouts, recognizable as a dimming of the lights.

**browser** — Software that provides clients with a simple, graphical interface to the Web.

**BSD (Berkeley Software Distribution)** — A UNIX distribution that originated at the University of California at Berkeley. The BSD suffix differentiates these distributions from AT&T distributions. No longer being developed at Berkeley, the last public release of BSD UNIX was version 4.4.

**bug** — A flaw in software or hardware that causes it to malfunction.

**bus** — 1) The single cable connecting all devices in a bus topology. 2) The type of circuit used by the system board to transmit data to components. Most new Pentium computers use buses capable of exchanging 32 or 64 bits of data. As the number of bits of data a bus handles increases, so too does the speed of the device attached to the bus.

**bus topology** — A topology in which a single cable connects all nodes on a network without intervening connectivity devices.

**byte** — Eight bits of information. In a digital signaling system, broadly speaking, one byte carries one piece of information.

# C

**cable checker** — A simple handheld device that determines whether cabling can provide connectivity. To accomplish this task, a cable checker applies a small voltage to each conductor at one end of the cable, then checks whether that voltage is detectable at the other end. It may also verify that voltage cannot be detected on other conductors in the cable.

**cable drop** — Fiber-optic or coaxial cable that connects a neighborhood cable node to a customer's house.

**cable modem** — A device that modulates and demodulates signals for transmission and reception via cable wiring.

**cable plant** — The hardware that constitutes the enterprise-wide cabling system.

**cable tester** — A handheld device that not only checks for cable continuity, but also ensures that the cable length is not excessive, measures the distance to a cable fault, measures attenuation along a cable, measures near-end crosstalk between wires, measures termination resistance and impedance for Thinnet cabling, issues pass/fail ratings for wiring standards, and stores and prints cable testing results.

**caching** — The process of saving frequently used data to an area of the physical memory so that it becomes more readily available for future requests. Caching accelerates the process of accessing the server because the operating system no longer needs to search for the requested data on the disk.

**call tracking system** — A software program used to document problems (also known as help desk software). Examples of popular call tracking systems include Clientele, Expert Advisor, Professional Help Desk, Remedy, and Vantive.

**capacity** — See *throughput*.

**Carrier Sense Multiple Access/Collision Avoidance (CSMA/CA)** — A network access method used on LocalTalk networks in which nodes on a shared communication channel signal their intent to transmit data before doing so, thus avoiding collisions.

**Carrier Sense Multiple Access/Collision Detection (CSMA/CD)** — Rules for communication used by shared Ethernet networks. In CSMA/CD each node waits its turn before transmitting data, to avoid interfering with other nodes' transmissions.

**CAT** — Abbreviation for the word "category" when describing a type of twisted-pair cable. For example, Category 3 unshielded twisted-pair cable may also be called CAT3. See *Category 1*, *Category 2*, *Category 3*, *Category 4*, *Category 5*, *Enhanced Category 5*, *Category 6*, and *Category 7*.

**Category 1 (CAT1)** — A form of UTP that contains two wire pairs. CAT1 is suitable for voice communications, but not for data. At most, it can carry only 20 Kbps of data.

**Category 2 (CAT2)** — A form of UTP that contains four wire pairs and can carry up to 4 Mbps of data. CAT2 is rarely found on modern networks, because most require higher throughput.

**Category 3 (CAT3)** — A form of UTP that contains four wire pairs and can carry up to 10-Mbps, with a possible bandwidth of 16 MHz. CAT3 has typically been used for 10-Mbps Ethernet or 4-Mbps Token Ring networks. Network administrators are gradually replacing CAT3 cabling with CAT5 to accommodate higher throughput. CAT3 is less expensive than CAT5.

**Category 4 (CAT4)** — A form of UTP that contains four wire pairs and can support up to 16-Mbps throughput. CAT4 may be used for 16-Mbps Token Ring or 10-Mbps Ethernet networks. It is guaranteed for data transmission up to 20 MHz and provides more protection against crosstalk and attenuation than CAT1, CAT2, or CAT3.

**Category 5 (CAT5)** — The most popular form of UTP for new network installations and upgrades to Fast Ethernet. CAT5 contains four wire pairs and supports up to 100-Mbps throughput and a 100 MHz signal rate. In addition to 100-Mbps Ethernet, CAT5 wiring can support other fast networking technologies, such as Asynchronous Transfer Mode (ATM) and Fiber Distributed Data Interface (FDDI).

**Category 5 enhanced (CAT5e)** — See *enhanced Category 5*.

**Category 6 (CAT6)** — A twisted-pair cable that contains four wire pairs, each wrapped in foil insulation. Additional foil insulation covers the bundle of wire pairs, and a fire-resistant plastic sheath covers the second foil layer. The foil insulation provides excellent resistance to crosstalk and enables CAT6 to support at least six times the throughput supported by regular CAT5.

**Category 7 (CAT7)** — A twisted-pair cable that contains multiple wire pairs, each separately shielded then surrounded by another layer of shielding within the jacket. CAT7 can support up to a 1-GHz signal rate. But because of its extra layers, it is less flexible than other forms of twisted-pair wiring.

**CD-ROM File System (CDFS)** — The read-only file system used to access resources on a CD. Windows 2000 supports this file system to allow CD-ROM file sharing.

**cell** — A packet of a fixed size. In ATM technology, a cell consists of 48 bytes of data plus a 5-byte header.

**certification** — The process of mastering material pertaining to a particular hardware system, operating system, programming language, or other software program, then proving your mastery by passing a series of exams.

**Certified NetWare Engineer (CNE)** — Professional certification established by Novell that demonstrates an in-depth understanding of Novell's networking software, including NetWare.

**change management system** — A process or program that provides support personnel with a centralized means of documenting changes made to the network. In smaller organizations, a change management system may be as simple as one document on the network to which networking personnel continually add entries to mark their changes. In larger organizations, it may consist of a database package complete with graphical interfaces and customizable fields tailored to the particular computing environment.

**channel** — A distinct communication path between two or more nodes, much like a lane is a distinct transportation path on a freeway. Channels may be separated either logically (as in multiplexing) or physically (as when they are carried by separate wires).

**child domain** — A domain found beneath another domain in a Windows 2000 domain tree.

**cipher text** — The unique data block that results when an original piece of data (such as text) is encrypted (for example, by using a key).

**CIR (committed information rate)** — The guaranteed minimum amount of bandwidth selected when leasing a frame relay circuit. Frame relay costs are partially based on CIR.

**circuit switching** — A type of switching in which a connection is established between two network nodes before they begin transmitting data. Bandwidth is dedicated to this connection and remains available until users terminate the communication between the two nodes.

**cladding** — The glass shield around the fiber core of a fiber-optic cable. Cladding acts as a mirror, reflecting light back to the core in patterns that vary depending on the transmission mode. This reflection allows fiber to bend around corners without impairing the light-based signal.

**class** — A type of object recognized by an NOS directory and defined in an NOS schema. Printers and users are examples of object classes.

**client** — A computer on the network that requests resources or services from another computer on a network. In some cases, a client could also act as a server. The term "client" may also refer to the user of a client workstation.

**Client Services for NetWare (CSNW)** — A Microsoft program that can be installed on Windows 2000 clients to enable them to access NetWare servers and make full use of the NetWare Directory System (NDS), its objects, files, directories, and permissions.

**client/server architecture** — The model of networking in which clients (typically desktop PCs) use a central server to share data, data storage space, and devices.

**client/server network** — A network based on the client/server architecture.

**client_hello** — In the context of SSL encryption, a message issued from the client to the server that contains information about what level of security the client's browser is capable of accepting and what type of encryption the client's browser can decipher (for example, RSA or Diffie-Hellman). The client_hello message also establishes a randomly generated number that uniquely identifies the client plus another number that identifies the SSL session.

**clustering** — See *server clustering.*

**CMOS (complementary metal oxide semiconductor)** — Firmware on a PC's system board that enables you to change its devices' configurations.

**coaxial cable** — A type of cable that consists of a central copper core surrounded by an insulator, a braided metal shielding, called braiding, and an outer cover, called the sheath or jacket. Coaxial cable, called "coax" for short, was the foundation for Ethernet networks in the 1980s and remained a popular transmission medium for many years.

**collapsed backbone** — A type of enterprise-wide backbone in which a router or switch acts as the single central connection point for multiple subnetworks.

**collision** — In Ethernet networks, the interference of one network node's data transmission with another network node's data transmission.

**collision domain** — A portion of a LAN encompassing devices that may cause and detect data collisions during transmission. Bridges and switches can logically define the boundaries of a collision domain.

**command interpreter** — A (usually text-based) program that accepts and executes system programs and applications on behalf of users. Often it includes the ability to execute a series of instructions that are stored in a file.

**communications server** — A server that runs communications services such as Windows NT's RAS or NetWare's NAS, also known as an access server or remote access server.

**CompTIA** — See *Computing Technology Industry Association.*

**Computing Technology Industry Association (CompTIA)** — An association of computer resellers, manufacturers, and training companies that sets industry-wide standards for computer professionals. CompTIA established and sponsors the A+ and Network+ (Net+) certifications.

**conduit** — Pipeline used to contain and protect the cabling. Conduit is usually made from metal.

**connection-oriented** — A feature of some protocols that requires the establishment of a connection between communicating nodes before the protocol will transmit data.

**connectionless** — A feature of some protocols that allows the protocol to service a request without requiring a verified session and without guaranteeing delivery of data.

**connectors** — The pieces of hardware that connect the wire to the network device, be it a file server, workstation, switch, or printer.

**container** — A logical receptacle for holding like objects in an NOS directory. Containers form the branches of the directory tree.

**container objects** — See *container.*

**context** — A kind of road map for finding an object in an NDS tree. A context is made up of an object's organizational unit names, arranged from most specific to most general, plus the organization name. Periods separate the organizational unit names in context.

**Controlled Access Unit (CAU)** — A connectivity device used on a Token Ring network. In addition to passing data between nodes, a CAU provides more flexibility and easier management of connected nodes than a MAU.

**convergence** — The use of networks to carry data, plus video and voice signals.

**convergence time** — The time it takes for a router to recognize a best path in the event of a change or network outage.

**core** — The central component of a fiber-optic cable, consisting of one or several pure glass fibers.

**core gateways** — Gateways that make up the Internet backbone. The Internet Network Operations Center (INOC) operates core gateways.

**cracker** — A person who uses his or her knowledge of operating systems and utilities to intentionally damage or destroy data or systems.

**crossover cable** — A twisted-pair patch cable in which the termination locations of the transmit and receive wires on one end of the cable are reversed.

**crosstalk** — A type of interference caused by signals traveling on nearby wire pairs infringing on another pair's signal.

**CSU (channel service unit)** — A device used with T-carrier technology that provides termination for the digital signal and ensures connection integrity through error correction and line monitoring.

**CSU/DSU** — A combination of a CSU (channel service unit) and a DSU (data service unit) that serves as the connection point for a T1 line at the customer's site.

**cut-through mode** — A switching mode in which a switch reads a frame's header and decides where to forward the data before it receives the entire packet. Cut-through mode is faster, but less accurate, than the other switching method, store and forward mode.

**Cyclic Redundancy Check (CRC)** — An algorithm used to verify the accuracy of data contained in a data frame.

# D

**D channel** — In ISDN, the "data" channel used to carry information about the call, such as session initiation and termination signals, caller identity, call forwarding, and conference calling signals.

**daisy chain** — A linked series of devices.

**data encryption standard (DES)** — A popular private key encryption technique that was developed by IBM in the 1970s.

**Data Link layer** — The second layer in the OSI Model. The Data Link layer bridges the networking media with the Network layer. Its primary function is to divide the data it receives from the Network layer into frames that can then be transmitted by the Physical layer.

**Data Link layer address** — See *MAC address*.

**data packet** — A discreet unit of information sent from one computer on a network to another.

**data propagation delay** — The length of time data take to travel from one point on the segment to another point. On Ethernet networks, CSMA/CD's collision detection routine cannot operate accurately if the data propagation delay is too long.

**daughter board** — See *expansion board*.

**daughter card** — See *expansion board*.

**DB-15** — A general term for connectors that use 15 metal pins to complete a connection between devices. "DB" stands for Data bus, while the number "15" indicates how many pins are used to make the connection.

**DB-9 connector** — A connector containing nine pins that is used on STP-based Token Ring networks.

**dedicated circuit** — A continuously available link between two access points that is leased from a communications provider, such as an ISP or telephone company.

**default gateway** — The gateway that first interprets a device's outbound requests, and then interprets its inbound requests to and from other subnets. In the postal service analogy, the default gateway is similar to a local post office.

**demand priority** — A method for data transmission used by 100BaseVG Ethernet networks. Each device on a star or hierarchical network sends a request to transmit to the central hub, which grants the requests one at a time. The hub examines incoming data packets, determines the destination node, and forwards the packets to that destination. Because demand priority runs on a star topology, no workstations except the source and destination can "see" the data. Data travel from one device to the hub, then to another device.

**demultiplexer (demux)** — A device that separates multiplexed signals once they are received and regenerates them in their original form.

**denial-of-service attack** — A security attack caused by a deluge of traffic that disables the victimized system.

**device driver** — Software that enables an attached device to communicate with the computer's operating system.

**device ID** — The second set of six characters that make up a network device's MAC address. The Device ID, which is added at the factory, is based on the device's model and manufacture date.

**dial-up** — A type of connection that uses modems at the transmitting and receiving ends and PSTN or other lines to access a network.

**dial-up networking** — The process of dialing into a LAN's access server or into an ISP. Dial-up Networking is also the name of the utility that Microsoft provides with its operating systems to achieve this type of connectivity.

**differential backup** — A backup method in which only data that have changed since the last backup are copied to a storage medium, and that information is marked for subsequent backup, regardless of whether it has changed.

**digital** — As opposed to analog signals, digital signals are composed of pulses that can have a value of only 1 or 0.

**digital certificate** — A password-protected and encrypted file that holds an individual's identification information, including a public key and a private key. The individual's public key is used to verify the sender's digital signature, and the private key allows individual to log onto a third-party authority who administers digital certificates.

**DIP (dual inline package) switch** — A small plastic toggle switch on a circuit board that can be flipped to indicate either an "on" or "off" status, which translates into a parameter setting.

**direct infrared transmission** — A type of infrared transmission that depends on the transmitter and receiver being within the line of sight of each other.

**directory** — In general, a listing that organizes resources and correlates them with their properties. In the context of network operating systems, a method for organizing and managing objects.

**Directory Services Migration Tool (DSMIGRATE)** — A tool provided with Windows 2000 Server that enables network administrators to migrate accounts, files, and permissions from a NetWare NDS directory to the Windows 2000 Active Server Directory.

**disaster recovery** — The process of restoring critical functionality and data to a network after an enterprise-wide outage that affects more than a single system or a limited group of users.

**disk mirroring** — A RAID technique in which data from one disk are automatically copied to another disk as the information is written.

**disk striping** — A simple implementation of RAID in which data are written in 64 KB blocks equally across all disks in the array.

**diskless workstations** — Workstations that do not contain hard disks, but instead rely on a small amount of read-only memory to connect to a network and to pick up their system files.

**distinguished name (DN)** — A long form of an object's name in Active Directory that explicitly indicates the object name, plus the names of its containers and domains. A distinguished name includes a domain component (DC), organizational unit (OU), and common name (CN). A client uses the distinguished name to access a particular object, such as a printer.

**distributed backbone** — A type of enterprise-wide backbone that consists of a number of hubs connected to a series of central hubs or routers in a hierarchy.

**DIX (Digital, Intel, and Xerox)** — A type of AUI connector used on Thicknet networks.

**domain** — (1) A group of networked devices that share a symbolic name according to Internet standards. For example, workstations used in the Whitehouse share the whitehouse.gov domain name. (2) In the context of Windows NT and Windows 2000 networking, a group of users, servers, and other resources that share account and security policies.

**domain account** — A type of user account on a Windows 2000 network that has privileges to resources across the domain onto which it is logged.

**domain controller** — A Windows 2000 server that contains a replica of the Active Directory database.

**domain local group** — A group on a Windows2000 network that allows members of one domain to access resources within that domain only.

**domain name** — The symbolic name that identifies a domain and identifies a group of network nodes. Usually, a domain name is associated with a company or other type of organization, such as a university or military unit.

**Domain Name System (DNS)** — A hierarchical way of tracking domain names and their addresses, devised in the mid-1980s. The DNS database does not rely on one file or even one server, but rather is distributed over several key computers across the Internet to prevent catastrophic failure if one or a few computers go down. DNS is a TCP/IP service that belongs to the Application layer of the OSI Model.

**domain tree** — A group of hierarchically arranged domains that share a common namespace in the Windows 2000 Active Directory.

**doskey** — A command used on MS-DOS and Windows systems that enables the user to recall (using the keyboard's arrow keys) and edit previously entered commands.

**dotted decimal notation** — The shorthand convention used to represent IP addresses and make them more easily readable by humans. In dotted decimal notation, a decimal number between 1 and 254 represents each binary octet. A period, or dot, separates each decimal.

**downstream** — A term used to describe data traffic that flows from a local carrier's POP to the customer. In asymmetrical communications, downstream throughput is usually much higher than upstream throughput. In symmetrical communications, downstream and upstream throughputs are equal.

**drop cable** — The cable that connects a device's Ethernet interface to a transceiver in a Thicknet network.

**DS0 (digital signal, level 0)** — The equivalent of one data or voice channel in T-carrier technology, as defined by ANSI physical layer standards. All other signal levels are multiples of DS0.

**DSL (digital subscriber line)** — A dedicated remote connectivity or WAN technology that uses advanced data modulation techniques to achieve extraordinary throughput over regular phone lines. DSL currently comes in seven different varieties, the most common of which is Asymmetric DSL (ADSL).

**DSL access multiplexer (DSLAM)** — A connectivity device located at a carrier's office that aggregates multiple DSL subscriber lines and connects them to a larger carrier or to the Internet backbone.

**DSL modem** — A device that demodulates an incoming DSL signal, extracting the information and passing it on to the data equipment (such as telephones and computers) and modulates an outgoing DSL signal.

**DSU (data service unit)** — A device used in T-carrier technology that converts the digital signal used by bridges, routers, and multiplexers into the digital signal used on cabling. Typically, a DSU is combined with a CSU in a single box, a CSU/DSU.

**duplex** — See *full-duplex.*

**dynamic IP address** — An IP address that is assigned to a device through DHCP and may change when the DHCP lease expires or is terminated.

**dynamic ARP table entry** — A record (of an IP address and its associated MAC address) created in an ARP table when a client makes an ARP request that cannot be satisfied by data already in the ARP table.

**Dynamic Host Configuration Protocol (DHCP)** — An application layer protocol in the TCP/IP suite that manages the dynamic distribution of IP addresses on a network. Using DHCP to assign IP addresses reduces the effort required to assign addresses and helps prevent duplicate-addressing problems.

**dynamic routing** — A method of routing that automatically calculates the best path between two nodes and accumulates this information in a routing table. If congestion or failures affect the network, a router using dynamic routing can detect the problems and reroute data through a different path. Most modern networks primarily use dynamic routing.

# E

**e-commerce** — A means of conducting business over the Web — be it in retailing, banking, stock trading, consulting, or training. Any buying and selling of products or services that occurs over the Internet belongs in the e-commerce category.

**echo reply** — The response signal sent by a device after another device pings it.

**echo request** — The request for a response generated when one device pings another device on the network.

**EIA (Electronic Industries Alliance)** — A trade organization composed of representatives from electronics manufacturing firms across the UnitedStates.

**electrically erasable programmable read-only memory (EEPROM)** — A type of ROM that is found on a circuit board and whose configuration information can be erased and rewritten through electrical pulses.

**electromagnetic interference (EMI)** — A type of interference that may be caused by motors, power lines, televisions, copiers, fluorescent lights, or other sources of electrical activity.

**encapsulation security payload (ESP)** — In the context of IPSec, a type of encryption that provides authentication of the IP packet's data payload through public key techniques. In addition, ESP also encrypts the entire IP packet for added security.

**encrypted virus** — A virus that is encrypted to prevent detection.

**encryption** — The use of an algorithm to scramble data into a format that can be read only by reversing the algorithm—decrypting the data—to keep the information private. The most popular kind of encryption algorithm weaves a key into the original data's bits, sometimes several times in different sequences, to generate a unique data block.

**enhanced CAT5 (CAT5e)** — A higher-grade version of CAT5 wiring that contains high-quality copper, offers a high twist ratio, and uses advanced methods for reducing crosstalk. Enhanced CAT5 can support a signaling rate of up to 200 MHz, double the capability of regular CAT5.

**Enhanced Interior Gateway Routing Protocol (EIGRP)** — A routing protocol developed in the mid-1980s by Cisco Systems that has a fast convergence time and a low network overhead, but is easier to configure and less CPU-intensive than OSPF. EIGRP also offers the benefits of supporting multiple protocols and limiting unnecessary network traffic between routers.

**enterprise** — An entire organization, including local and remote offices, a mixture of computer systems, and a number of departments. Enterprise-wide computing takes into account the breadth and diversity of a large organization's computer needs.

**enterprise-wide network** — A network that spans an entire organization and often services the needs of many diverse users. It may include many locations (as a WAN), or it may be confined to one location but include many different departments, floors, and network segments.

**Ethernet** — A networking technology originally developed at Xerox in 1970 and improved by Digital Equipment Corporation, Intel, and Xerox. Today, four types of Ethernet technology are used on LANs, with each type being governed by a set of IEEE standards.

**Ethernet 802.2 frame** — See *IEEE 802.3 frame*.

**Ethernet 802.3 frame** — See *Novell proprietary 802.3 frame*.

**Ethernet II frame** — The original Ethernet frame type developed by Digital, Intel, and Xerox, before the IEEE began to standardize Ethernet. Ethernet II lacks Logical Link Control layer information but contains a 2-byte type field to identify the upper-layer protocol contained in the frame. It supports TCP/IP, AppleTalk, IPX/SPX, and other higher layer protocols.

**expansion board** — A circuit board used to connect a device to a computer's system board.

**expansion card** — See *expansion board*.

**expansion slots** — Openings on a computer's system board that contain multiple electrical contacts into which the expansion board can be inserted.

**explicit one-way trust** — A type of trust relationship in which two domains that belong to different NOS directory trees are configured to trust each other.

**extended attributes** — Attributes beyond the basic Read, Write, System Hidden, and Archive attrevutes supported by FAT.HPFS supports extended attributes.

**Extended Industry Standard Architecture (EISA)** — A 32-bit bus that is compatible with older ISA devices (because it shares the same length and pin configuration as the ISA bus), but that uses an extra layer of pins (resulting in a deeper, two-layered slot connector) for a second 16 bits to achieve faster throughput. The EISA bus was introduced in the late 1980s to compete with IBM's MCA bus.

**extended network prefix** — The combination of an address's network and subnet information. By interpreting an address's extended network prefix, a device can determine the subnet to which an address belongs.

**external network number** — Another term for the network address portion of an IPX/SPX address.

# F

**fail-over** — The capability for one component (such as a NIC or server) to assume another component's responsibilities without manual intervention.

**failure** — A deviation from a specified level of system performance for a given period of time. A failure occurs when something doesn't work as promised or as planned.

**Fast Ethernet** — A type of Ethernet network that is capable of 100-Mbps throughput. 100BaseT and 100BaseFX are both examples of Fast Ethernet.

**FAT32 (32-bit File Allocation Table)** — An enhanced version of FAT that accommodates the use of long filenames and smaller allocation units on a disk. FAT32 makes more efficient use of disk space than the original FAT and is therefore faster and can handle larger files.

**FAT16 (16-bit File Allocation Table)** — A file system designed for use with early DOS- and Windows-based computers that allocates file system space in 16-bit units. Compared to FAT32, FAT16 is less desirable because of its partition size, file naming, fragmentation, speed, and security limitations.

**fault** — The malfunction of one component of a system. A fault can result in a failure.

**fault tolerance** — The capacity for a system to continue performing despite an unexpected hardware or software malfunction.

**Federal Communications Commission (FCC)** — The regulatory agency that sets standards and policy for telecommunications transmission and equipment in the United States.

**Fiber Distributed Data Interface (FDDI)** — A networking standard originally specified by ANSI in the mid-1980s and later refined by ISO. FDDI uses a dual fiber-optic ring to transmit data at speeds of 100 Mbps. It was commonly used as a backbone technology in the 1980s and early 1990s, but lost favor as fast Ethernet technologies emerged in the mid-1990s. FDDI provides excellent reliability and security.

**fiber-optic cable** — A form of cable that contains one or several glass fibers in its core. Data are transmitted via pulsing light sent from a laser or light-emitting diode through the central fiber (or fibers). Outside the central fiber, a layer of glass called cladding acts as a mirror, reflecting light back to the core in patterns that vary depending on the transmission mode. Outside the cladding, a plastic buffer protects the core and absorbs any light that might escape. Outside the buffer, strands of Kevlar provide further protection from stretching and damage. A plastic jacket surrounds the Kevlar strands.

**fiber-optic modem (FOM)** — A demultiplexer used on fiber networks that employ wave division multiplexing. The fiber-optic modem separates the multiplexed signals into individual signals according to their different wavelengths.

**Fibre Channel** — A distinct network transmission method that relies on fiber-optic media and its own, proprietary protocol. Fibre Channel is capable of 1-Gbps (and soon, 2-Gbps) throughput.

**file server** — A specialized server that enables clients to share applications and data across the network.

**file services** — The function of a file server that allows users to share data files, applications, and storage areas.

**file system** — An operating system's method of organizing, managing, and accessing its files through logical structures and software routines.

**File Transfer Protocol (FTP)** — An application layer protocol in the TCP/IP protocol suite that manages file transfers between TCP/IP hosts.

**file-infected virus** — A virus that attaches itself to executable files. When the infected executable file runs, the virus copies itself to memory. Later, the virus will attach itself to other executable files.

**filtering database** — A collection of data created and used by a bridge that correlates the MAC addresses of connected workstations with their locations. A filtering database is also known as a forwarding table.

**firewall** — A specialized device (typically a router, but possibly only a PC running special software) that selectively filters or blocks traffic between networks. A firewall may be strictly hardware-based, or it may involve a combination of hardware and software.

**firmware** — A combination of hardware and software. The hardware component of firmware is a read-only memory (ROM) chip that stores data established at the factory and possibly changed by configuration programs that can write to ROM.

**flashing** — A security attack in which an Internet user sends commands to another Internet user's machine that cause the screen to fill with garbage characters. A flashing attack will cause the user to terminate his or her session.

**flavor** — Term used to refer to the different implementations of a particular UNIX-like system. For example, the different flavors of Linux include Red Hat, Caldera, and Mandrake.

**flow control** — A method of gauging the appropriate rate of data transmission based on how fast the recipient can accept data.

**forest** — In the context of Windows 2000 Server, a collection of domain trees that use different namespaces. A forest allows for trust relationships to be established between trees.

**Format Prefix** — A variable-length field at the beginning of an IPv6 address that indicates what type of address it is (for example, unicast, anycast, or multicast).

**forwarding table** — See *filtering database*.

**fox and hound** — Another term for the combination of devices known as a tone generator and a tone locator. The tone locator is considered the hound because it follows the tone generator (the fox).

**fractional T1** — An arrangement that allows organizations to use only some channels on a T1 line and pay for only the channels actually used.

**frame** — A package for data that includes not only the raw data, or "payload," but also the sender's and receiver's network addresses and control information.

**Frame Check Sequence (FCS)** — The field in a data frame responsible for ensuring that data carried by the frame arrives intact. FCS uses an algorithm, such as CRC, to accomplish this verification.

**frame relay** — An updated, digital version of X.25 that relies on packet switching. Because it is digital, frame relay supports higher bandwidth than X.25, offering a maximum of 45-Mbps throughput. It provides the basis for much of the world's Internet connections. On network diagrams, the frame relay system is often depicted as a cloud.

**FreeBSD** — An open source software implementation of the Berkeley Software Distribution version of the UNIX system.

**freely distributable** — A term used to describe software with a very liberal copyright. Often associated with open source software.

**frequency** — The number of times that a signal's amplitude changes over a fixed period of time, expressed in cycles per second, or hertz (Hz).

**frequency modulation (FM)** — A method of data modulation in which the frequency of the carrier signal is modified by the application of the data signal.

**full backup** — A backup in which all data on all servers are copied to a storage medium, regardless of whether the data are new or changed.

**full-duplex** — A type of transmission in which signals may travel in both directions over a medium simultaneously. May also be called, simply, "duplex."

**fully qualified domain name (FQDN)** — In TCP/IP addressing, the combination of a host and domain name that together uniquely identify a device.

# G

**gateway** — A combination of networking hardware and software that connects two dissimilar types of networks. Gateways perform connectivity, session management, and data translation, so they must operate at multiple layers of the OSI Model.

**Gateway Services for NetWare (GSNW)** — A Windows 2000 service that acts as a translator between the Windows 2000 and NetWare client redirector services. With GSNW installed, a Windows 2000 server can access files and other shared resources on any NetWare server on a network.

**General Public License** — The copyright that applies to freely distributable versions of UNIX and specifies that the source code must be made available to anyone receiving the system.

**ghosts** — Frames that are not actually data frames, but rather aberrations caused by a repeater misinterpreting stray voltage on the wire. Unlike true data frames, ghosts have no starting delimiter.

**giants** — Packets that exceed the medium's maximum packet size. For example, any Ethernet packet that is larger than 1518 bytes is considered a giant.

**global group** — A group on a Windows 2000 network that allows members of one domain to access resources within that domain as well as resources from other domains in the same forest.

**globally unique identifier (GUID)** — A 128-bit number generated and assigned to an object upon its creation in the Windows 2000 Active Directory. Network applications and services use an object's GUID to communicate with it.

**globbing** — A form of filename substitution, similar to the use of wildcards in Windows and DOS.

**GNU** — The name given to the free software project to implement a complete source code implementation of UNIX, the collection of UNIX-inspired utilities and tools that are included with Linux distributions and other free software UNIX systems. The acronym within an acronym stands for "GNUs Not UNIX."

**gopher** — A text-based utility that allows you to navigate through a series of menus to find and read specific files.

**grandfather-father-son** — A backup rotation scheme that uses daily (son), weekly (father), and monthly (grandfather) backup sets.

**graphical user interface (GUI)** — A pictorial representation of computer functions and elements that, in the case of network operating systems, enables administrators to more easily manage files, users, groups, security, printers, and other issues.

**group** — A means of collectively managing users' permissions and restrictions applied to shared resources. Groups form the basis for resource and account management for every type of network operating system, not just Windows 2000 Server. Many network administrators create groups according to department or, even more specifically, according to job function within a department.

**Guest** — A user account with very limited privileges that is created during the installation of a network operating system.

# H

**hacker** — A person who masters the inner workings of operating systems and utilities in an effort to better understand them. A hacker is distinguished from a cracker in that a cracker will attempt to exploit a network's vulnerabilities for malicious purposes.

**half-duplex** — A type of transmission in which signals may travel in both directions over a medium, but in only one direction at a time.

**handshake protocol** — One of several protocols within SSL, and perhaps the most significant. As its name implies, the handshake protocol allows the client and server to authenticate (or introduce) each other and establishes terms for how they will securely exchange data during an SSL session.

**hard disk redundancy** — See *Redundant Array of Inexpensive Disks (RAID)*.

**Hardware Compatibility List (HCL)** — A list of computer components proven to be compatible with Windows 2000 Server. The HCL appears on the same CD as your Windows 2000 Server software and on Microsoft's Web site.

**head-end** — A cable company's central office, which connects cable wiring to many nodes before it reaches customers' sites.

**hertz (Hz)** — A measure of frequency equivalent to the number of amplitude cycles per second.

**heuristic scanning** — A type of virus scanning that attempts to identify viruses by discovering "virus-like" behavior.

**hierarchical file system** — The organization of files and directories (or folders) on a disk partition in which directories may contain files and other directories. When displayed graphically, this organization resembles a tree-like structure.

**hierarchical hybrid topology** — A network topology in which devices are divided into separate layers according to their priority or function.

**High-Performance File System (HPFS)** — A file system designed for IBM's OS/2 operating system that offers greater efficiency and reliability than does FAT. HPFS is rarely used but can be supported by Windows 2000 servers.

**High-Speed Token Ring (HSTR)** — A standard for Token Ring networks that operate at 100 Mbps.

**hop** — A term used to describe each trip data take from one connectivity device to another.

**host** — 1) A computer connected to a network that uses the TCP/IP protocol. 2) A type of computer that enables resource sharing by other computers on the same network.

**host file** — A text file that associates TCP/IP host names with IP addresses. On Windows 9x, NT, and 2000 platforms, the host file is called "lmhosts" On UNIX platforms the file is called "hosts" and is located in the /etc directory.

**host name** — A symbolic name that describes a TCP/IP device.

**hosts** — Name of the DNS host file found on a UNIX computer. The hosts file is usually found in the /etc directory.

**hot swappable** — A characteristic that enables identical components to be interchanged (or swapped) while a machine is still running (hot). Once installed, hot swappable components automatically assume the functions of their counterpart if it suffers a fault.

**HOWTO** — A series of brief, highly focused documents giving Linux system details. The people responsible for the Linux Documentation Project centrally coordinate the HOWTO papers (see *www.linuxhq.com/ldp/howto/HOWTO-INDEX/ howtos.html*).

**HP-UX** — Hewlett-Packard's proprietary implementation of the UNIX system.

**HTTPS** — The URL prefix that indicates that a Web page requires its data to be exchanged between client and server using SSL encryption. HTTPS uses the TCP port number 443, rather than port 80 (the port that normal HTTP uses).

**hub** — A multiport repeater containing multiple ports to interconnect multiple devices. Unless they are used on a peer-to-peer network, hubs also contain an uplink port, one port that connects to a network's backbone. Hubs regenerate digital signals.

**Hurd** — The kernel in the GNU operating system. While many UNIX and Linux systems include GNU utilities such as the EMACS editor or the GNU C compiler, the Hurd is the only operating system kernel that can currently be called a GNU kernel.

**hybrid fiber-coax (HFC)** — A link that consists of fiber cable connecting the cable company's offices to a node location near the customer and coaxial cable connecting the node to the customer's house. HFC upgrades to existing cable wiring are required before current TV cable systems can serve as WAN links.

**hybrid topology** — A complex combination of the simple physical topologies.

**Hypertext Markup Language (HTML)** — The language that defines formatting standards for Web documents.

**Hypertext Transport Protocol (HTTP)** — The language that Web clients and servers use to communicate. HTTP forms the backbone of the Web.

# I

**i-node** — A UNIX file system information storage area that holds all details about a file. This information includes the size, access rights, date and time of creation, and a pointer to the actual contents of the file.

**ICA (Independent Computing Architecture) client** — A remote access client developed by Citrix Systems, Inc. that enables remote users to use virtually any LAN application over any type of connection, public or private. The ICA client is especially well suited to slower connections, as it exchanges only keystrokes, mouse clicks, and screen updates with the server. The ICA client requires that Citrix's server software run on the access server.

**IEEE (Institute of Electrical and Electronic Engineers)** — An international society composed of engineering professionals. Its goals are to promote development and education in the electrical engineering and computer science fields.

**IEEE 802.3 frame** — A popular Ethernet frame type used on IPX/SPX networks. The defining characteristics of its data portion are the source and destination service access points that belong to the Logical Link Control layer, a sublayer of the Data Link layer. Also called LLC or, in Novell lingo, Ethernet 802.2.

**IEEE 802.3 SNAP frame** — A rarely used Ethernet frame type that is an adaptation of IEEE 802.3 and Ethernet II. SNAP stands for Sub-Network Access Protocol. The SNAP portion of the frame contains the three Logical Link Control fields (DSAP, SSAP, and Control). The Organization ID (OUI) field provides a method of identifying the type of network on which the frame is running. In addition, Ethernet SNAP frames carry Ethernet type information, just as an Ethernet II frame does.

**ifconfig** — A TCP/IP configuration and management utility used with UNIX systems (similar to the ipconfig utility used on Windows NT and 2000 systems).

**incremental backup** — A backup in which only data that have changed since the last backup are copied to a storage medium.

**indirect infrared transmission** — A type of infrared transmission in which signals bounce off walls, ceilings, and any other objects in their path. Because indirect infrared signals are not confined to a specific pathway, they are not very secure.

**Industry Standard Architecture (ISA)** — The original PC bus, developed in the early 1980s to support an 8-bit and later 16-bit data transfer capability. Although an older technology, ISA buses are still used to connect serial devices, such as mice or modems, in new PCs.

**infrared** — A type of data transmission in which infrared light signals are used to transmit data through space, similar to the way a television remote control sends signals across the room. Networks may use two types of infrared transmission: direct or indirect.

**integrity** — The soundness of a network's files, systems, and connections. To ensure integrity, you must protect your network from anything that might render it unusable, such as corruption, tampering, natural disasters, and viruses.

**integrity checking** — A method of comparing the current characteristics of files and disks against an archived version of these characteristics to discover any changes. The most common example of integrity checking involves a checksum.

**intelligent hub** — A hub that possesses processing capabilities and can therefore interpret and manage data traffic, rather than simply regenerating signals as a simple hub would do.

**Internet** — A complex WAN that connects LANs around the globe.

**Internet Control Message Protocol (ICMP)** — A core protocol in the TCP/IP suite that notifies the sender that something has gone wrong in the transmission process and that packets were not delivered.

**Internet Corporation for Assigned Names and Numbers (ICANN)** — The non-profit corporation currently designated by the U.S. government to maintain and assign IP addresses.

**Internet Key Exchange (IKE)** — The first phase of IPSec authentication, which accomplishes key management. IKE is a service that runs on UDP port 500. Once IKE has established the rules for the type of keys two nodes will use, IPSec invokes its second phase, encryption.

**Internet Mail Access Protocol (IMAP)** — A mail storage and manipulation protocol that depends on SMTP's transport system and improves upon the shortcomings of POP. The most current version of IMAP is version 4 (IMAP4). IMAP4 can (and eventually will) replace POP without the user having to change e-mail programs. The single biggest advantage IMAP4 has relative to POP is that it allows users to store messages on the mail server, rather than always having to download them to the local machine.

**Internet Protocol (IP)** — A core protocol in the TCP/IP suite that belongs to the Internet layer of the TCP/IP model and provides information about how and where data should be delivered. IP is the subprotocol that enables TCP/IP to internetwork.

**Internet services** — Services that enable a network to communicate with the Internet, including World Wide Web servers and browsers, file transfer capabilities, Internet addressing schemes, security filters, and a means for directly logging on to other computers.

**Internet telephony** — The provision of telephone service over the Internet.

**internetwork** — To traverse more than one LAN segment and more than one type of network through a router.

**Internetwork Packet Exchange (IPX)** — A core protocol of the IPX/SPX suite that operates at the Network layer of the OSI Model and provides routing and internetwork services, similar to IP in the TCP/IP suite.

**Internetwork Packet Exchange/Sequenced Packet Exchange (IPX/SPX)** — A protocol originally developed by Xerox, then modified and adopted by Novell in the 1980s for the NetWare network operating system.

**interrupt** — A wire through which a device issues voltage, thereby signaling a request for the processor's attention.

**interrupt request (IRQ)** — A message sent to the computer that instructs it to stop what it is doing and pay attention to something else. IRQ is often used (informally) to refer to the interrupt request number.

**interrupt request number (IRQ number)** — The unique number assigned to each interrupt request in a computer. Interrupt request numbers range from 0 to 15, and many PC devices reserve specific numbers for their use alone.

**IntraNetWare** — Another term for NetWare version 4.11, the version in which support for Internet services was first introduced.

**intrusion detection** — The process of monitoring the network for unauthorized access to its devices.

**IP address** — A logical address used in TCP/IP networking. This unique 32-bit number is divided into four groups of octets, or 8-bit bytes, that are separated by periods.

**IP datagram** — The IP portion of a TCP/IP frame that acts as an envelope for data, holding information necessary for routers to transfer data between subnets.

**IP next generation (IPng)** — See *IP Version 6*.

**IP Security Protocol (IPSec)** — A Layer 3 protocol that defines encryption, authentication, and key management for TCP/IP transmissions. IPSec is an enhancement to IPv4 and native to IPv6. IPSec is unique among authentication methods in that it adds security information to the header of all IP packets.

**IP spoofing** — A security attack in which an outsider obtains internal IP addresses, then uses those addresses to pretend that he or she has authority to access a private network from the Internet.

**IP version 6 (IPv6)** — A new standard for IP addressing that will replace the current IP version 4 (IPv4). Most notably, IPv6 uses a newer, more efficient header in its packets and allows for 128-bit source and destination IP addresses. The use of longer addresses will allow for more total IP addresses to be in circulation.

**ipconfig** — The TCP/IP configuration and management utility for use with Windows NT or Windows 2000 systems.

**IPX address** — An address assigned to a device on an IPX/SPX network.

**ISDN (Integrated Services Digital Network)** — An international standard, established by the ITU, for transmitting data over digital lines. Like PSTN, ISDN uses the telephone carrier's lines and dial-up connections, but it differs from PSTN in that it exclusively uses digital lines andswitches.

**ISO (International Organization for Standardization)** — A collection of standards organizations representing 130 countries with headquarters located in Geneva, Switzerland. Its goal is to establish international technological standards to facilitate the global Exchange of information and barrier-free trade.

**ITU (International Telecommunication Union)** — A United Nations agency that regulates international telecommunications, including radio and TV frequencies, satellite and telephony specifications, networking infrastructure, and tariffs applied to global communication. It also provides developing countries with technical expertise and equipment to advance these nations' technological bases.

# J

**jabber** — A device that handles electrical signals improperly, usually affecting the rest of the network. A network analyzer will detect a jabber as a device that is always retransmitting, effectively bringing the network to a halt. A jabber usually results from a bad NIC. Occasionally, it can be caused by outside electrical interference.

**jamming** — A part of CSMA/CD in which, upon detecting a collision, a station issues a special 32-bit sequence to indicate to all nodes on an Ethernet segment that its previously transmitted frame has suffered a collision and should be considered faulty.

**jumper** — A small, removable piece of plastic that contains a metal receptacle that fits over a pair of pins on a circuit board to complete a circuit between those two pins. By moving the jumper from one set of pins to another set of pins, you can modify the board's circuit, thereby giving it different instructions on how to operate.

# K

**Kerberos** — A cross-platform authentication protocol that uses key encryption to verify the identity of clients and to securely exchange information once a client logs onto a system. It is an example of a private key encryption service.

**kernel** — The core of an operating system, such as UNIX or NetWare. The kernel, which is loaded into memory as the computer starts, oversees all critical server processes.

**kernel modules** — Portions of the Linux kernel that you can load and unload to add or remove functionality on a running Linux system.

**key** — A series of characters that is combined with a block of data during that data's encryption. In order to decrypt the resulting data, the recipient must also possess the key.

**key distribution center (KDC)** — In Kerberos terminology, the server that runs the authentication service and the ticket granting service in order to issue keys and tickets to clients. On a Windows 2000 network, a user's domain controller serves as his KDC.

**key management** — The method whereby two nodes using key encryption agree on common parameters for the keys they will use in order to encrypt data.

**key pair** — The combination of a public and private key used to decipher data that has been encrypted using public key encryption.

# L

**LAN** — See *local area network.*

**LAN Emulation (LANE)** — A method for transporting Token Ring or Ethernet frames over ATM networks. LANE encapsulates incoming Ethernet or Token Ring frames, then converts them into ATM cells for transmission over an ATM network.

**LAN topology** — The physical layout, or pattern, of nodes on a local area network(LAN).

**LANalyzer** — Novell's network monitoring software package. LANalyzer can act as a standalone program on a Windows 9x or 2000 workstation or as part of the ManageWise suite of network management tools on a NetWare server. LANalyzer offers the following capabilities: discovery of all network nodes on a segment, continuous monitoring of network traffic, alarms that are tripped when traffic conditions meet preconfigured thresholds (for example, if usage exceeds 70%), and the capturing of traffic to and from all or selected nodes.

**late collisions** — Collisions that take place outside the normal window in which collisions are detected and redressed. Late collisions are usually caused by a defective station (such as a card, or transceiver) that is transmitting without first verifying line status or by failure to observe the configuration guidelines for cable length, which results in collisions being recognized too late.

**latency** — The delay between the transmission of a signal and its receipt.

**layer** — (1) In the context of hierarchical topologies, the division between one set of devices and another set of devices on a network; (2) A portion of the OSI Model that corresponds to specific processes involved in data communication between two computers.

**Layer 2 Forwarding (L2F)** — A Layer 2 protocol similar to PPTP that provides tunneling for other protocols and can work with the authentication methods used by PPP. L2F was developed by Cisco Systems and requires special hardware on the host system end. It can encapsulate protocols to fit more than just the IP format, unlike PPTP.

**Layer 2 Tunneling Protocol (L2TP)** — A Layer 2 tunneling protocol developed by a number of industry consortia. L2TP is an enhanced version of L2F. Like L2F, it supports multiple protocols; unlike L2F, it does not require costly hardware upgrades to implement. L2TP is optimized to work with the next generation of IP (IPv6) and IPSec (the Layer 3 IP encryption protocol).

**Layer 3 switch** — A switch capable of interpreting data at Layer 3 (Network layer) of the OSI Model.

**Layer 4 switch** — A switch capable of interpreting data at Layer 4 (Transport layer) of the OSI Model.

**lease** — The agreement between a DHCP server and client on how long the client will borrow a DHCP-assigned IP address. As network administrator, you configure the duration of the lease (in the DHCP service) to be as short or long as necessary, from a matter of minutes to forever.

**leased lines** — Permanent dedicated connections established through a public telecommunications carrier and billed to customers on a monthly basis.

**license tracking** — Determining how many copies of a single application are currently in use on the network.

**Lightweight Directory Access Protocol (LDAP)** — A standard protocol for accessing network directories.

**line noise** — Fluctuations in voltage levels caused by other devices on the network or by electromagnetic interference.

**Linux** — A freely distributable implementation of the UNIX system. Finnish computer scientist Linus Torvalds originally developed it.

**LLC frame** — See *IEEE 802.3 frame.*

**lmhosts** — A host file on a Windows-based computer that maps IP addresses to host names and aliases.

**load balancing** — An automatic distribution of traffic over multiple links, hard disks, or processors intended to optimize responses.

**Lobe Attachment Module (LAM)** — A device that attaches to a CAU to expand the capacity of that device. LAMs typically allow up to 20 devices to plug into each CAU receptacle.

**local account** — A type of user account on a Windows 2000 network that has rights to the resources managed by the server the user has logged onto.

**local area network (LAN)** — A network of computers and other devices that is confined to a relatively small space, such as one building or even one office.

**local collisions** — Collisions that occur when two or more stations are transmitting simultaneously. Excessively high collision rates within the network can usually be traced to cable or routing problems.

**local computer** — The computer on which you are actually working (as opposed to a remote computer).

**local loop** — The part of a phone system that connects a customer site with a public carrier's POP. Some WAN transmission methods, such as ISDN, are suitable for only the local loop portion of the network link.

**LocalTalk** — A logical topology designed by Apple Computer, Inc. especially for networking Macintosh computers. LocalTalk uses the CSMA/CA network access method, and its throughput is limited to a maximum of 230 Kbps. Because of its throughput limitations, LocalTalk has been replaced by Ethernet on most modern Macintosh-based networks.

**logical address** — See *Network layer addresses*.

**Logical Link Control (LLC) sublayer** — The upper sublayer in the Data Link layer. The LLC provides a common interface and supplies reliability and flow control services.

**logical topology** — A networking technology defined by its Data Link layer data packaging and Physical layer signaling techniques. Also known as network transport system or access method.

**loopback address** — An IP address reserved for communicating from a node to itself (used mostly for testing purposes). The value of the loopback address is always 127.0.0.1.

**loopback plug** — A connector used for troubleshooting that plugs into a port (for example, a serial, parallel, or RJ-45 port) and crosses over the transmit line to the receive line, allowing outgoing signals to be redirected back into the computer for testing.

# M

**MAC address** — A number that uniquely identifies a network node. The manufacturer hard-codes the MAC address on the NIC. This address is composed of the Block ID and Device ID.

**macro viruses** — A newer type of virus that takes the form of a word-processing or spreadsheet program macro, which may execute when a word-processing or spreadsheet program is in use.

**MacTCP** — A version of the TCP/IP protocol supplied with LocalTalk.

**mail services** — Network services that manage the storage and transfer of e-mail between users on a network. In addition to sending, receiving, and storing mail, mail services can include intelligent e-mail routing capabilities, notification, scheduling, indexing, document libraries, and gateways to other mail servers.

**MAN** — See *metropolitan area network*.

**managed hub** — See *intelligent hub*.

**management services** — Network services that centrally administer and simplify complicated management tasks on the network. Examples of management services include license tracking, security auditing, asset management, addressing management, software distribution, traffic monitoring, load balancing, and hardware diagnosis.

**manual pages (man pages)** — UNIX online documentation. This documentation describes the use of the commands and the programming interface to the UNIX system.

**Media Access Control (MAC) sublayer** — The lower sublayer of the Data Linklayer. The MAC appends the physical address of the destination computer onto the frame.

**media access unit (MAU)** — The type of transceiver used on a Thicknet network to connect network nodes to the backbone.

**media filter** — A device that enables two types of cables or connectors to be linked.

**member server** — A type of server on a Windows 2000 network that does not hold directory information and therefore cannot authenticate users.

**memory range** — A hexadecimal number that indicates the area of memory that the network adapter and CPU will use for exchanging, or buffering, data. As with IRQs, some memory ranges are reserved for specific devices—most notably, the system board.

**mesh network** — An enterprise-wide topology in which routers are interconnected with other routers so that at least two pathways connect each node.

**mesh WAN topology** — A WAN topology that consists of many directly interconnected locations forming a complex mesh.

**message switching** — A type of switching in which a connection is established between two devices in the connection path; one device transfers data to the second device, then breaks the connection. The information is stored and forwarded from the second device once a connection between that device and a third device on the path is established.

**metropolitan area network (MAN)** — A network that connects clients and servers in multiple buildings within a limited geographic area. For example, a network connecting multiple city government buildings around the city's center.

**MIB (management information base)** — A collection of data used by management programs (which may be part of the network operating system or a third-party program) to analyze network performance and problems.

**MicroChannel Architecture (MCA)** — IBM's proprietary 32-bit bus for personal computers, introduced in 1987 and later replaced by the more standard EISA and PCI buses.

**Microsoft Certified Systems Engineer (MCSE)** — A professional certification established by Microsoft that demonstrates in-depth knowledge about Microsoft's products, including Windows 98 and Windows 2000.

**Microsoft Management Console (MMC)** — A graphical network management interface used with Windows 2000 Server.

**Microsoft Message Queueing (MSMQ)** — An API used in a network environment. MSMQ stores messages sent between nodes in queues then forwards them to their destination based on when the link to the recipient is available.

**middleware** — Software that sits between the client and server in a 3-tier architecture. Middleware may be used as a messaging service between clients and servers, as a universal query language for databases, or as means of coordinating processes between multiple servers that need to work together in servicing clients.

**mirroring** — See *server mirroring*.

**modem** — A device that modulates analog signals into digital signals at the transmitting end for transmission over telephone lines, and demodulates digital signals into analog signals at the receiving end.

**modular hub** — A type of hub that provides a number of interface options within one chassis. Similar to a PC, a modular hub contains a system board and slots accommodating different adapters. These adapters may connect to other types of hubs, routers, WAN links, or to both Token Ring and Ethernet network backbones. They may also connect the modular hub to management workstations or redundant components, such as an extra power supply.

**modular router** — A router with multiple slots that can hold different interface cards or other devices so as to provide flexible, customizable network interoperability.

**modulation** — A technique for formatting signals in which one property of a simple, carrier wave is modified by the addition of a data signal during transmission.

**Monitor** — An NLM that enables the system administrator to view server parameters such as protocols, bindings, system resources, and loaded modules. In many cases, it also allows the system administrator to modify these parameters.

**multi-master replication** — The technique of replicating an Active Directory database to multiple domain controllers so they each have the same data and the same privileges to modify that data. Multi-master replication is used within a domain tree.

**multicast address** — A type of address in the IPv6 that represents multiple interfaces, often on multiple nodes. An IPv6 multicast address begins with the following hexadecimal field: FF0x, where x is a character that identifies the address's group scope.

**multicasting** — A means of transmission in which one device sends data to a specific group of devices (not the entire network segment) in a point-to-multipoint fashion. Multicasting can be used for teleconferencing or videoconferencing over the Internet, for example.

**multimeter** — A simple instrument that can measure multiple characteristics of an electric circuit, including its resistance and voltage.

**multimode fiber** — A type of fiber-optic cable that contains a core with a diameter between 50 and 100 microns, over which many pulses of light generated by a light emitting diode (LED) travel at different angles. Because light is being reflected many different ways in a multimode fiber cable, the waves become less easily distinguishable the longer they travel. Thus, multimode fiber is best suited for shorter distances than single-mode fiber.

**multiplexer (mux)** — A device that separates a medium into multiple subchannels and issues signals to each of those subchannels.

**multiplexing** — A form of transmission that allows multiple signals to simultaneously travel over one medium.

**multiprocessing** — The technique of splitting tasks among multiple processors to expedite the completion of any single instruction.

**multiprotocol network** — A network that uses more than one protocol.

**Multistation Access Unit (MAU)** — A device on a Token Ring network that regenerates signals; equivalent to a hub.

**multitasking** — The ability of a processor to perform multiple activities in a brief period of time (often seeming simultaneous to the user).

# N

**n-series connector (n connector)** — A type of connector used on Thicknet networks in which a screw-and-barrel arrangement securely connects coaxial cables to devices.

**name server** — A server that contains a database of TCP/IP host names and their associated IP addresses. A name server supplies a resolver with the requested information. If it cannot resolve the IP address, the query passes to a higher-level name server.

**name space** — The database of Internet IP addresses and their associated names distributed over DNS name servers worldwide.

**narrowband** — A type of radiofrequency transmission in which signals travel over a single frequency. The same method is used by radio and TV broadcasting stations, and signals can be easily intercepted and decoded.

**nbtstat** — A TCP/IP troubleshooting utility that provides information about NetBIOS names and their addresses. If you know the NetBIOS name of a workstation, you can use nbtstat to determine its IP address.

**NDS eDirectory** — Novell's integration tool for Windows 2000 networks. It works with the NetWare 5.x operating systems and Windows 2000 servers to enable the Windows 2000 domains to appear as container objects in NWAdmin.

**NDS tree** — A logical representation of how resources are grouped by NetWare in the enterprise.

**negative frame sequence checks** — The result of the cyclic redundancy checksum (CRC) generated by the originating node not matching the checksum calculated from the data received. It usually indicates noise or transmission problems on the LAN interface or cabling. A high number of (non-matching) CRCs usually results from excessive collisions or a station transmitting bad data.

**NetBIOS** — See *Network Basic Input Output System*.

**NetBIOS Enhanced User Interface (NetBEUI)** — Microsoft's adaptation of the IBM NetBIOS protocol. NetBEUI expands on NetBIOS by adding an Application layer component. NetBEUI is a fast and efficient protocol that consumes few network resources, provides excellent error correction and requires little configuration.

**netstat** — A TCP/IP troubleshooting utility that displays statistics and the state of current TCP/IP connections. It also displays ports, which can signal whether services are using the correct ports.

**NetWare 3.x** — The group of NetWare versions that includes versions 3.0, 3.1, and 3.2.

**NetWare 4.x** — The group of NetWare versions that includes versions 4.0, 4.1, and 4.11.

**NetWare 5.x** — The group of NetWare versions that includes versions 5.0, 5.1, and 5.11.

**NetWare Administrator utility (NWAdmin)** — The graphical NetWare utility thatallows administrators to manage objects in the NDS tree from a Windows workstation.

**NetWare Core Protocol (NCP)** — One of the core protocols of the IPX/SPX suite. NCP handles requests for services, such as printing and file access, between clients and servers.

**NetWare Directory Services (NDS)** — A system of managing multiple servers and their resources, including users, volumes, groups, profiles, and printers. The NDS model is similar to Active Directory in Windows 2000. In NDS, every networked resource is treated as a separate object with distinct properties.

**NetWare loadable modules (NLMs)** — Routines that enable the server to run programs and services. Each NLM consumes some of the server's memory and processor resources (at least temporarily). The kernel requires many NLMs to run NetWare's core operating system.

**network** — A group of computers and other devices (such as printers) that are connected by some type of transmission media, usually wire or cable.

**network access method** — See *access method*.

**network adapter** — A synonym for NIC (network interface card). The device that enables a workstation, server, printer, or other node to connect to the network. Network adapters belong to the Physical layer of the OSI Model.

**network address** — See *Network layer addresses*.

**network address translation (NAT)** — A technique in which private (or hidden) IP addresses are assigned a public IP address by an IP gateway, thus masking their true origin.

**network analyzer** — A portable, hardware-based tool that a network manager connects to the network expressly to determine the nature of network problems. Network analyzers can typically interpret data up to Layer 7 of the OSI Model.

**network architect** — A professional who designs networks, performing tasks that range from choosing basic components (such as cabling type) to figuring out how to make those components work together (by, for example, choosing the correct protocols).

**network attached storage (NAS)** — A device or set of devices attached to a client/server network that is dedicated to providing highly fault-tolerant access to large quantities of data. NAS depends on traditional network transmission methods such as Ethernet.

**Network Basic Input Output System (NetBIOS)** — A protocol designed by IBM to provide Transport and Session layer services for applications running on small, homogeneous networks.

**network interface card (NIC)** — The device that enables a workstation to connect to the network and communicate with other computers. NICs are manufactured by several different companies and come with a variety of specifications that are tailored to the workstation's and the network's requirements.

**Network layer** — The third layer in the OSI Model. The Network layer translates network addresses into their physical counterparts and decides how to route data from the sender to the receiver.

**Network layer addresses** — Addresses that reside at the Network level of the OSI Model, follow a hierarchical addressing scheme, and can be assigned through operating system software.

**Network Monitor (NetMon)** — A software-based network monitoring tool that comes with Windows NT Server 4.0 or Windows 2000. Its capabilities include capturing network data traveling from one or many segments, capturing frames sent by or to a specified node, reproducing network conditions by transmitting a selected amount and type of data, detecting any other running copies of NetMon, and generating statistics about network activity.

**network monitor** — A software-based tool that continually monitors traffic on the network from a server or workstation attached to the network. Network monitors typically can interpret up to Layer 3 of the OSI Model.

**Network News Transfer Protocol (NNTP)** — The protocol that supports the process of reading newsgroup messages, posting new messages, and transferring news files between news servers.

**network operating system (NOS)** — The software that runs on a server and enables the server to manage data, users, groups, security, applications, and other networking functions. The most popular network operating systems are Microsoft's Windows NT, Windows 2000, UNIX, and Novell's NetWare.

**Network Termination 1 (NT1)** — A device used on ISDN networks that connects the incoming twisted-pair wiring with the customer's ISDN terminal equipment.

**Network Termination 2 (NT2)** — An additional connection device required on PRI to handle the multiple ISDN lines between the customer's network termination connection and the local phone company's wires.

**Network Time Protocol (NTP)** — A simple TCP/IP protocol that is used to synchronize the clocks of computers on a network. NTP belongs to the Application layer of the TCP/IP Model and depends on UDP.

**network transport system** — See *logical topology*.

**network virus** — A type of virus that takes advantage of network protocols, commands, messaging programs, and data links to propagate itself. Although all viruses could theoretically travel across network connections, network viruses are specially designed to attack network vulnerabilities.

**Network+ (Net+)** — Professional certification established by CompTIA that verifies broad, vendor-independent networking technology skills such as an understanding of protocols, topologies, networking hardware, and network troubleshooting.

**New Technology File System (NTFS)** — A file system developed by Microsoft for use with its Windows NT and Windows 2000 operating systems. NTFS integrates reliability, compression, the ability to handle massive files, system security, and fast access. Most Windows 2000 Server partitions employ either FAT32 or NTFS.

**newsgroups** — An Internet service similar to e-mail that provides a means of conveying messages, but in which information is distributed to a wide group of users at once rather than from one user to another.

**NFS** — Network File System. A client/server application that allows you to view, store and update files on a remote computer as though they were on your own computer. Can be used to install Linux.

**node** — A computer or other device connected to a network which has a unique address and is capable of sending or receiving data.

**noise** — Unwanted signals, or interference, from sources near network cabling, such as electrical motors, power lines and radar.

**NOS** — See *network operating system*.

**Novell proprietary 802.3 frame** — The original NetWare Ethernet frame type and the default frame type for networks running NetWare versions lower than 3.12. It supports only the IPX/SPX protocol. Sometimes called 802.3 "raw," because its data portion contains no control bits.

**nslookup** — A TCP/IP utility on Windows NT, Windows 2000, and UNIX systems that allows you to look up the DNS host name of a network node by specifying its IP address, or vice versa. This ability is useful for verifying that a host is configured correctly and for troubleshooting DNS resolution problems.

**NWConv** — A utility provided with Windows 2000 that converts (migrates) an existing NetWare server's user account, file, and other information to a Windows 2000 server.

# O

**object** — A representation of a thing or person associated with the network that belongs in the NOS directory. Objects include users, printers, groups, computers, data files, and applications.

**object class** — See *Class*.

**octet** — One of the four 8-bit bytes that are separated by periods and together make up an IP address.

**ohmmeter** — A device used to measure resistance in an electrical circuit.

**online backup** — A technique in which data are backed up to a central location over the Internet.

**online UPS** — A power supply that uses the A/C power from the wall outlet to continuously charge its battery, while providing power to a network device through its battery.

**open shortest path first (OSPF)** — A routing protocol that makes up for some of the limitations of RIP and can coexist with RIP on a network.

**open source software** — Term used to describe software that is distributed without any restriction and whose source code is freely available. See also *freely distributable*.

**Open Systems Interconnection (OSI) Model** — A model for understanding and developing computer-to-computer communication developed in the 1980s by ISO. It divides networking architecture into seven layers: Physical, Data Link, Network, Transport, Session, Presentation, and Application.

**optical loss** — The degradation of a light signal on a fiber-optic network.

**optical time domain reflectometer (OTDR)** — A time domain reflectometer specifically made for use with fiber optic networks. It works by issuing a light-based signal on a fiber-optic cable and measuring the way in which the signal bounces back (or reflects) to the OTDR.

**Orange Book** — A rigorous security specification for computer operating systems published in 1985 by the U.S. Department of Defense.

**Organizational unit (OU)** — A container within an NOS directory used to group objects wih similar characteristics or priviledges.

**OSI Model** — See *Open Systems Interconnection Model*.

**overhead** — The nondata information that must accompany data in order for a signal to be properly routed and interpreted by the network.

# P

**Packet Internet Groper (PING)** — A TCP/IP troubleshooting utility that can verify that TCP/IP is installed, bound to the NIC, configured correctly, and communicating with the network. PING uses ICMP to send echo request and echo reply messages that determine the validity of an IP address.

**packet switching** — A type of switching in which data are broken into packets before they are transported. In packet switching, packets can travel any path on the network to their destination, because each packet contains a destination address and sequencing information.

**packet-filtering firewall** — A router that operates at the Data Link and Transport layers of the OSI Model, examining the header of every packet of data that it receives to determine whether that type of packet is authorized to continue to its destination. Packet-filtering firewalls are also called screening firewalls.

**padding** — Bytes added to the data (or information) portion of an Ethernet frame to make sure this field is at least 46 bytes in size. Padding has no effect on the data carried by the frame.

**page file** — A file on the hard disk that is used for virtual memory.

**paging** — The process of moving blocks of information, called pages, between RAM and into a page file on disk.

**parallel backbone** — The most robust enterprise-wide topology. This variation on the collapsed backbone arrangement consists of more than one connection from the central router or switch to each network segment.

**parity** — The mechanism used to verify the integrity of data by making the number of bits in a byte sum to either an odd or even number.

**parity error checking** — The process of comparing the parity of data read from a disk with the type of parity used by the system.

**passive hub** — A hub that simply amplifies and retransmits signals over the network.

**patch** — A correction, improvement, or enhancement to part of a software program, often distributed at no charge by software vendors to fix a bug in their code or to add slightly more functionality.

**patch cable** — A relatively short section (usually between 3 and 50 feet) of twisted-pair cabling, with connectors on both ends, that connects network devices to data outlets.

**patch panel** — A wall-mounted panel of data receptors into which cross-connect patch cables from the punch-down block are inserted.

**PC Card** — See *PCMCIA*.

**PCMCIA** — An interface developed in the early 1990s by the Personal Computer Memory Card International Association to provide a standard interface for connecting any type of device to a portable computer. PCMCIA slots may hold modem cards, network interface cards, external hard disk cards, or CD-ROM cards. PCMCIA cards are also known as PC Cards or credit card adapters.

**peer-to-peer communication** — A simple means of networking computers using a single cable. In peer-to-peer communication, no single computer has more authority than another and each computer can share its resources with other computers.

**peer-to-peer network** — A network in which computers communicate directly with other computers on a single segment of cable and share each others' data and devices. By default, no computer in a peer-to-peer network has more authority than another, and every computer can use resources from every other computer.

**peer-to-peer topology** — A WAN with single interconnection points for each location.

**per seat** — A Windows 2000 Server licensing mode that requires a license for every client capable of connecting to the Windows 2000 server.

**per server** — A Windows 2000 Server licensing mode that allows a limited number of clients to access the server simultaneously. (The number is determined by your Windows 2000 Server purchase agreement.) The restriction applies to the number of concurrent connections, rather than specific clients. Per server mode is the most popular choice for installing Windows 2000 Server.

**Peripheral Component Interconnect (PCI)** — A 32-, 64-, or 128-bit bus introduced in its original form in the 1990s. The PCI bus is the network adapter connection type used for nearly all new PCs. It's characterized by a shorter length than ISA, MCA, or EISA cards, but a much faster data transmission capability.

**phase** — A point or stage in a wave's progress overtime.

**physical address** — See *MAC address*.

**Physical layer** — The lowest, or first, layer of the OSI Model. The Physical layer contains the physical networking media, such as cabling and connectors.

**physical memory** — The RAM chips installed on the computer's system board that provide dedicated memory to that computer.

**physical topology** — The physical layout of a network. A physical topology depicts a network in broad scope; it does not specify devices, connectivity methods, or addresses on the network. Physical topologies are categorized into three fundamental geometric shapes: bus, ring, and star. These shapes can be mixed to create hybrid topologies.

**PING** — See *Packet Internet Groper*.

**pinging** — The process of sending an echo request signal from one node on a TCP/IP network to another, using the PING utility.

**pipe** — The facility in a UNIX system that enables you to combine commands to form new commands. It is one of the most powerful facilities of the UNIX system.

**pipeline** — A series of two or more UNIX commands connected together with pipe symbols.

**plain old telephone service (POTS)** — See *PSTN*.

**plenum** — The area above the ceiling tile or below the subfloor in a building.

**point of presence (POP)** — The place where the two telephone systems meet—either a long-distance carrier with a local telephone company or a local carrier with an ISP's facility.

**point-to-point** — A data transmission that involves one transmitter and one receiver.

**Point-to-Point Protocol (PPP)** — A communications protocol that enables a workstation to connect to a server using a serial connection. PPP can support multiple Network layer protocols, can use both asynchronous and synchronous communications, and does not require much (if any) configuration on the client workstation.

**Point-to-Point Tunneling Protocol (PPTP)** — A Layer 2 protocol developed by Microsoft that encapsulates PPP so that any type of data can traverse the Internet masked as pure IP transmissions. PPTP supports the encryption, authentication, and LAN access services provided by RAS. Instead of users having to dial directly into an access server, they can dial into their ISP using PPTP and gain access to their corporate LAN over the Internet.

**polymorphic virus** — A type of virus that changes its characteristics (such as the arrangement of its bytes, size, and internal instructions) every time it is transferred to a new system, making it harder to identify.

**POP** — See *Post Office Protocol* or *point of presence*.

**port** — The address on a host where an application makes itself available to incoming data.

**port number** — A unique number associated with a process running on a computer. For example, 23 is the standard port number associated with the Telnet utility.

**Post Office Protocol (POP)** — A TCP/IP subprotocol that provides centralized storage for e-mail messages. In the postal service analogy, POP is like the post office that holds mail until it can be delivered.

**preemptive multitasking** — The type of multitasking supported by NetWare, UNIX, and Windows 2000 Server that actually performs one task at a time, allowing one program to use the processor for a certain period of time, then suspending that program to allow another program to use the processor.

**Presentation layer** — The sixth layer of the OSI Model. The Presentation layer serves as a translator between the application and the network. Here data are formatted in a schema that the network can understand, with the format varying according to the type of network used. The Presentation layer also manages data encryption and decryption, such as the scrambling of system passwords.

**Pretty Good Privacy (PGP)** — A key-based encryption system for e-mail that uses a two-step verification process.

**PRI (Primary Rate Interface)** — A type of ISDN that uses 23 bearer channels and one 64-Kbps data channel as represented by the following notation: 23B + D. PRI is less commonly used by individual subscribers than BRI, but it may be used by businesses and other organizations needing more throughput.

**principal** — In Kerberos terminology, a user.

**print services** — The network service that allows printers to be shared by several users on a network.

**printer queue** — A logical representation of a networked printer's functionality. To use a printer, clients must have access to the printer queue.

**private key encryption** — A type of key encryption in which the sender and receiver have private keys, which only they know. Data encryption standard (DES), which was developed by IBM in the 1970s, is a popular example of a private key encryption technique. Private key encryption is also known as symmetric encryption.

**process** — A routine of sequential instructions that runs until it has achieved its goal. For example, a spreadsheet program is–a process.

**promiscuous mode** — The feature of a network adapter card that allows a device driver to direct it to pick up all frames that pass over the network—not just those destined for the node served by the card.

**proprietary UNIX** — Any implementation of UNIX for which the source code is either unavailable or available only by purchasing a licensed copy from Caldera International and Tarantella, Inc. (costing as much as millions of dollars).

**protected mode** — A manner in which NetWare runs services in a separate memory area from the operating system. Running services in protected mode prevents one rogue routine from taking the server down. As a result, the service and its supporting routines cannot harm critical server processes.

**protocol** — The rules a network uses to transfer data. Protocols ensure that data is transferred whole, in sequence, and without error from one node on the network to another.

**protocol analyzer** — See *network analyzer*.

**proxy server** — A network host that runs a proxy service. Proxy servers may also be called gateways.

**proxy service** — A software application on a network host that acts as an intermediary between the external and internal networks, screening all incoming and outgoing traffic and providing one address to the outside world, instead of revealing the addresses of internal LAN devices.

**PSTN (Public Switched Telephone Network)** — The network of typical telephone lines that has been evolving for 100 years and still services most homes.

**public key encryption** — A form of key encryption in which data are encrypted using two keys: one is a key known only to a user, and the other is a key associated with the user and can be obtained from a public source, such as a public key server. Some examples of public key algorithms include RSA (named after its creators, Rivest, Shamir, and Adleman), Diffie-Hellman, and Elliptic-curve cryptography. Public key encryption is also known as asymmetric encryption.

**public-key server** — A publicly available host (such as an Internet host) that provides free access to a list of users' public keys (for use in public key encryption).

**punch-down block** — A panel of data receptors into which horizontal cabling from the workstations is inserted.

**PVC (permanent virtual circuit)** — A point-to-point connection over which data may follow any number of different paths, as opposed to a dedicated line that follows a predefined path. X.25, frame relay, and some forms of ATM use PVCs.

# Q

**quality of service (QoS)** — The result of standards for delivering data within a certain period of time after their transmission. For example, ATM networks can supply four QoS levels, from a "best effort" attempt for noncritical data to a guaranteed, real-time transmission for time-sensitive data.

# R

**radiofrequency (RF)** — A type of transmission that relies on signals broadcast over specific frequencies, in the same manner as radio and TV broadcasts. RF may use narrowband or spread spectrum technology.

**radiofrequency interference (RFI)** — A kind of interference that may be generated by motors, power lines, televisions, copiers, fluorescent lights, or broadcast signals from radio or TV towers.

**RAID** — See *Redundant Array of Inexpensive Disks*.

**RAID Level 0** — An implementation of RAID in which data are written in 64 KB blocks equally across all disks in the array.

**RAID Level 1** — An implementation of RAID that provides redundancy through disk mirroring, in which data from one disk are automatically copied to another disk as the information is written.

**RAID Level 3** — An implementation of RAID that uses disk striping for data and parity error correction code on a separate parity disk.

**RAID Level 5** — The most popular, highly fault-tolerant, data storage technique in use today, RAID Level 5 writes data in small blocks across several disks. At the same time, it writes parity error checking information among several disks.

**real-time** — The term used to describe an operating system that at least one of the following includes two characteristics: the ability to respond to external events (for example, a change in temperature), and an ability to respond to those events deterministically—with predictable response time (for example, turning on a heating element within three microseconds).

**reassembly** — The process of reconstructing data units that have been segmented.

**redirector** — A service that runs on a client workstation and determines whether the client's request should be handled by the client or the server.

**redundancy** — The use of more than one identical component for storing, processing, or transporting data.

**Redundant Array of Inexpensive Disks (RAID)** — A server redundancy measure that uses shared, multiple physical or logical hard disks to ensure data integrity and availability. Some RAID designs also increase storage capacity and improve performance. See also *disk striping*, and *disk mirroring*.

**regeneration** — The process of retransmitting a digital signal. Regeneration, unlike amplification, repeats the pure signal, with none of the noise it has accumulated.

**relative distinguished name (RDN)** — An attribute of the object that identifies an object separately from its related container(s) and domain. For most objects, the relative distinguished name is the same as its common name (CN) in the distinguished name convention.

**release** — The act of terminating a DHCP lease.

**remote access** — A method for connecting and logging onto a LAN from a workstation that is remote, or not physically connected, to the LAN. Remote access can be accomplished one of three ways: by using a modem to dial directly into the LAN; by using a modem to dial directly to a workstation; or by using an Internet connection with a Web interface. Remote access may complete a connection via public or private lines.

**remote access server** — A combination of software and hardware that provides a central access point for multiple users to dial into a network.

**Remote Access Service (RAS)** — One of the simplest dial-in servers. This software is included with Windows 2000 Server. Note that "RAS" is pronounced *razz*.

**Remote Authentication Dial-In User Service (RADIUS)** — A server that offers authentication services to the network's access server (which may run the Windows NT or 2000 RAS or Novell's NAS, for example). RADIUS provides a single, centralized point of authentication for dial-in users and is often used by ISPs.

**remote computer** — The computer that you are controlling or working on via a network connection.

**remote control** — A remote access method in which the remote user dials into a workstation that is directly attached to a LAN. Software running on both the remote user's computer and the LAN computer allows the remote user to "take over" the LAN workstation.

**remote node** — A client that has dialed directly into a LAN's remote access server. The LAN treats a remote node like any other client on the LAN, allowing the remote user to perform the same functions he or she could perform while in the office.

**remote user** — A person working on a computer in a different geographical location from the LAN's server.

**repeater** — A device used to regenerate a digital signal.

**replication** — The process of copying Active Directory data to multiple domain controllers. This ensures redundancy so that in case one of the domain controllers fails, clients can still log onto the network, be authenticated, and access resources.

**resistance** — The opposition to an electric current. Resistance of a wire is a factor of its size and molecular structure.

**resolver** — Any host on the Internet that needs to look up domain name information.

**resource record** — The element of a DNS database stored on a name server that contains information about TCP/IP host names and their addresses.

**resources** — The devices, data, and data storage space provided by a computer, whether standalone or shared.

**restore** — The process of retrieving files from a backup if the original files are lost or deleted.

**Reverse Address Resolution Protocol (RARP)** — The reverse of ARP. RARP allows the client to send a broadcast message with the MAC address of a device and receive the device's IP address in reply.

**RFI** — See *radiofrequency interference*.

**ring topology** — A network layout in which each node is connected to the two nearest nodes so that the entire network forms a circle. Data are transmitted unidirectionally around the ring. Each workstation accepts and responds to packets addressed to it, then forwards the other packets to the next workstation in the ring.

**ring WAN topology** — A WAN topology in which each site is connected to two other sites so that the entire WAN forms a ring pattern. This architecture is similar to the LAN ring topology, except that a WAN ring topology connects locations rather than local nodes.

**risers** — The backbone cabling that provides vertical connections between floors of a building.

**RJ-45** — The standard connector used with shielded twisted-pair and unshielded twisted-pair cabling. "RJ" stands for registered jack.

**root** — A highly privileged user ID that has all rights to create, delete, modify, move, read, write, or execute files on a system. This term may specifically refer to the administrator on a UNIX-based network.

**root domain** — In Windows 2000 networking, the single domain from which child domains branch out in a domain tree.

**root server** — A DNS server maintained by ICANN (in North America) that is an authority on how to contact the top-level domains, such as those ending with .com, .edu, .net, .us, and so on. ICANN maintains 13 root servers around the world.

**routable** — Protocols that can span more than one LAN segment because they carry Network layer and addressing information that can be interpreted by a router.

**route** — To direct data between networks based on addressing, patterns of usage, and availability of network segments.

**router** — A multiport device that can connect dissimilar LANs and WANs running at different transmission speeds and using a variety of protocols. In addition, a router can determine the best path for data transmission and perform advanced management functions. Routers operate at the Network layer (Layer 3) or higher of the OSI Model. They are intelligent, protocol-dependent devices.

**Routing Information Protocol (RIP)** — The oldest routing protocol that is still widely used. RIP does not work in very large network environments where data may have to travel through more than 16 routers to reach their destination (for example, on the Internet). And, compared to other routing protocols, RIP is slower and less secure.

**routing protocols** — Protocols that assist routers in efficiently managing information flow. For instance, routing protocols determine the best path for data to take between nodes.

**routing switch** — Another term for a Layer 3 or Layer 4 switch. A routing switch is a hybrid between a router and a switch and can therefore interpret data from Layer 2 and either Layer 3 or Layer 4.

**runts** — Packets that are smaller than a logical topology's minimum packet size. For instance, any Ethernet packet that is smaller than 64 bytes is considered a runt.

# S

**sag** — See *brownout*.

**Samba** — An open source software package that provides complete Windows 2000-style file and printer sharing facility.

**schema** — The description of object types, or classes, and their required and optional attributes that are stored in an NOS's directory.

**screening firewall** — See *packet-filtering firewall*.

**SDH (Synchronous Digital Hierarchy)** — The international equivalent of SONET.

**security audit** — An assessment of an organization's security vulnerabilities. A security audit should be performed at least annually and preferably quarterly or sooner if the network has undergone significant changes. For each risk found, it should rate the severity of a potential breach, as well as its likelihood.

**segment** — A part of a LAN that is logically separated from other parts of the LAN and that shares a fixed amount of traffic capacity.

**segmentation** — The process of decreasing the size of data units when moving data from a network segment that can handle larger data units to a network segment that can handle only smaller data units.

**self-healing** — A characteristic of dual-ring topologies that allows them to automatically reroute traffic along the backup ring if the primary ring becomes severed.

**Sequenced Packet Exchange (SPX)** — One of the core protocols in the IPX/SPX suite. SPX belongs to the Transport layer of the OSI Model and works in tandem with IPX to ensure that data are received whole, in sequence, and error free.

**sequencing** — The process of assigning a placeholder to each piece of a data block to allow the receiving node's Transport layer to reassemble the data in the correct order.

**serial backbone** — The simplest kind of backbone, consisting of two or more hubs connected to each other by a single cable.

**Serial Line Internet Protocol (SLIP)** — A communications protocol that enables a workstation to connect to a server using a serial connection. SLIP can support only asynchronous communications and IP traffic, and requires some configuration on the client workstation.

**server** — A computer on the network that manages shared resources. Servers usually have more processing power, memory, and hard disk space than clients. They run network operating software that can manage not only data, but also users, groups, security, and applications on the network.

**server clustering** — A fault-tolerance technique that links multiple servers together to act as a single server. In this configuration, clustered servers share processing duties and appear as a single server to users. If one server in the cluster fails, the other servers in the cluster will automatically take over its data transaction and storage responsibilities.

**server console** — The network administrator's primary interface to a NetWare server. Unlike Windows NT, the NetWare server interface is not entirely graphical. NetWare 4.x offers only text-based server menus at the console. NetWare 5.0 allows you to access commands through either a text-based or graphical menu system.

**server mirroring** — A fault-tolerance technique in which one server duplicates the transactions and data storage of another, identical server. Server mirroring requires a link between the servers and software running on both servers so that the servers can continually synchronize their actions and take over in case the other fails.

**server-based network** — A network that uses special computers, known as servers, to process data for and facilitate communication between the other computers on the network. See *client/server network*.

**server_hello** — In the context of SSL encryption, a message issued from the server to the client that confirms the information the server received in the client_hello message and agrees to certain terms of encryption based on the options the client supplied. Depending on the Web server's preferred encryption method, the server may choose to use issue your browser a public key or a digital certificate at this time.

**Service Access Point (SAP)** — A feature of Ethernet networks that identifies a node or internal process that uses the LLC protocol. Each process between a source and destination node on the network may have a unique SAP.

**Service Advertising Protocol (SAP)** — A core protocol in the IPX/SPX suite that works in the Application, Presentation, Session, and Transport layers of the OSI Model and runs directly over IPX. NetWare servers and routers use SAP to advertise to the entire network which services they can provide.

**service pack** — A significant patch to Windows NT or 2000 Server software.

**services** — The features provided by a network.

**session** — A connection for data exchange between two parties. The term "session" is most often used in the context of terminal and mainframe communications.

**session key** — In the context of Kerberos authentication, a key issued to both the client and service by the authentication service that uniquely identifies their session.

**Session layer** — The fifth layer in the OSI Model. The Session layer establishes and maintains communication between two nodes on the network. It can be considered the traffic "cop" for network communications.

**shared Ethernet** — A version of Ethernet in which all the nodes share a common channel and a fixed amount of bandwidth.

**sheath** — The outer cover, or jacket, of a cable.

**shell** — Another term for command interpreter.

**shielded twisted-pair (STP)** — A type of cable containing twisted wire pairs that are not only individually insulated, but also surrounded by a shielding made of a metallic substance such as foil. The shielding acts as an antenna, converting the noise into current (assuming that the wire is properly grounded). This current induces an equal, yet opposite current in the twisted pairs it surrounds. The noise on the shielding mirrors the noise on the twisted pairs, and the two cancel each other out.

**signal bounce** — A phenomenon caused by improper termination on a bus network in which signals travel endlessly between the two ends of the network, preventing new signals from getting through.

**signal level** — An ANSI standard for T-carrier technology that refers to its Physical layer electrical signaling characteristics. DS0 is the equivalent of one data or voice channel. All other signal levels are multiples of DS0.

**signature scanning** — The comparison of a file's content with known virus signatures (unique identifying characteristics in the code) in a signature database to determine whether the file is a virus.

**Simple Mail Transfer Protocol (SMTP)** — A protocol within the TCP/IP suite that is responsible for moving e-mail messages between one mail server and another.

**Simple Network Management Protocol (SNMP)** — A communication protocol used to manage devices on a TCP/IP network.

**simplex** — A type of transmission in which signals may travel in only one direction over a medium.

**single point of failure** — A device or connection on a network that, were it to fail, could cause the entire network to stop functioning.

**single-mode fiber** — A type of fiber-optic cable with a core of less than 10 microns in diameter that carries light pulses along a single data path from one end of the cable to another. Single-mode fiber can carry data faster and farther than multimode fiber. However, single-mode fiber is more expensive than multimode fiber.

**site license** — A type of software license that, for a fixed price, allows any number of users in one location to legally access an application.

**snap-in** — An administrative tool, such as Computer Management, that can be added to the Microsoft Management Console (MMC).

**sneakernet** — The only means of exchanging data without using a network. Sneakernet requires that data be copied from a computer to a floppy disk, carried (presumably by someone wearing sneakers) to another computer, then copied from the floppy disk onto the second computer.

**sniffer** — A laptop equipped with a special network adapter and software that performs network analysis. Unlike laptops that may have a network monitoring tool installed, sniffers typically cannot be used for other purposes, because they don't depend on a desktop operating system such as Windows.

**Sniffer Portable** — Network analyzer software from Network Associates that provides data capture and analysis, node discovery, traffic trending, history, alarm tripping, and utilization prediction.

**social engineering** — Manipulating relationships to circumvent network security measures and gain access to a system.

**socket** — A logical address assigned to a specific process running on a computer. A socket forms a virtual connection between the host and client.

**software distribution** — The process of automatically transferring a data file or program from the server to a client on the network.

**Solaris** — Sun Microsystems' proprietary implementation of the UNIX system.

**SONET (Synchronous Optical Network)** — A WAN technology that provides data transfer rates ranging from 64 Kbps to 39.8 Gbps, using the same time division multiplexing technique used by T-carriers. SONET is the best choice for linking WANs between North America, Europe, and Asia, because it can link directly using the different standards used in different countries.

**source code** — Computer instructions written in a programming language that is readable by humans. Source code must be translated into a form that is executable by the machine, typically called binary code (for the sequence of zeros and ones) or target code.

**source-route bridging** — A type of bridging in which the bridge polls the network to determine the best path for data between two points. Source-route bridging is not susceptible to circular routing and, for this reason, is particularly well-suited to WANs.

**spanning tree algorithm** — A technique used in bridging that can detect circular traffic patterns and modify the way multiple bridges work together in order to avoid such patterns.

**spike** — A single (or short-lived) jump in a measure of network performance, such as utilization.

**spread spectrum** — A type of radiofrequency transmission in which lower-level signals are distributed over several frequencies simultaneously. Spread spectrum RF is more secure than narrowband RF.

**SSL (Secure Sockets Layer)** — A method of encrypting TCP/IP transmissions—including Web pages and data entered into Web forms—en route between the client and server using public key encryption technology.

**SSL session** — In the context of SSL encryption, an association between the client and server that is defined by an agreement on a specific set of encryption techniques. An SSL session allows the client and server to continue to exchange data securely as long as the client is still connected to the server. SSL sessions are established by the SSL handshake protocol.

**stackable hub** — A type of hub designed to be linked with other hubs in a single telecommunications closet. Stackable hubs linked together logically represent one large hub to the network.

**standalone computer** — A computer that uses programs and data only from its local disks and that is not connected to a network.

**standalone hub** — A type of hub that serves a workgroup of computers that are separate from the rest of the network. A standalone hub may be connected to another hub by a coaxial, fiber-optic, or twisted-pair cable. Such hubs are not typically connected in a hierarchical or daisy-chain fashion.

**standards** — Documented agreements containing technical specifications or other precise criteria that are used as guidelines to ensure that materials, products, processes, and services suit their intended purpose.

**standby UPS** — A power supply that provides continuous voltage to a device by switching virtually instantaneously to the battery when it detects a loss of power from the wall outlet. Upon restoration of the power, the standby UPS switches the device to use A/C power again.

**star topology** — A physical topology in which every node on the network is connected through a central device, such as a hub. Any single physical wire on a star network connects only two devices, so a cabling problem will affect only two nodes. Nodes transmit data to the hub, which then retransmits the data to the rest of the network segment where the destination node can pick it up.

**star WAN topology** — A WAN topology that mimics the arrangement of star LANs. A single site acts as the central connection point for several other locations.

**star-wired bus topology** — A hybrid topology in which groups of workstations are connected in a star fashion to hubs that are networked via a single bus.

**star-wired ring topology** — A hybrid topology that uses the physical layout of a star and the token-passing data transmission method.

**static ARP table entry** — A record (of an IP address and its associated MAC address) that is manually entered in the ARP table using the ARP utility.

**static IP address** — An IP address that is manually assigned to a device and remains constant until it is manually changed.

**static routing** — A technique in which a network administrator programs a router to use specific paths between nodes. Since it does not account for occasional network congestion, failed connections, or device moves, static routing is not optimal.

**statistical multiplexing** — A method of multiplexing in which each node on a network is assigned a separate time slot for transmission, based on the node's priority and need.

**stealth virus** — A type of virus that hides itself to prevent detection. Typically, stealth viruses disguise themselves as legitimate programs or replace part of a legitimate program's code with their destructive code.

**storage area network (SAN)** — A distinct network of multiple storage devices and servers that provides fast, highly available, and highly fault-tolerant access to large quantities of data for a client/server network. SAN uses a proprietary network transmission method (such as Fibre Channel) rather than a traditional network transmission method such as Ethernet.

**store and forward mode** — A method of switching in which a switch reads the entire data frame into its memory and checks it for accuracy before transmitting it. While this method is more time-consuming than the cut-through method, it allows store and forward switches to transmit data more accurately.

**straight-through cable** — A twisted-pair patch cable in which the wire terminations in both connectors follow the same scheme.

**structured cabling** — A method for uniform, enterprise-wide, multivendor cabling systems specified by the TIA/EIA 568 Commercial Building Wiring Standard. Structured cabling is based on a hierarchical design using a high-speed backbone.

**subchannel** — One of many distinct communication paths established when a channel is multiplexed or modulated.

**subnet mask** — A special 32-bit number that, when combined with a device's IP address, informs the rest of the network as to what kind of subnet the device is on.

**subnets** — In an internetwork, the individual networks that are joined together by routers.

**subnetting** — The process of subdividing a single class of network into multiple, smaller networks.

**subprotocols** — Small, specialized protocols that work together and belong to a protocol suite.

**surge** — A momentary increase in voltage due to distant lightning strikes or electrical problems.

**SVC (switched virtual circuit)** — Logical, point-to-point connections that rely on switches to determine the optimal path between sender and receiver. ATM technology uses SVCs.

**swap file** — See *page file*.

**switch** — 1) A connectivity device that logically subdivides a network into smaller, individual segments. Most switches operate at the Data Link layer of the OSI Model. They interpret MAC address information to determine whether to filter (discard) or forward packets they receive. 2) The letters or words added to a command that allow you to customize a utility's output. Switches are usually preceded by a hyphen or a forward slash character.

**switched Ethernet** — An Ethernet model that enables multiple nodes to simultaneously transmit and receive data and individually take advantage of more bandwidth because they are assigned separate logical network segments through switching.

**switching** — A component of a network's logical topology that manages how packets are filtered and forwarded between nodes on the network.

**symmetric encryption** — A method of encryption that requires the same key to encode the data as is used to decode the cipher text.

**symmetric multiprocessing** — A method of multiprocessing that splits all operations equally among two or more processors. Windows 2000 Server supports this type of multiprocessing.

**symmetrical** — A characteristic of transmission technology that provides equal throughput for data traveling both upstream and downstream and is suited to users who both upload and download significant amounts of data.

**symmetrical DSL** — A variation of DSL that provides equal throughput both upstream and downstream between the customer and the carrier.

**synchronous** — A transmission method in which data being transmitted and received by nodes must conform to a timing scheme.

**System V** — The proprietary version of UNIX, originally developed at AT&T Bell Labs, currently distributed by Caldera International and Tarantella, Inc.

# T

**T-carriers** — The term for any kind of leased line that follows the standards for T1s, fractional T1s, T1Cs, T2s, T3s, or T4s.

**T1** — A T-carrier technology that provides 1.544-Mbps throughput and 24 channels for voice, data, video, or audio signals. T1s may use shielded or unshielded twisted-pair, coaxial cable, fiber-optic, or microwave links. Businesses commonly use T1s to connect to their ISP, and phone companies typically use at least one T1 to connect their central offices.

**T3** — A T-carrier technology that can carry the equivalent of 672 channels for voice, data, video, or audio, with a maximum data throughput of 44.736 Mbps (typically rounded up to 45 Mbps for purposes of discussion). T3s require either fiber-optic or microwave transmission media.

**TCP segment** — The portion of a TCP/IP packet that holds TCP data fields and becomes encapsulated by the IP datagram.

**TCP/IP core protocols** — The subprotocols of the TCP/IP suite.

**teleconnector** — A transceiver used on LocalTalk networks. The teleconnector is linked to the node's serial port on one side, and to the wall jack on the other side.

**Telnet** — A terminal emulation protocol used to log on to remote hosts using the TCP/IP protocol. Telnet resides in the Application layer of the TCP/IP suite.

**terminal** — A device with little (if any) of its own processing or disk capacity that depends on a host to supply it with applications and data-processing services.

**Terminal Access Controller Access Control System (TACACS)** — A centralized authentication system for remote access servers that is similar to RADIUS.

**terminal adapter (TA)** — Devices used to convert digital signals into analog signals for use with ISDN phones and other analog devices. Terminal adapters are sometimes called ISDN modems.

**terminal equipment (TE)** — Devices that connect computers to the ISDN line. Terminal equipment may include standalone devices or cards (similar to the network adapters used on Ethernet and Token Ring networks) or ISDN routers.

**Thicknet** — A type of coaxial cable, also known as thickwire Ethernet, that is a rigid cable approximately 1-cm thick. Thicknet was used for the original Ethernet networks. Because it is often covered with a yellow sheath, Thicknet is also called "yellow Ethernet." IEEE has designated Thicknet as 10Base5 Ethernet, with the "10" representing its throughput of 10 Mbps, the "Base" standing for baseband transmission, and the "5" representing the maximum segment length of a Thicknet cable, 500 m.

**thickwire Ethernet** — See *Thicknet*.

**thin client** — A type of software that enables a client to accomplish functions over a network while utilizing little of the client workstation's resources and, instead, relying on the server to carry the processing burden.

**thin Ethernet** — See *Thinnet*.

**Thinnet** — A type of coaxial cable, also known as thin Ethernet, that was the most popular medium for Ethernet LANs in the 1980s. Like Thicknet, Thinnet is rarely used on modern networks. IEEE has designated Thinnet as 10Base2 Ethernet, with the "10" representing its data transmission rate of 10 Mbps, the "Base" representing the fact that it uses baseband transmission, and the "2" roughly representing its maximum segment length of 185 m.

**thread** — A well-defined, self-contained subset of a process. Using threads within a process enables a program to efficiently perform related, multiple, simultaneous activities. Threads are also used to enable processes to use multiple processors on SMP systems.

**throughput** — The amount of data that a medium can transmit during a given period of time. Throughput is usually measured in megabits (1,000,000 bits) per second, or Mbps. The physical nature of every transmission medium determines its potential throughput.

**ticket** — In Kerberos terminology, a temporary set of credentials that a client uses to prove that its identity has been validated by the authentication service.

**ticket granting service (TGS)** — In Kerberos terminology, an application that runs on the key distribution center that issues ticket granting tickets to clients so that they need not request a new ticket for each new service they want to access.

**ticket granting ticket (TGT)** — In Kerberos terminology, a ticket that enables a user to be accepted as a validated principal by multiple services.

**tiered WAN topology** — A WAN topology in which sites are connected in star or ring formations and interconnected at different levels with the interconnection points organized into layers.

**time division multiplexing (TDM)** — A method of multiplexing that assigns a time slot in the flow of communications to every node on the network and in that time slot, carries data from that node.

**time domain reflectometer (TDR)** — A high-end instrument for testing the qualities of a cable. It works by issuing a signal on a cable and measuring the way in which the signal bounces back (or reflects) to the TDR.

**time-dependent virus** — A virus programmed to activate on a particular date. This type of virus, also known as a "time bomb," can remain dormant and harmless until its activation date arrives.

**time-sharing system** — A computing system to which users must attach directly so as to use the shared resources of the computer.

**TLS (Transport Layer Security)** — A version of SSL being standardized by the Internet Engineering Task Force (IETF). With TLS, IETF aims to create a version of SSL that will encrypt UDP as well as TCP transmissions. TLS, which will likely be supported by new Web browsers, uses slightly different encryption algorithms than SSL, but otherwise is very similar to the most recent version of SSL.

**token** — A special control frame that indicates to the rest of the network that a particular node has the right to transmit data.

**token passing** — A means of data transmission in which a 3-byte packet, called a token, is passed around the network in a round-robin fashion.

**Token Ring** — A networking technology developed by IBM in the 1980s. It relies upon direct links between nodes and a ring topology, using tokens to allow nodes to transmit data.

**Token Ring media filter** — A device that enables a DB-9 cable and a type 1 IBM cable to be connected.

**tone generator** — A small electronic device that issues a signal on a wire pair. When used in conjunction with a tone locator, it can help locate the termination of a wire pair.

**tone locator**—A small electronic device that emits a tone when it detects electrical activity on a wire pair. When used in conjunction with a tone generator, it can help locate the termination of a wire pair.

**top-level domain (TLD)** — The highest-level category used to distinguish domain names—for example, .org, .com, .net. A TLD is also known as the domain suffix.

**topology** — The physical layout of a computer network.

**traceroute (or tracert)** — A TCP/IP troubleshooting utility that uses ICMP to trace the path from one networked node to another, identifying all intermediate hops between the two nodes. Traceroute is useful for determining router or subnet connectivity problems.

**traffic** — The data transmission and processing activity taking place on a computer network at any given time.

**traffic monitoring** — Determining how much processing activity is taking place on a network or network segment and notifying administrators when a segment becomes overloaded.

**transceiver (transmitter/receiver)** — A device that both transmits and receives signals. Since a transceiver is concerned with applying signals to the wire, it belongs in the Physical layer of the OSI Model. Many different types of transceivers exist in networking.

**translational bridging** — A type of bridging in which bridges can not only forward packets, but also translate packets between one logical topology and another. For instance, translational bridging can connect Token Ring and Ethernet networks.

**transmission** — In networking, the application of data signals to a medium or the progress of data signals over a medium from one point to another.

**Transmission Control Protocol (TCP)** — A core protocol of the TCP/IP suite. TCP belongs to the Transport layer and provides reliable data delivery services.

**transmission media** — The means through which data are transmitted and received. Transmission media may be physical, such as wire or cable, or atmospheric (wireless), such as radio waves.

**transparent bridging** — The method of bridging used on most Ethernet networks.

**Transport layer** — The fourth layer of the OSI Model. The Transport layer is primarily responsible for ensuring that data are transferred from point A to point B (which may or may not be on the same network segment) reliably and without errors.

**tree** — A logical representation of multiple, hierarchical levels in a directory. It is called a tree because the whole structure shares a common starting point (the root) and from that point extends branches (or containers), which may extend additional branches, and so on.

**Trivial File Transfer Protocol (TFTP)** — A TCP/IP Application layer protocol that enables file transfers between computers. Unlike FTP, TFTP relies on UDP at the Transport layer and does not require a user to log onto the remote host.

**Trojan horse** — A program that disguises itself as something useful but actually harms your system.

**trust relationship** — The relationship between two domains on a Windows 2000 or Windows NT network that allows a domain controller from one domain to authenticate users from the other domain.

**tunneling** — The process of encapsulating one protocol to make it appear as another type of protocol.

**twist ratio** — The number of twists per meter or foot in a twisted-pair cable.

**twisted-pair (TP)** — A type of cable similar to telephone wiring that consists of color-coded pairs of insulated copper wires, each with a diameter of 0.4 to 0.8mm, twisted around each other and encased in plastic coating.

**two-way transitive trust** — The security relationship between domains in the same domain tree in which one domain grants every other domain in the tree access to its resources and, in turn, that domain can access other domains' resources. When a new domain is added to a tree, it immediately shares a two-way trust with the other domains in the tree.

**type 1 IBM connector** — A type of Token Ring connector that uses interlocking tabs that snap into an identical connector when one is flipped upside-down, making for a secure connection. Type 1 IBM connectors are used on STP-based Token Ring networks.

**typeful** — A way of denoting an object's context in which the Organization and Organizational Unit designators ("O" and "OU," respectively) are included. For example, OU=Inv.OU=Ops.OU=Corp.O=Sutkin.

**typeless** — A way of denoting an object's context in which the Organization and Organizational Unit designators ("O" and "OU," respectively) are omitted. For example, Inv.Ops.Corp.Sutkin.

# U

**unicast address** — A type of IPv6 address that represents a single interface on a device. An IPv6 unicast address begins with either FFC0 or FF80.

**Uniform Resource Locator (URL)** — A standard means of identifying every Web page, which specifies the service used, its server's host name, and its HTML page or script name.

**uninterruptible power supply (UPS)** — A battery-operated power source directly attached to one or more devices and to a power supply (such as a wall outlet), which prevents undesired features of the power source from harming the device or interrupting its services.

**Universal Disk Format (UDF)** — A file system used on CD-ROMs and digital video disc (DVD) media.

**universal group** — A group on a Windows 2000 network that allows members from one domain to access resources in multiple domains and forests.

**unqualified host name** — A TCP/IP host name minus its prefix and suffix.

**unshielded twisted-pair (UTP)** — A type of cabling that consists of one or more insulated wire pairs encased in a plastic sheath. As its name implies, UTP does not contain additional shielding for the twisted pairs. As a result, UTP is both less expensive and less resistant to noise than STP.

**upgrade** — A major change to the existing code in a software program, which may or may not be offered free from a vendor and may or may not be comprehensive enough to substitute for the original program.

**upstream** — A term used to describe data traffic that flows from a customer's site to the local carrier's POP. In symmetrical communications, upstream throughput is usually much lower than downstream throughput. In symmetrical communications, upstream and downstream throughputs are equal.

**USB (universal serial bus) port** — A standard external bus that can be used to connect multiple types of peripherals, including modems, mice, and network adapters, to a computer. The original USB standard was capable of transmitting only 12 Mbps of data; a new standard is capable of transmitting 480 Mbps of data.

**user** — A person who uses a computer.

**User Datagram Protocol (UDP)** — A core protocol in the TCP/IP suite that sits in the Transport layer, between the Internet layer and the Application layer of the TCP/IP model. UDP is a connectionless transport service.

**user principal name (UPN)** — The preferred Active Directory naming convention for objects when used in informal situations. This name looks like a familiar Internet address, including the positioning of the domain name after the @ sign. UPNs are typically used for e-mail and related Internet services.

**user principal name (UPN) suffix** — The portion of a universal principal name (in Windows 2000 Active Directory's naming conventions) that follows the @ sign.

# V

**vampire tap** — A connector used on Thicknet MAUs that pierces a hole in the coaxial cable, thus completing a connection between the metal tooth in the vampire tap and the copper core of the cable.

**vault** — A large tape storage library.

**virtual circuits** — Connections between network nodes that, while based on potentially disparate physical links, logically appear to be direct, dedicated links between those nodes.

**virtual local area network (VLAN)** — A network within a network that is logically defined by grouping its devices' switch ports in the same broadcast domain. A VLAN can consist of servers, workstations, printers, routers, or any other network device you can connect to a switch.

**virtual memory** — Memory that is logically carved out of space on the hard disk and added to physical memory (RAM).

**virtual private network (VPN)** — A logically constructed WAN that uses existing public transmission systems. VPNs can be created through the use of software or combined software and hardware solutions. This type of network allows an organization to carve out a private WAN on the Internet (or, less commonly over leased lines) that serves only its offices, while keeping the data secure and isolated from other (public) traffic.

**virus** — A program that replicates itself so as to infect more computers, either through network connections or through floppy disks passed among users. Viruses may damage files or systems or simply annoy users by flashing messages or pictures on the screen or by causing the keyboard to beep.

**virus hoax** — A rumor, or false alert, about a dangerous, new virus that could supposedly cause serious damage to your workstation.

**Voice over IP (VoIP)** — The provision of telephone service over a TCP/IP network. (Pronounced "voyp".) One form of VoIP is Internet telephony.

**volt** — Measurement used to describe the degree of pressure an electrical current exerts on a conductor.

**volt-amp (VA)** — A measure of electrical power. A volt-amp is the product of the voltage and current (measured in amps) of the electricity on a line.

**voltage** — The pressure (sometimes informally referred to as the strength) of an electrical current.

**voltmeter** — Device used to measure voltage (or electrical pressure) on an electricalcircuit.

# W

**WAN** — See *wide area network.*

**WAN link** — The line that connects one location on a WAN with another location.

**WAN topology** — The physical layout, or pattern, of locations on a wide area network (WAN).

**wavelength** — The distance between corresponding points on a wave's cycle. Wavelength is inversely proportional to frequency.

**wavelength division multiplexing (WDM)** — A multiplexing technique in which each signal on a fiber-optic cable is assigned a different wavelength, which equates to its own subchannel. Each wavelength is modulated with a data signal. In this manner multiple signals can be simultaneously transmitted in the same direction over a length of fiber.

**Webcasting** — A broadcast transmission from one Internet-attached node to multiple other Internet-attached nodes.

**well-known ports** — TCP/IP port numbers 0 to 1023, so called because they were long ago assigned by Internet authorities to popular services (for example, FTP and Telnet), and are therefore well known and frequently used.

**wide area network (WAN)** — A network connecting geographically distinct locations, which may or may not belong to the same organization. The Internet is an example of a very large WAN.

**Windows Internet Naming Service (WINS)** — A service that resolves NetBIOS names with IP addresses. WINS is used exclusively with systems that use NetBIOS—therefore, it is usually found on Windows-based systems.

**winipcfg** — The TCP/IP configuration and management utility for use with Windows 9x systems. Winipcfg differs from ipconfig in that it supplies a graphical user interface.

**wireless** — Networks that transmit signals through the atmosphere via infrared or RF signaling.

**wizard** — A simple graphical program that assists the user in performing complex tasks, such as configuring a NIC on a server.

**workgroup** — A group of interconnected computers that share each others' resources without relying on a central file server.

**workstation** — A computer that typically runs a desktop operating system and connects to a network.

**World Wide Web (WWW or Web)** — A collection of internetworked servers that share resources and exchange information according to specific protocols and formats.

**worm** — An unwanted program that travels between computers and across networks. Although worms do not alter other programs as viruses do, they may carry viruses.

# X

**X.25** —An analog packet switched WAN technology optimized for long-distance data transmission and standardized by the ITU in the mid-1970s. X.25 can support 2-Mbps throughput. It was originally developed and used for communications between mainframe computers and remote terminals.

**xDSL** — Term used to refer to all varieties of DSL.

# Z

**zone** — The group of machines managed by a DNS server.

# INDEX

private networks and, 96, 97
proxies and, 146–147
RAS and, 110
routers and, 46–47
switching technologies and, 98, 99
TCP/IP and, 60
troubleshooting, 180–181
Layer 2 Tunneling Protocol (L2TP),
114–115
Layer 3 switches, 68, 69
layers
Application layer, 48–49, 58–59, 76,
80, 86, 87, 90
basic description of, 56–59
Data Link layer, 12–13, 15, 17–18,
44, 54, 56, 68, 69
identifying, 58–59, 68–69
LLC (Logical Link Control)
sublayer, 12–13, 54
MAC (Media Access Control)
sublayer, 12–14, 16–18, 54–55
Network layer, 48, 49, 56, 68,
144–145
Physical layer, 12–13, 42, 50, 56, 57,
68, 101, 164, 184–185
Presentation layer, 58–59, 64, 68
Session layer, 48, 49, 64, 68, 69,
58–59
Transport layer, 58–59, 60, 62–63,
68, 70–73, 76–77, 81, 144–145
LEDs
basic description of, 42, 43
interpreting, 170–171
link, 42, 43
legacy networks, 64
Linux, 120–121, 128–129, 166–167
LLC (Logical Link Control) sublayer,
12–13, 54
LocalTalk, 126–127
logical network topologies, recognizing,
2–11

# M

MAC (Media Access Control) sublayer,
12–14, 54–55. *See also* Mac
addresses
basic description of, 12
Token Ring networks and, 16–17
wireless topologies and, 18

Mac addresses. *See also* MAC (Media
Access Control) sublayer
ARP and, 156
basic description of, 54
BOOTP and, 84
bridges and, 44, 45
identifying, 54–55
IPX/SPX and, 62
OSI Model and, 57, 68, 69
valid, examples of, 54–55
Macintosh, 126–127, 132–133. *See also*
AppleTalk
connecting to, configuring, 166–167
IPX/SPX and, 62
TCP/IP and, 60
MacTCP, 132–133
mainframes, 48
MAUs (Multistation Access Units)
basic description of, 42–43
connecting with, 40
hubs and, distinction between, 43
memory
areas, assigning, 125
routers and, 46
mesh topology, 6–7
MIB (Management Information
Base), 90
MIT (Massachusetts Institute of
Technology), 118
modem(s)
cable, 162
basic description of, 52–53
DSL, 162
pools, 58

# N

NAS (network attached storage),
136–137
NAT (network address translation),
88–89, 96, 97
NBTSTAT, 152–153
n-connectors, 30
NDS (NetWare Directory Service), 122
NetBEUI (NetBIOS Enhanced User
Interface)
basic description of, 64–65
routers and, 46, 47
NetBIOS. *See also* NetBEUI (NetBIOS
Enhanced User Interface)
names, 64, 65, 150, 152

NetBEUI and, relationship of, 64, 65
WINS and, 86
Netscape
Communicator, 76, 116
FTP site, 73
NETSTAT, 152–153
NetWare (Novell)
basic description of, 122–123
connecting to, configuring, 166–167
Directory Service (NDS), 122
IPX/SPX and, 62, 63
Loadable Modules (NLM), 122
TCP/IP and, 60
network adapters, 50. *See also* NICs
(Network Interface Cards)
Network layer
basic description of, 56
firewalls and, 144–145
gateways and, 48, 49, 68
routers and, 68
NICs (Network Interface Cards), 15, 62
10Base2 Ethernet and, 28
10Base5 Ethernet and, 30
10BaseFX Ethernet and, 32–33
10BaseT Ethernet and, 24
basic description of, 50–51
CSMA/CD and, 14
diagnostic utilities for, 54
Gigabit Ethernet and, 34
LEDs and, 170–171
MAC addresses and, 54, 55
OSI Model and, 68
selecting, 150
troubleshooting, 182
wireless topologies and, 10, 11
NLMs (NetWare Loadable
Modules), 122
Node(s)
10Base5 Ethernet and, 30–31
bus topologies and, 5
CSMA/CD and, 14
failures, 3, 5, 9
ICS and, 88–89
IDs, 66
IP addresses and, 92
IPX/SPX and, 62
ring topologies and, 9
token passing and, 8
Token Ring networks and, 16
wireless topologies and, 10–11, 18

Novell NetWare
   basic description of, 122–123
   connecting to, configuring, 166–167
   Directory Service (NDS), 122
   IPX/SPX and, 62, 63
   Loadable Modules (NLM), 122
   TCP/IP and, 60
NSLOOKUP, 156–157
NT1 (Network Termination 1)
   device, 50
NTFS (New Technology File
   System), 124
NTP (Network Time Protocol), 80–81

# O

OC (Optical Carrier) level, 106, 107
octets, 92–93
Open Transport, 132
OpenView, 90, 91
OSI (Open Systems Interconnection)
   Model. *See also* layers
   basic description of, 12, 56–59
   gateways and, 48, 49
   HTTP and, 76–77
   hubs and, 42
   IPSec and, 114–115
   LLC standards and, 12, 13
   NetBIOS and, 64, 65
   NICs and, 50
   routers and, 46–47
   switches and, 44
   Telnet and, 78–79
   TCP/IP and, 60
   wireless topologies and, 19
OTDRs (optical time domain
   reflectometers), 168–169

# P

packet filtering
   bridges and, 44, 45
   firewalls, 144–145
packet switching, 98–99
partial-mesh topology, 6–7
passwords, 58
P channel, 100
PCMCIA slots, 52
PCs (personal computers). *See also*
   Windows (Microsoft)
   gateways and, 48

Gigabit Ethernet and, 34
ICS and, 88
modems and, 52
peer-to-peer networks, 64
Physical layer, 12–13, 42, 68
   basic description of, 12, 56, 57
   ISDN and, 101
   NICs and, 50
   troubleshooting, 164, 184–185
physical topology. *See also* topologies
   basic description of, 2–3
   recognizing, 2–11
Ping, 80–81, 154–155, 172–173
PnP (Plug and Play), 150
POP3 (Post Office Protocol, Version 3)
   basic description of, 74–75, 82
   ports, 82
   servers, 74
port(s)
   backbone, 42, 43
   basic description of, 82
   COM1, 52
   COM3, 52
   FTP, 82–83
   HTTP, 76–77, 82–83
   numbers, 82–83
   POP3, 82
   SMTP, 82–83
   switches and, 44
   TCP, 76, 82–83
   Telnet, 78, 82–83
   UDP, 82–83
   uplink, 42, 43
   USB, 52
   well-known, identifying, 82–83
POTS (plain old telephone service),
   162–163
PPP (Point-to-Point Protocol), 112–113
PPTP (Point-to-Point Tunneling
   Protocol), 112–113
Presentation layer
   basic description of, 58–59
   gateways and, 68
   NetBIOS and, 64
PRI (Primary Rate Interface), 100
printers, 2, 40, 67
private
   -key encryption, 118–119
   networks, 96–97, 114–115

protocols. *See also* IP (Internet Protocol;
   TCP/IP (Transmission Control
   Protocol/Internet Protocol)
   ARP (Address Resolution Protocol),
   80–81, 156–157
   BOOTP (Bootstrap Protocol), 84–85
   differentiating between, 66–67
   DHCP (Dynamic Host
   Configuration Protocol), 84–85, 92,
   150–151, 174–175
   FTP (File Transfer Protocol), 72–73,
   82–83
   HTTP (HyperText Transfer
   Protocol), 76–77, 82–83, 116
   HTTPS (Secure HTTP), 76–77,
   116, 117
   ICMP (Internet Control Message
   Protocol), 80–81
   IMAP (Internet Mail Access
   Protocol), 74–75
   IPSec (Internet Protocol Security),
   96, 114–115
   L2TP (Layer 2 Tunneling Protocol),
   114–115
   NTP (Network Time Protocol),
   80–81
   POP3 (Post Office Protocol, Version
   3), 74–75
   PPP (Point-to-Point Protocol),
   112–113
   PPTP (Point-to-Point Tunneling
   Protocol), 112–113
   SMTP (Simple Mail Transfer
   Protocol), 74–75, 82–83
   SNMP (Simple Network
   Management Protocol), 90–91
   TCP (Transmission Control
   Protocol), 60, 70, 76, 78, 80,
   82–83, 116
   TFTP (Trivial File Transfer
   Protocol), 72–73
   UDP (User Datagram Protocol),
   70–71, 80, 82–83, 116
proxies, 146–147
PSTN, 52, 98–101
   basic description of, 96–97
   ISDN and, 101
   RAS and, 110
   switching technologies and, 98, 99
   troubleshooting, 164–165

Professional, 5
RAS and, 110–111
TCP/IP and, 60
Telnet and, 78
Windows 2000 Server (Microsoft),
    124–125
Windows for Workgroups
    (Microsoft), 64
Windows ME (Microsoft), 88
Windows NT (Microsoft)
    basic capabilities of, identifying,
    124–125

RAS and, 110
Server, 86
TCP/IP and, 60
WINIPCFG, 54, 158–159
WINS (Windows Internet Naming
    System)
    basic description of, 86–87,
    150–151
    predicting the impact of, 174–175
    servers, 174
wireless topology, 10–11, 18–19, 50

## X

X.25 circuits, 104
xDSL, 162
Xerox, 40, 62, 63

## Z

zones, 66